Oracle APEX Best Practices

Accentuate Oracle APEX development with proven best practices

Learco Brizzi

Iloon Ellen-Wolff

Alex Nuijten

[PACKT] enterprise
professional expertise distilled
PUBLISHING

BIRMINGHAM - MUMBAI

Oracle APEX Best Practices

First published: October 2012

Production Reference: 1181012

Published by Packt Publishing Ltd.

Livery Place
35 Livery Street
Birmingham B3 2PB, UK.

ISBN 978-1-84968-400-2

www.packtpub.com

Cover Image by Sandeep Babu (sandyjb@gmail.com)

Credits

Authors
Learco Brizzi
Iloon Ellen-Wolff
Alex Nuijten

Reviewers
Dimitri Gielis
Surachart Opun
Michel van Zoest

Acquisition Editors
Dilip Venkatesh
Dhwani Devatar

Lead Technical Editor
Susmita Panda

Technical Editors
Prasad Dalvi
Lubna Shaikh

Project Coordinators
Yashodhan Dere
Jovita Pinto

Proofreader
Aaron Nash

Indexers
Tejal Soni
Hemangini Bari

Graphics
Valentina Dsilva
Aditi Gajjar

Production Coordinator
Nilesh R. Mohite

Cover Work
Nilesh R. Mohite

About the Authors

Learco Brizzi received his MSc in Informatics in 1993 and then he started working with the early versions of Oracle Forms (3.0), Reports (1.1), and Designer (1.2.1). When WebDB was launched, he created his first steps towards building Internet applications. When APEX (HTMLDB) hit the market, he saw the potential of this tool and built a complete music download store with it in 2004, including integration with e-mail, reports, and payment service providers. This was one of the very first serious applications ever built with APEX. Nowadays, Learco is dedicated to the APEX and PL/SQL development. He is a very enthusiastic technician, trainer of advanced APEX courses, presenter at conferences, organizer of seminars, committee member of the OGh (Oracle user group in Holland) and member of the editorial-committee for the Oracle magazine *OGh Visie*. Together with a companion Learco started his own company, Itium, in 1999, which specializes in Oracle technology. In May 2010, Learco was awarded the Oracle ACE membership. You can contact Learco at `lbrizzi@itium.nl`.

I would like to thank my wife Judith, and my children Emma (my nine-year-old daughter) and Dante (my six-year-old son) for their patience and support they gave me while writing this book. Most of the work had to be done in the evenings and weekends (our family time together).

For me this was the first time I wrote a book and didn't know what to expect. I didn't expect that it would take so much time, but it was fun to do and I learned a lot of new things about Oracle and APEX as well.

I would also like to thank my fellow writers Alex and Iloon. Together we were a great team and kept each other sharp.

Last but not least I would like to thank the editors of the book who had good comments and suggestions on our material.

Iloon Ellen-Wolff started working with Oracle 21 years ago, employed by several software houses in the Netherlands. Her experience goes back to Oracle Forms version 2 and Report Writer.

Almost 14 years ago, she started working for Oracle Support Services for the developer competency (Oracle Forms, Oracle Reports, SQL Developer, and Application Express), assisting customers by solving their software-related problems.

During those years, she applied the knowledge she had gained in many ways such as coaching new engineers, team leading, teaching the Application Express courses, and seminars for Oracle University.

Aside from being a very senior team member with excellent troubleshooting and customer skills, in Oracle Support, she acts as Advanced Resolution Engineer.

One of her responsibilities in Oracle Support is Global Technical Lead Application Express. She works closely with Sustaining Engineering, Product Development, and Product Management of the Application Express team.

Starting last year, she is now involved in the Oracle Cloud project. She is member of the *platform as a service* readiness team. Involved in testing Application Express in the Cloud and being a trainer in this area, she enjoys the challenge to prepare her engineers for the Cloud and ultimately to support Oracle customers in the very near future!

Besides that, she is a frequent speaker for different Oracle User Groups about Application Express, SQL Developer, and Oracle Public Cloud.

I would like to take the opportunity to thank the Application Express development team and particularly Joel Kallman as Development Director for the continuing effort to make Application Express an excellent product.

I'd also like to thank my husband, Albert Ellen, for assisting me in getting the layout right and supporting me in writing this book. Of course, it took a big amount of time to achieve this goal.

I would also like to thank co-authors on this book, Alex and Learco.

Alex Nuijten works as a database developer and Expertise Lead (database development) for AMIS Services BV in Nieuwegein, The Netherlands. Besides his consultancy work, he conducts training classes, mainly in SQL and PL/SQL. Alex has been a speaker at numerous international conferences, such as ODTUG, Oracle Open World, UKOUG, IOUG, OGh, and OBUG. He is also a frequent contributor at the *Oracle Technology Network* forum for SQL and PL/SQL. He has written many articles in Oracle-related magazines, and at regular intervals he writes about Oracle database development on the *AMIS Technology Blog* (`technology.amis.nl`), as well as on his own blog, *Notes on Oracle* (`nuijten.blogspot.com`). In August 2010, Alex was awarded the Oracle ACE Director membership.

I think this may be the hardest section to write. There are so many people that inspired me and from whom I have learned so much along the way. And each one of them helped me in writing my chapters. It would be impossible to try to name you all and therefore do injustice to the ones I let slip. My colleagues, fellow members of the OTN forums and in the ACE program, the bloggers, the Oracle user groups all over the globe, basically everyone I ever dealt with—a big thank you to you all.

There are still some people I have to name in this section explicitly.

Let me start by thanking my co-authors, Iloon and Learco. Writing this book was quite a journey. Thank you for allowing me to join you with this adventure, it was a great experience.

Without the technical reviewers, this book would have looked totally different. Thank you, Dimitri Gielis, Surachart Opun, and Michel van Zoest, for your feedback and suggestions on improving the quality of the book. Any outstanding errors in my chapters are, of course, my own.

Without the continuing support of my wife Rian, son Tim, and daughter Lara, I could never have worked on this. Preparing presentations, writing articles and chapters take an enormous amount of time and my family understands this, and they are alright with it. I could never do all that without you, I love you so much.

Finally I would like to thank the Packt editorial and production teams who have worked on this book, especially Yashodhan Dere, Susmita Panda, Dilip Venkatesh, Dhwani Devatar, and Jovita Pinto.

About the Reviewers

Dimitri Gielis was born in 1978. Together with his family he lives in Leuven, Belgium.

At an early age, Dimitri started experimenting with computers (Apple II and IBM XT), and he quickly got to know that he would like to work with computers and especially with databases all his life.

In 2000, Dimitri began his career working as a consultant for Oracle Belgium where he came across almost every Oracle product. His main expertise was in the database area, but at that time he was also exposed to HTMLDB, which was renamed as Oracle Application Express later on. From the very start he liked the Oracle database and APEX so much that he never stopped working with it. Dimitri then switched to another company to create an Oracle team and do pre-sales, to later create and manage an Oracle Business Unit.

In 2007, Dimitri co-founded APEX Evangelists (`http://www.apex-evangelists.com`), together with John Scott. APEX Evangelists is a company that specializes in providing training, development, and consulting specifically for the Oracle Application Express product.

On his blog (`http://dgielis.blogspot.com`), he shares his thoughts and experience about Oracle, and especially, Oracle Application Express.

Dimitri is a frequent presenter at OBUG Connect, IOUG Collaborate, ODTUG Kaleidoscope, UKOUG conference, and Oracle Open World. He likes to share his experience and meet other people. He's also President of the **OBUG** (**Oracle Benelux User Group**) APEX SIG.

In 2008, Dimitri became an Oracle ACE Director. Oracle ACE Directors are known for their strong credentials as Oracle community enthusiasts and advocates.

In 2009, Dimitri received the APEX Developer of the year award by Oracle Magazine.

In 2012, Dimitri was part of the LA OTN Tour where he presented different APEX topics.

You can contact Dimitri at `dimitri.gielis@apex-evangelists.com`.

Surachart Opun has been working on Oracle products for over seven years. He has worked with Internet Service Provider Business for over eight years. He is Oracle ACE, OCE RAC 10*g*, and OCP 10*g* and 11*g*. He has experience in implementation, migration, and management of Oracle Database in telecommunication business and so on. He has spent time in helping people who are interested in the Oracle products as contributor. He is working on APEX since version 3 and has worked on APEX implementation and migration.

His blog is at `http://surachartopun.com`.

Michel van Zoest was born in 1976. He currently lives in Bergambacht, The Netherlands with his wife, two daughters, and son.

In 2000, he started working as an Oracle Consultant. He now has more than 12 years of experience in building (web) applications by using the Oracle technologies such as Oracle (web) Forms, Oracle Designer, MOD_PLSQL, ADF, SOA Suite, and of course, APEX.

Michel was one of the first Oracle Application Express Developer Certified Experts in the world.

He currently works at Whitehorses in The Netherlands and runs his own blog at `http://www.aboutapex.com`. As well as that, he blogs at the company website at `http://blog.whitehorses.nl` and he regularly writes Whitebook articles (in Dutch) for Whitehorses.

Michel is also one of the authors of the *Oracle APEX 4.0 Cookbook* published by Packt in December 2010.

You can contact Michel via his website or by emailing him at `michel.van.zoest@whitehorses.nl`.

Table of Contents

Preface **1**
Chapter 1: Prepare and Build **7**
History and background **7**
Installing APEX **9**
Runtime or full development environment 10
Build status 10
Tablespaces 10
Converting runtime environment into a full development environment and vice versa 11
Choosing a web server **12**
OHS 13
EPG 13
APEX Listener 14
Creating a second administrator **16**
APEX web interface 17
Command line 18
Other accounts 19
Database **19**
Data model 19
Creating the database objects 21
Other tools 22
PL/SQL usage 23
Creating a workspace **23**
Creating administrators, developers, and users 24
User Interface Defaults **25**
Attribute Dictionary 25
Table Dictionary 25
Creating User Interface Defaults 26
Page Zero **29**

Structure of multiple applications 30
Subscribe and publish 30
Creating a framework 32
Master and template application 33
Login application—optional 33
System application—optional 35
Deploying 36
Template workspace 36
Creating applications 36
List of values 36
Mapping the model to pages 37
Base tables 38
Master detail 40
Intersection 42
Simple report 46
Other pages 46
Summary 46
Chapter 2: Leveraging the Database 47
Instrumentation 48
Efficient lookup tables 52
Single-table hash clusters 53
Index-organized tables 59
Analytic functions 61
Syntax overview 61
Examples 64
Running totals 64
Visualizing the window 66
Accessing values from other records 67
Another way of accessing other rows in the result set 69
Ranking—top N 70
Stringing it all together 72
Caveats 73
Aggregate functions 77
Grouping sets 78
Rollup 81
Cube 83
Identifying the totals and subtotals with grouping 84
Offloading your frontend and scheduling a job 86
One-off job 86
Pipelined table functions 91
Pipelined table functions in APEX 93
Using images 95
Searching the contents of documents 97
Summary 100

Chapter 3: Printing **101**
Printing architecture **102**
What is planned for the future version of APEX Listener? 102
Installation and configuration of the Apache FOP report server **103**
How to configure Apache FOP 105
Business Intelligence Publisher 109
Installation of Business Intelligence Publisher Version 11 109
Simple print test using BI Publisher 111
How to debug or troubleshoot printing issues **112**
How to check if network services are enabled **113**
Creating a report with BI Publisher **115**
Creating the report query 115
Designing the report layout 116
Downloading XML data 117
Designing with the RTF template (MS Word) 117
Uploading the report layout 118
Linking the report to your application 119
How to create a report that can deliver output in different formats **120**
How to add a chart to a report **122**
Creating a chart in a report 123
How to add dynamic images to a report **125**
Print API **130**
How to bypass the 32K limit **133**
Alternatives to use for PDF printing **133**
Integration with Oracle Reports 133
Integration with Cocoon 134
Integration with JasperReports 135
Architecture 135
Plugins **135**
Reports 2 PDF 135
Embedded PDF 136
Summary **136**
Chapter 4: Security **137**
Securing Oracle Application Express for administrators **138**
Protecting the database environment 138
Virtual Private Database **139**
VPD policy 139
VPD and Application Context 144
Implementing VPD in APEX 148
What to do when you get a runtime exception 149

Securing the web listener 151
HTTP server 151
Embedded PL/SQL gateway 153
Oracle Application Express Listener 154
Enabling SSL for the web server 155
Security considerations when installing Oracle Application Express 156
Runtime installation 156
Access Control Lists (ACLs) 157
Enabling builders in Oracle Application Express 158
Session timeout 159
Instance level 159
Application level 160
Password complexity rules 161
Patching strategy 162
Security considerations for the developer 162
Browser attacks 163
Cross-site scripting (XSS) 163
Protecting HTML regions and other static areas 165
Protecting dynamic output 165
Protecting reports regions 165
Protecting form items 165
SQL injection 166
Insecure use of variables 167
Correct use of Bind variables 169
SYS.DBMS_ASSERT 169
Security attributes 170
Authentication 170
Authorization 174
Database schema 179
URL tampering 179
Session state protection against URL tampering 179
Browser security attributes 183
Cache 183
Embed in Frames 183
Database session 184
Authorization and authentication plugin 184
Secure items in an application 185
Item encryption 186
Hidden items protection 186
Items of type password 187
File upload items 188
Managing instance security 188
Application data 189
Fake input 189
Saving state before branching 191

Utilities 191
Application dashboard 191
How to check the security of your application 192
Oracle Application Express Advisor 192
Third-party tools to check on security 193
Summary 194
Chapter 5: Debugging and Troubleshooting 195
Debugging an APEX page 195
Instrumentation of the APEX code 201
APEX_APPLICATION.G_DEBUG 202
The debug Advanced Programming Interface (API) 202
The APEX debug message 202
APEX_DEBUG_MESSAGE.LOG_MESSAGE 204
WWV_FLOW_API.SET_ENABLE_APP_DEBUGGING 205
APEX and Oracle SQL Developer 205
Remote debugging 209
Steps to be performed in APEX 210
JavaScript console wrapper 211
Installation of the console wrapper 211
Web development tools 213
Firebug 214
APEX and Firebug 215
Debugging dynamic actions 215
Yslow 216
Error handling 217
Logging and tracing 217
Enabling/disabling logging 219
Reports in Application Express that facilitate troubleshooting 220
Application Express Advisor 221
Summary 223
Chapter 6: Deploy and Maintain 225
Package your application, or not? 226
Version control 231
Subversion 232
Deploying the database packages 235
Deploying the APEX application 239
Using the APEX environment 239
Using the command-line interface 245
Housekeeping the APEX repository 248

Being active and proactive **249**
Feedback 249
Activate feedback 250
Processing entered feedback 252
Weighted page performance 255
Summary **258**
Appendix A: Database Cloud Service and APEX 4.2 **259**
Oracle Public Cloud **259**
Packaged applications 260
Plan for the future 260
RESTful web services 261
The RESTful Web Services wizard 262
Data load feature (SQL Workshop/utilities/data load) 267
Summary **267**
Index **269**

Preface

Have you ever wanted to create real-world database applications? In this book, you will not only get APEX best practices, but will also take into account the total environment of an APEX application and benefit from it. Many examples are given based on a simple but appealing case.

This book will guide you through the development of real-world applications. It will give you a broader view of APEX. The various aspects include setting up an APEX environment, testing and debugging, security, and getting the best out of SQL and PL/SQL.

In six distinct chapters, you will learn about different features of Oracle APEX as well as SQL and PL/SQL.

Do you maximize the capabilities of Oracle APEX? Do you use all the power that SQL and PL/SQL have to offer? Do you want to learn how to build a secure, fully functional application? Then this is the book you'll need.

Oracle APEX Best Practices is where practical development begins!

What this book covers

Chapter 1, Prepare and Build, discusses different aspects of setting up an Application Express (APEX) environment. Among others, we'll take a look at installing APEX, performing preparational tasks before actually building applications, and transforming the data model into initial screens. We will also discuss some guidelines and best practices for these phases.

Chapter 2, Leveraging the Database, explains various subjects related to an APEX environment. These subjects include instrumentation, efficient lookup tables, analytic and aggregate functions, offloading long running programs, and so on.

Chapter 3, Printing, deals with different aspects of printing in Oracle Application Express. In this chapter, we will discuss the two most used architectures in Application Express printing, using Apache FOP and Business Intelligence Publisher. Then, we will see how to install and configure both Apache FOP and Business Intelligence Publisher.

Chapter 4, Security, describes how to provide security for Oracle Application Express. In this chapter, we will discuss the responsibilities of an administrator. We will also discuss security aspects for developers.

Chapter 5, Debugging and Troubleshooting, discusses various subjects such as debugging in APEX, remote debugging using Oracle SQL Developer, reports available in Application Express for troubleshooting, and so on.

Chapter 6, Deploy and Maintain, discusses the deployment and maintenance of an APEX environment. In this chapter, we will discuss various topics such as considerations regarding packaging the application, version control, and so on.

Appendix, Database Cloud Service and APEX 4.2, discusses Oracle Public Cloud and the Application Express features in the Database Cloud Service and APEX 4.2.

What you need for this book

You will require following software:

- SQL Developer version 3.2 or higher
- Application Express 4.1.1 or higher
- APEX Listener with GlassFish, OC4J, or WebLogic
- BI Publisher (version 10 or version 11) and/or FOP

Who this book is for

This book is filled with best practices on how to make the most of Oracle APEX. Developers beginning with application development as well as those who are experienced will benefit from this book. You will need to have basic knowledge of SQL and PL/SQL to follow the examples in this book.

Conventions

In this book, you will find a number of styles of text that distinguish between different kinds of information. Here are some examples of these styles, and an explanation of their meaning.

Code words in text are shown as follows: "These settings can also be set manually with the `APEX_INSTANCE_ADMIN` API."

A block of code is set as follows:

```
BEGIN
  wwv_flow_api.set_security_group_id
  (p_security_group_id=>10);
  wwv_flow_fnd_user_api.create_fnd_user(
    p_user_name      => 'second_admin',
    p_email_address => 'email@company.com',
    p_web_password  => 'second_admin_password') ;
END;
/
COMMIT
/
```

Any command-line input or output is written as follows:

```
@apexins tablespace_apex tablespace_files tablespace_temp images
```

New terms and **important words** are shown in bold. Words that you see on the screen, in menus or dialog boxes for example, appear in the text like this: "Select the appropriate settings for **Disable Administrator Login** and **Disable Workspace Login**."

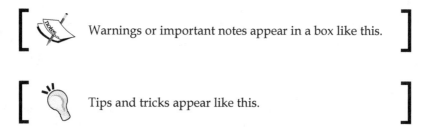

> Warnings or important notes appear in a box like this.

> Tips and tricks appear like this.

Reader feedback

Feedback from our readers is always welcome. Let us know what you think about this book—what you liked or may have disliked. Reader feedback is important for us to develop titles that you really get the most out of.

To send us general feedback, simply send an e-mail to `feedback@packtpub.com`, and mention the book title via the subject of your message.

If there is a book that you need and would like to see us publish, please send us a note in the **SUGGEST A TITLE** form on `www.packtpub.com` or e-mail `suggest@packtpub.com`.

If there is a topic that you have expertise in and you are interested in either writing or contributing to a book, see our author guide on `www.packtpub.com/authors`.

Customer support

Now that you are the proud owner of a Packt book, we have a number of things to help you to get the most from your purchase.

Downloading the example code

You can download the example code files for all Packt books you have purchased from your account at `http://www.PacktPub.com`. If you purchased this book elsewhere, you can visit `http://www.PacktPub.com/support` and register to have the files e-mailed directly to you.

Errata

Although we have taken every care to ensure the accuracy of our content, mistakes do happen. If you find a mistake in one of our books—maybe a mistake in the text or the code—we would be grateful if you would report this to us. By doing so, you can save other readers from frustration and help us improve subsequent versions of this book. If you find any errata, please report them by visiting `http://www.packtpub.com/support`, selecting your book, clicking on the **errata submission form** link, and entering the details of your errata. Once your errata are verified, your submission will be accepted and the errata will be uploaded on our website, or added to any list of existing errata, under the Errata section of that title. Any existing errata can be viewed by selecting your title from `http://www.packtpub.com/support`.

Piracy

Piracy of copyright material on the Internet is an ongoing problem across all media. At Packt, we take the protection of our copyright and licenses very seriously. If you come across any illegal copies of our works, in any form, on the Internet, please provide us with the location address or website name immediately so that we can pursue a remedy.

Please contact us at `copyright@packtpub.com` with a link to the suspected pirated material.

We appreciate your help in protecting our authors, and our ability to bring you valuable content.

Questions

You can contact us at `questions@packtpub.com` if you are having a problem with any aspect of the book, and we will do our best to address it.

1
Prepare and Build

In this chapter, we will discuss different aspects of setting up an **Application Express** (**APEX**) environment. Among others, we'll take a look at installing APEX, performing preparational tasks before actually building applications, and transforming the data model into initial screens. We will also discuss some guidelines and best practices for these phases. You'll get a lot of new ideas for structuring and building your applications.

Before doing that we will take a brief look at the history and background of APEX.

History and background

APEX is a very powerful development tool, which is used to create web-based database-centric applications. The tool itself consists of a schema in the database with a lot of tables, views, and PL/SQL code. It's available for every edition of the database. The techniques that are used with this tool are PL/SQL, HTML, CSS, and JavaScript.

Before APEX there was WebDB, which was based on the same techniques. WebDB became part of Oracle Portal and disappeared in silence. The difference between APEX and WebDB is that WebDB generates packages that generate the HTML pages, while APEX generates the HTML pages at runtime from the repository. Despite this approach APEX is amazingly fast.

Because the database is doing all the hard work, the architecture is fairly simple. We only have to add a web server. We can choose one of the following web servers:

- Oracle HTTP Server (OHS)
- Embedded PL/SQL Gateway (EPG)
- APEX Listener

APEX became available to the public in 2004 and then it was part of version 10*g* of the database. At that time it was called **HTMLDB** and the first version was 1.5. Before HTMLDB, it was called Oracle Flows, Oracle Platform, and Project Marvel. Throughout the years many versions have come out and at the time of writing the current version is 4.1.1. These many versions prove that Oracle has continuously invested in the development and support of APEX. This is important for the developers and companies who have to make a decision about which techniques to use in the future. According to Oracle, as written in their statement of direction, new versions of APEX will be released at least annually. The following screenshot shows the home screen of the current version of APEX:

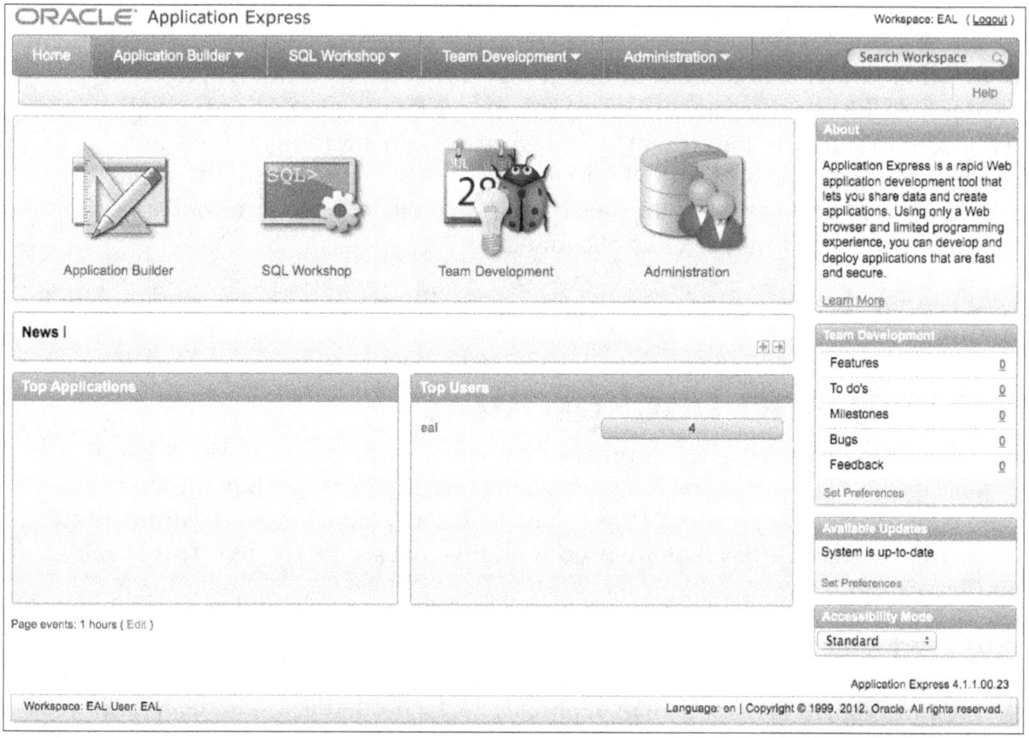

Home screen of APEX

For the last few years, there is an increasing interest in the use of APEX from developers. The popularity came mainly from developers who found themselves comfortable with PL/SQL and wanted to easily enter the world of web-based applications. Oracle gave ADF a higher priority, because APEX was a no cost option of the database and with ADF (and all the related techniques and frameworks from Java), additional licenses could be sold.

Especially now Oracle has pointed out APEX as one of the important tools for building applications in their Oracle Database Cloud Service, this interest will only grow. APEX shared a lot of the characteristics of cloud computing, even before cloud computing became popular. These characteristics include:

- Elasticity
- Roles and authorization
- Browser-based development and runtime
- RESTful web services (**REST** stands for **Representational State Transfer**)
- Multi-tenant
- Simple and fast to join

APEX has outstanding community support, witnessed by the number of posts and threads on the Oracle forum. This forum is the most popular after the database and PL/SQL.

Oracle itself has some websites, based on APEX. Among others there are the following:

- `http://asktom.oracle.com`
- `http://shop.oracle.com`
- `http://cloud.oracle.com`

Oracle uses quite a few internal APEX applications.

Oracle also provides a hosted version of APEX at `http://apex.oracle.com`. Users can sign up for free for a workspace to evaluate and experiment with the latest version of APEX. This environment is for evaluations and demonstrations only, there are no guarantees! `Apex.oracle.com` is a very popular service—more than 16,000 workspaces are active. To give an idea of the performance of APEX, the server used for this service used to be a Dell Poweredge 1950 with two Dual Core Xeon processors with 16 GB.

To get a jumpstart with developing real-life APEX applications, we have written this book and provided you with some best practices. These practices don't have to be appropriate in all situations, see them as guidelines. This book is not intended as a *point and click* starters guide and assumes a basic understanding of APEX, PL/SQL, HTML, and CSS.

Installing APEX

In this section, we will discuss some additional considerations to take care of while installing APEX. The best source for the installation process is the *Installation Guide of APEX*.

Runtime or full development environment

On a production database, the runtime environment of APEX should be installed. This installation lacks the Application Builder and the SQL Workshop. Users can run applications, but the applications cannot be modified. The runtime environment of APEX can be administered using SQL*Plus and SQL Developer. The (web interface) options for importing an application, which are only available in a full development environment, can be used manually with the `APEX_INSTANCE_ADMIN` API. See the reference guide for details. Using a runtime environment for production is recommended for security purposes, so that we can be certain that installed applications cannot be modified by anyone.

On a development environment the full development environment can be installed with all the features available to the developers.

Build status

Besides the environment of APEX itself, the applications can also be installed in a similar way. When importing or exporting an application the **Run Application Only** or **Run and Build Application** options can be selected.

Changing an application to **Run Application Only** can be done in the Application Builder by choosing **Edit Application Properties**. Changing the **Build Status** to **Run and Build Application** can only be done as the admin user of the workspace `internal`. In the APEX Administration Services, choose **Manage Workspaces** and then select **Manage Applications | Build Status**. Also refer to *Chapter 6, Deploy and Maintain*.

Another setting related to the **Runtime Only** option could be used in the APEX Administration Services at instance level. Select **Manage Instance** and then select **Security**. Setting the property **Disable Workspace Login** to **yes**, acts as setting a Runtime Only environment, while still allowing instance administrators to log in to the APEX Administration Services.

Tablespaces

Following the install guide for the full development environment, at a certain moment, we have to run the following command, when logged in as `SYS` with the `SYSDBA` role, on the command line:

```
@apexins tablespace_apex tablespace_files tablespace_temp images
```

The command is explained as follows:

- `tablespace_apex` is the name of the tablespace that contains all the objects for the APEX application user.
- `tablespace_files` is the name of the tablespace that contains all the objects for the APEX files user.
- `tablespace_temp` is the name of the temporary tablespace of the database.
- `images` will be the virtual directory for APEX images. Oracle recommends using `/i/` to support the future APEX upgrades.

For the runtime environment, the command is as follows:

```
@apxrtins tablespace_apex tablespace_files tablespace_temp images
```

In the documentation, `SYSAUX` is given as an example for both `tablespace_apex` and `tablespace_files`. There are several reasons for not using `SYSAUX` for these tablespaces, but to use our own instead:

- `SYSAUX` is an important tablespace of the database itself
- We have more control over sizing and growth
- It is easier for a DBA to manage tablespace placement
- Contention in the `SYSAUX` tablespace is less occurring
- It's easier to clean-up older versions of APEX
- And last but not least, it's only an example

Converting runtime environment into a full development environment and vice versa

It's always possible to switch from a runtime to a production environment and vice versa. If you want to convert a runtime to a full development environment log in as `SYS` with the `SYSDBA` role and on the command line type `@apxdvins.sql`. For converting a full development to a runtime environment, type `@apxdevrm`—but export websheet applications first. For more details see the installation guide.

Another way to restrict user access can be accomplished by logging in to the APEX Administration Services, where we can (among others) manage the APEX instance settings and all the workspaces. We can do that in two ways:

- `http://server:port/apex/apex_admin`: Log in with the administrator credentials
- `http://server:port/apex/`: Log in to the workspace internal, with the administrator credentials

After logging in, perform the following steps:

1. Go to **Manage Instance**.
2. Select **Security**.
3. Select the appropriate settings for **Disable Administrator Login** and **Disable Workspace Login**. These settings can also be set manually with the `APEX_INSTANCE_ADMIN` API. See the reference guide for details.

Choosing a web server

When using a web-based development and runtime environment, we have to use a web server.

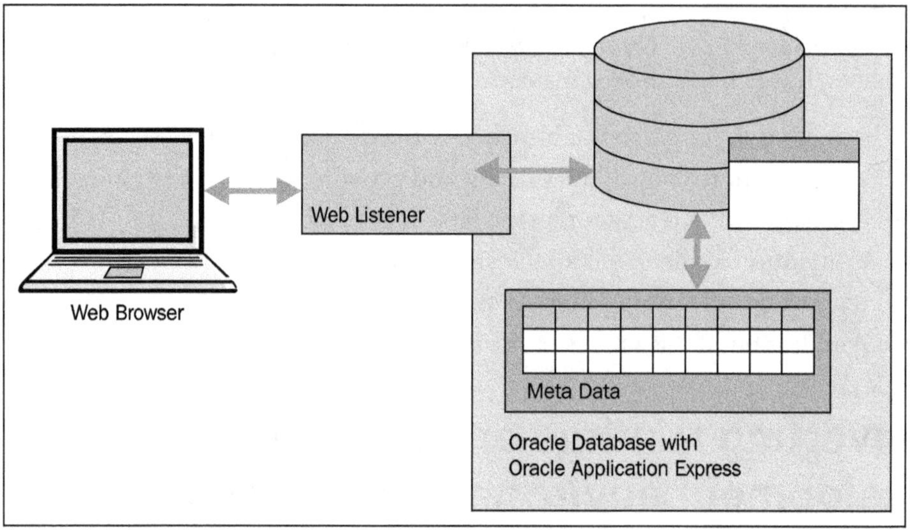

Architecture of APEX

The choice of a web server and the underlying architecture of the system has a direct impact on performance and scalability. Oracle provides us with three choices:

- **Oracle HTTP Server (OHS)**
- **Embedded PL/SQL Gateway (EPG)**
- **APEX Listener**

Simply put, the web server maps the URL in a web browser to a procedure in the database. Everything the procedure prints with `sys.htp package`, is sent to the browser of the user. This is the concept used by tools such as WebDB and APEX.

OHS

The OHS is the oldest of the three. It's based on the Apache HTTP Server and uses a custom Apache Module named as `mod_plsql`:

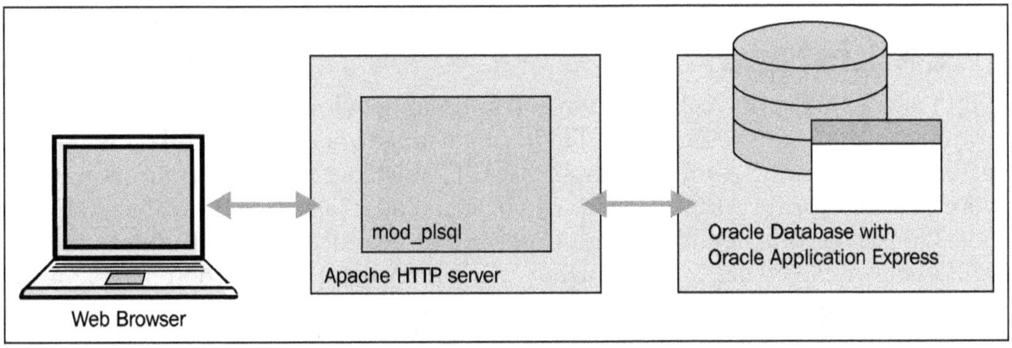

Oracle HTTP Server

In release 10*g* of the database, OHS was installed with the database on the same machine. Upward to the release 11*g*, this is not the case anymore. If you want to install the OHS, you have to install the web tier part of WebLogic. If you install it on the same machine as the database, it's free of extra licence costs. This installation takes up a lot of space and is rather complex, compared with the other two. On the other hand, it's very flexible and it has a proven track record. Configuration is done with the text files.

EPG

The EPG is part of XML DB and lives inside the database. Because everything is in the database, we have to use the `dbms_xdb` and `dbms_epg` PL/SQL packages to configure the EPG. Another implication is that all images and other files are stored inside the database, which can be accessed with PL/SQL or FTP, for example:

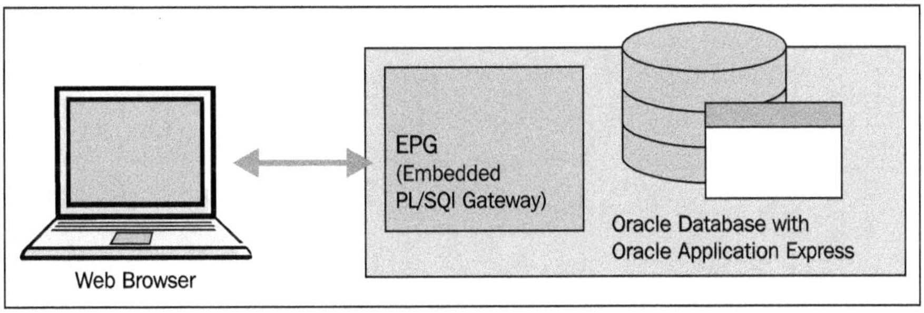

Embedded PL/SQL gateway

The architecture is very simple. It's not possible to install the EPG on a different machine than the database. From a security point of view, this is not the recommended architecture for real-life Internet applications and in most cases the EPG is used in development, test, or other internal environments with few users.

APEX Listener

APEX Listener is the newest of the three, it's still in development and with every new release more features are added to it. In the latest version, RESTful APIs can be created by configuring resource templates. APEX Listener is a Java application with a very small footprint. APEX Listener can be installed in a standalone mode, which is ideal for development and testing purposes. For production environments, the APEX Listener can be deployed by using a J2EE compliant Application Server such as Glassfish, WebLogic, or Oracle Containers for J2EE:

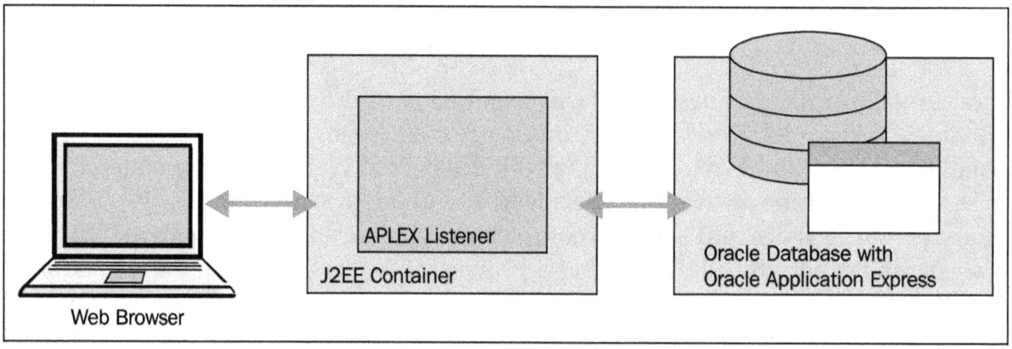

APEX Listener

Configuration of the APEX Listener is done in a browser. With some extra configuration, uploading of Excel into APEX collections can be achieved. In future release, other functionalities, such as OAuth 2.0 and ICAP virus scanner integration, have been announced.

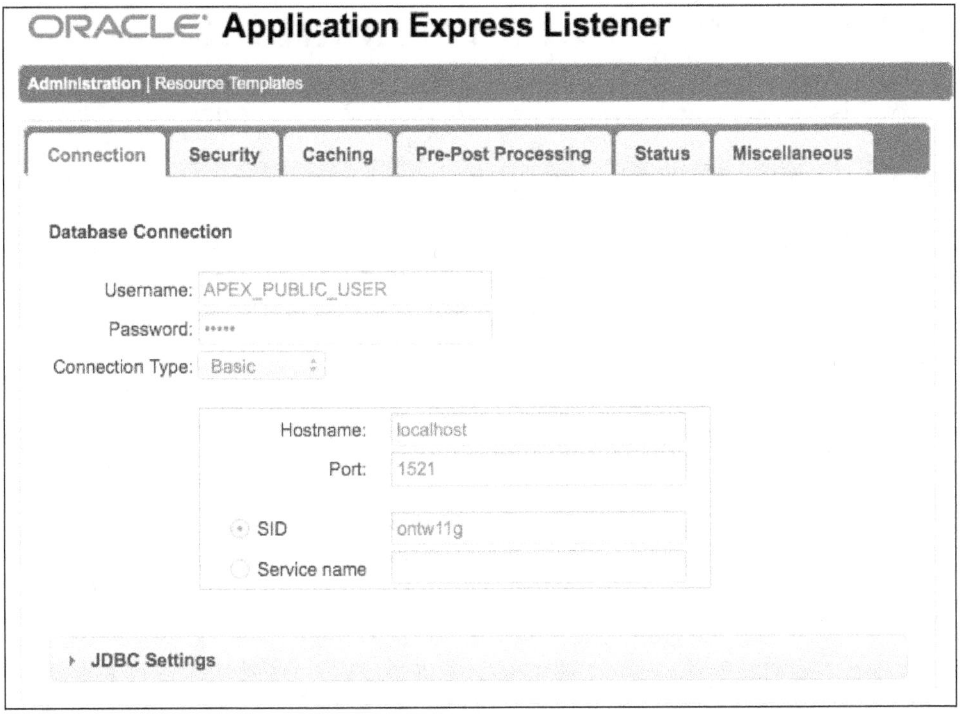

Configuration options of the APEX Listener

Like OHS, an architectural choice can be made if we want to install APEX Listener on the same machine as the database. For large public applications, it's better to use a separate web server.

Many documents and articles have been written about choosing the right web server. If you read between the lines, you'll see that Oracle more or less recommends the use of APEX Listener. Given the functionality, enhanced security, file caching, flexibility of deployment possibilities, and feature announcements makes it the best choice.

Creating a second administrator

When installing APEX, by default the workspace `Internal` with the administrator user `Admin` is created. Some users know more than the average end user. Also, developers have more knowledge than the average user. Imagine that such users try to log in to either the APEX Administration Services or the normal login page with the workspace `Internal` and administrator `Admin`, and consequently use the wrong password. As a consequence, the Admin account would be locked after a number of login attempts. This is a very annoying situation, especially when it happens often. Big companies and APEX Hosting companies with many workspaces and a lot of anonymous users or developers may suffer from this. Fortunately there is an easy solution, creating a second administrator account.

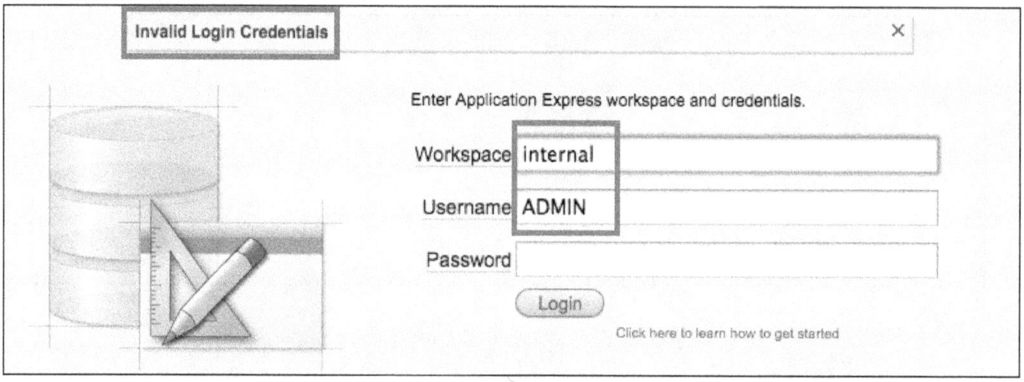

Login attempt in workspace Internal as Admin

If the account is already locked, we have to unlock it first. This can be easily done by running the `apxchpwd.sql` script, which can be found in the main Apex directory of the unzipped installation file of APEX:

1. Start SQL*Plus and connect as `sys` with the `sysdba` role.
2. Run the script by entering `@apxchpwd.sql`.
3. Follow the instructions and enter a new password.

Now we are ready to create a second administrator account. This can be done in two ways, using the web interface or the command line.

APEX web interface

Follow these steps to create a new administrator, using the browser.

First, we need to log in to the APEX Administrator Services at `http://server:port/apex/`. Log in to the workspace `Internal`, with the administrator credentials.

After logging in, perform the following steps:

1. Go to **Manage Workspaces**.
2. Select **Existing Workspaces**.
3. You can also select the edit icon of the workspace `Internal` to inspect the settings. You cannot change them. Select **Cancel** to return to the previous screen.
4. Select the workspace `Internal` by clicking on the name.
5. Select **Manage Users**. Here you can see the user `Admin`.
6. You can also select the user `Admin` to change the password. Other settings cannot be changed. Select **Cancel** or **Apply Changes** to return to the previous screen.
7. Select **Create User**. Make sure that **Internal** is selected in the **Workspace** field and `APEX_xxxxxx` is selected in **Default Schema**, and that the new user is an administrator. `xxxxxx` has to match your APEX scheme version in the database, for instance, **APEX_040100**.
8. Click on **Create** to finish.

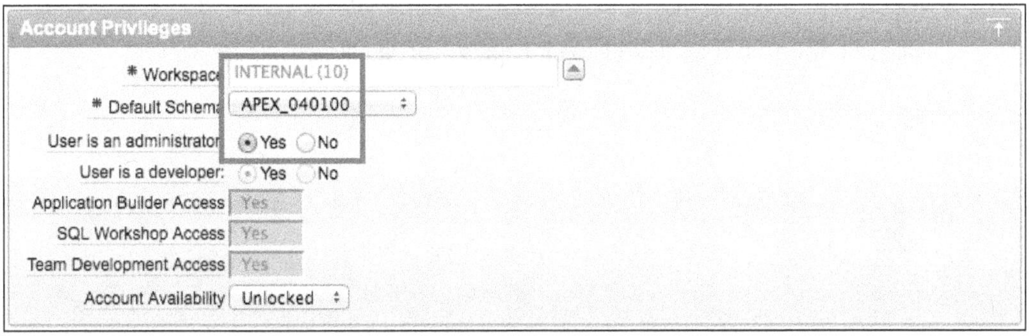

Settings for the new administrator

Command line

When we still have access, we can use the web interface of APEX. If not we can use the command line:

1. Start SQL*Plus and connect as `SYS` with the `SYSDBA` role.
2. Unlock the `APEX_xxxxxx` account by issuing the following command:

   ```
   alter user APEX_xxxxxx account unlock;
   ```

3. Connect to the `APEX_xxxxxx` account. If you don't remember your password, you can just reset it, without impacting the APEX instance.
4. Execute the following (use your own username, e-mail, and password):

   ```
   BEGIN
     wwv_flow_api.set_security_group_id
     (p_security_group_id=>10);
     wwv_flow_fnd_user_api.create_fnd_user(
       p_user_name     => 'second_admin',
       p_email_address => 'email@company.com',
       p_web_password  => 'second_admin_password') ;
   END;
   /
   COMMIT
   /
   ```

5. The new administrator is created. Connect again as `SYS` with the `SYSDBA` role and lock the account again with the following command:

   ```
   alter user APEX_xxxxxx account lock;
   ```

6. Now you can log in to the `Internal` workspace with your newly created account and you'll be asked to change your password.

Other accounts

When an administrator of a developer workspace loses his/her password or has a locked account, you can bring that account back to life by following these steps:

1. Log in to the APEX Administrator Services.
2. Go to **Manage Workspace**.
3. Select **Existing Workspaces**.
4. Select the workspace.
5. Select **Manage Users**.
6. Select the user, change the password, and unlock the user.

A developer or an APEX end user account can be managed by the administrator of the workspace from the workspace itself. Follow these steps to do so:

1. Log in to the workspace.
2. Go to **Administration**.
3. Select the user, change the password, and unlock the user.

Database

We have set up the APEX environment, now let's focus on the database. For means of consistency and maintainability, it's a good practice to use standards and guidelines. In this section, we will describe some standards and guidelines for data modeling, database objects, and PL/SQL usage.

Data model

When the requirements are clear, we can create a data model. A data model provides the structure, definition, and format of the data.

We will translate the requirements into tables, columns, and relations. It will be the single point of truth of our system. Because our whole system is built upon this model, it's very important to spend sufficient time on it. A data model is also a great means to communicate with your customers and among developers about the system and design of the database. When a database is well designed, it can be easily maintained for future development.There are a number of **Computer Aided Software Engineering (CASE)** tools that you can use to create a data model. Besides data modeling, some of these CASE tools can also be used to maintain all the PL/SQL packages, functions, procedures, and trigger code that we use in our applications. Oracle itself provides Oracle Designer and Data Modeler from SQL Developer. The following diagram shows Data Modeler. One of the advantages of using such a tool is the ability to generate and reverse engineer the database creation scripts in an intuitive graphical manner.

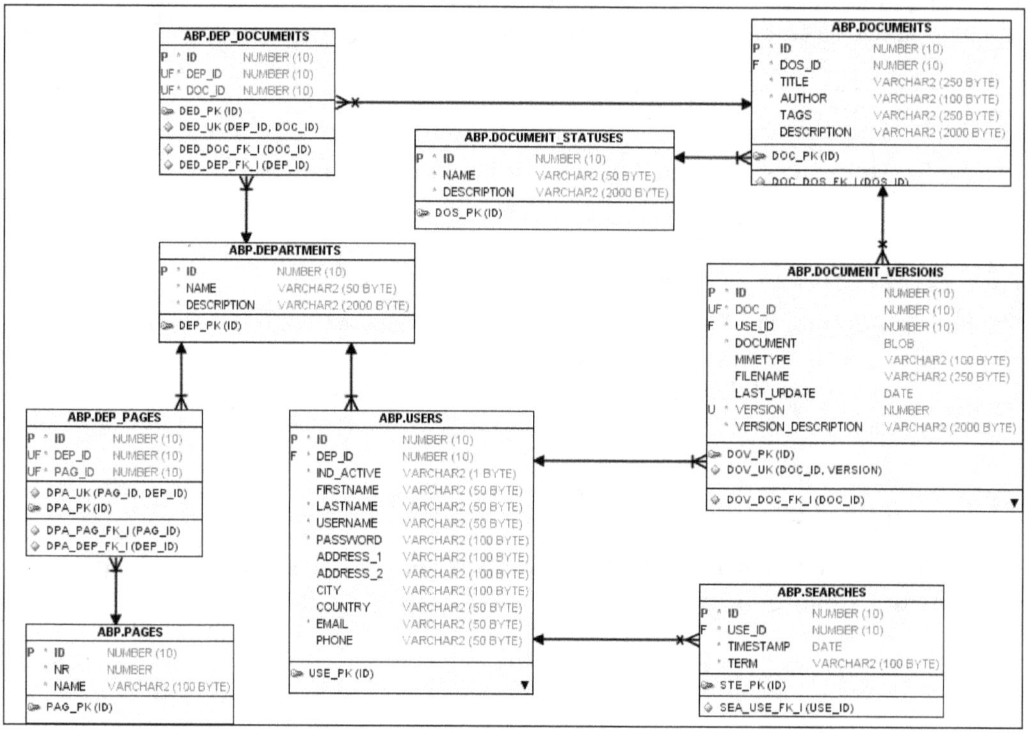

SQL Developer Data Modeler

Relations between the tables are always in a one-to-many relationship; for example, a user can perform one or more searches. We can use colors to differentiate between tables that have a lot of mutations and tables that don't have any. Those tables can be candidates for creating lists of values (discussed later in this chapter).

A great example of standards and guidelines is Oracle's well-documented CDM RuleFrame. Database modeling standards and guidelines can be as follows:

- Table names are written in plural.
- Check constraints will be used for short domains on columns. If they are long or not know yet, we use a lookup table.
- The primary key is always named as `id`. This is useful when we want to write reusable generic code.
- For each table we define a short three- or four-letter alias.
- Foreign key column names are constructed as follows:
    1. The alias of the join table name is postfixed with `id`.
    2. For every foreign key we define an index.
- We use database triggers to populate the primary keys and use one sequence that will be used to populate all the primary keys. For the triggers, a script such as the following can be used for all tables:

```
CREATE OR REPLACE TRIGGER doc_bir
BEFORE INSERT ON documents
FOR EACH ROW
BEGIN
  :new_id := NVL(:new_id,all_seq.NEXTVAL);
END;
/
```

- An alternative to triggers and sequence is the use of `sys_guid()`. On the Internet, a lot of information about the pros and cons for both approaches is available. Define all the `id` columns as the `RAW(16)` columns and use `sys_guid()` as a default value for the `id` column. For example:

```
CREATE TABLE t
  ( id       RAW(16) DEFAULT sys_guid() PRIMARY KEY
  , column_a VARCHAR2(10)
  , column_b VARCHAR2(10)
  ...
  )
  /
```

Creating the database objects

The first thing we have to do is create the database schema, which will hold the database objects. We can use the SQL Workshop of APEX for creating the database objects, but its use is very limited compared to the specialized CASE tools.

The following objects can be created in the application schema:

- Tables
- Primary keys
- Unique constraints
- Foreign keys
- Indexes on the foreign keys
- Other indexes
- Sequences
- Scripts for insert and update triggers on the tables to generate an ID
- Other objects (packages, materialized views, and so on)

Other tools

Beside the tools for creating a model, we need some tools during the further development process, tools for accessing the database easily, and tools for web development. Without going into detail, we will just name a few tools that you can use.

Examples of database tools are:

- Toad
- SQL Developer
- PL/SQL Developer

Tools for web development, HTML, CSS, and JavaScript are as follows:

- Aptana
- Firebug
- Web Developer
- Internet Explorer Developer Tools
- Built-in tools in the browser

Miscellaneous tools:

- Versioning tools
- Performance measurement tools
- GUI design tools

Refer to *Chapter 5, Debugging and Troubleshooting* for the details on other tools.

PL/SQL usage

We use the following guidelines regarding PL/SQL:

- Keep PL/SQL in APEX to an absolute minimum
- Try to store all your PL/SQL in packages in the database
- Replace PL/SQL blocks in APEX with simple calls to the functions and procedures in those packages.

This approach has the following advantages:

- Easier to debug
- Higher maintainability, due to more structure
- Better reusability possible
- Don't deploy an application each time there is a change in PL/SQL
- Easier to tune

Creating a workspace

We have installed APEX and the database objects, now we have to create a workspace that will hold our applications. A workspace is linked to one or more schemas in the database. Workspaces can contain zero or more applications. An application in a workspace can access all the objects of the workspace schemas. The following diagram explains the relation between workspaces and applications:

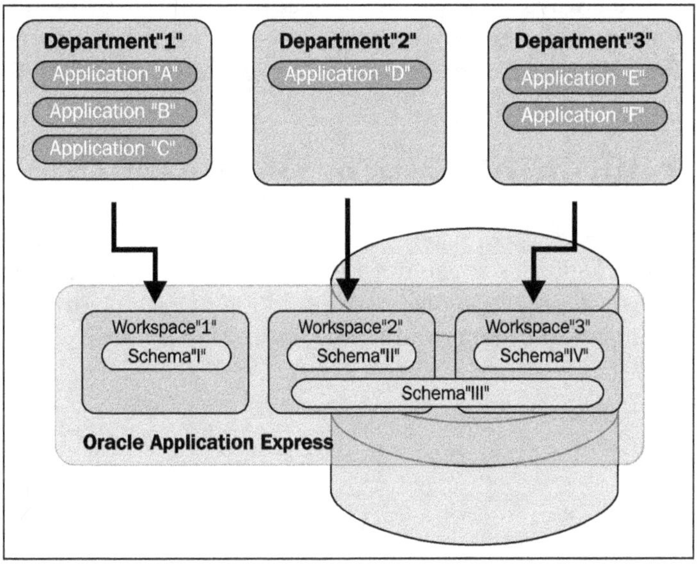

Relationship between workspaces and applications

If security issues are expected, it is possible to create a dedicated empty schema for the workspace and grant access to only the database objects that are needed for that schema. Applications in that workspace can only access the objects that have been granted to the schema.

When we want to create a workspace we have to log in to the APEX Administration Services. In APEX there are two special workspaces. Internal as mentioned before is, as the name implies, the internal workspace used by APEX itself. There is also another workspace called `com.oracle.apex.repository`, which is used for themes.

Once logged in to the Internal workspace, we see the screen shown in the following screenshot:

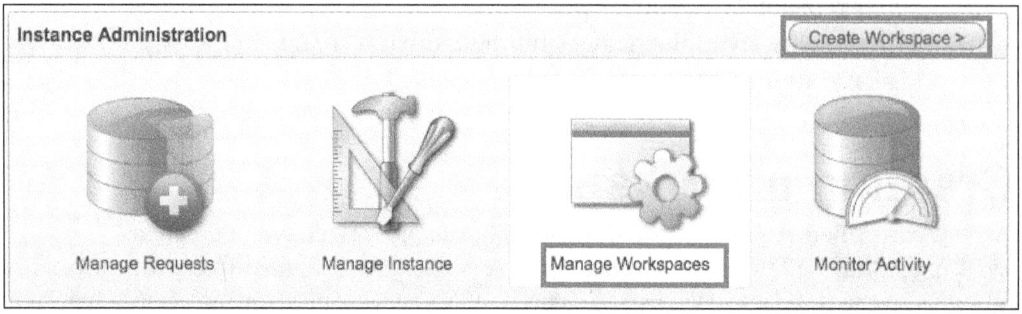

Creating a workspace

We have two possible ways to create a workspace: directly by using the button or indirectly through the **Manage Workspaces** option, where we have to click on **Create Workspace**. After filling in the details in the wizard, the workspace will be created.

Creating administrators, developers, and users

When creating a workspace, we also need to create an administrator for the workspace. If the workspace is in place, we could log in to the workspace as the administrator and add other administrators, developers, and end users.

User Interface Defaults

After creating the workspace and users, it's the moment to use the User Interface Defaults possibilities in APEX—do not start building applications immediately. This option isn't used very much in practice, but it's a very useful utility. With User Interface Defaults, we populate initial values and control the appearance and behavior of items when using them in reports and items (in forms). User Interface Defaults can accelerate your development and result in less repetition of tasks in APEX. You can compare its possibilities with table and column properties in Oracle Designer.

User Interface Defaults don't work retroactively; they only apply to newly built objects. User Interface Defaults can provide consistency across multiple pages for all the applications in our workspace. It's also possible to export and import the User Interface Defaults, to use them in another workspace.

APEX provides two types of dictionaries for this purpose:

- Attribute Dictionary
- Table Dictionary

Attribute Dictionary

The Attribute Dictionary consists of a simple set of attributes. The definitions are matched only by column name, and a particular definition can be shared amongst several columns by creating synonyms.

Table Dictionary

In the Table Dictionary, the defaults are defined by table and column combinations. The Table Dictionary is more specific than the Attribute Dictionary, because more properties can be defined in this one. When processed during the use of a creation wizard for a region or item, an entry in the Table Dictionary takes priority over an entry in the Attribute Dictionary. On table level, we can define some region defaults. It's also possible to migrate the Table Dictionary to the more generic Attribute Dictionary. When migrating, you lose some default properties that don't exist in the Attribute Dictionary (for instance the list of values information).

Another functionality of the Table Dictionary is the use of Column Groups. Related columns within a table can be grouped together. In forms, these groups appear as separate regions and in the single row view of interactive reports.

Creating User Interface Defaults

User Interface Defaults can be defined at the workspace level. Follow these steps to get there:

1. From the **Home** screen, select **SQL Workshop**.
2. Select **Utilities**.
3. Then, select **User Interface Defaults**.

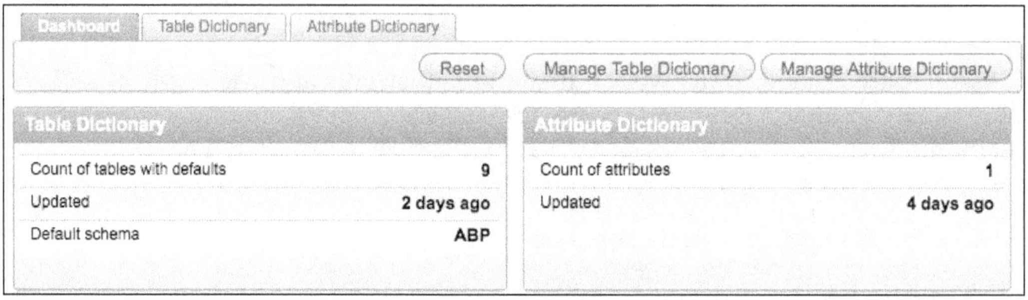

User Interface Defaults Dashboard

On this screen, you'll see the **Dashboard** tab of the User Interface Defaults. You can also see the tabs for **Table Dictionary** and **Attribute Dictionary**.

The simplest way to start using User Interface Defaults is to synchronize the database tables with the Table Dictionary. New tables and columns from the database are added to the Data Dictionary that doesn't exist yet, as well as table and columns that don't exist in the database anymore as they are removed from the Table Dictionary.

After selecting a table entry, we see the following screen:

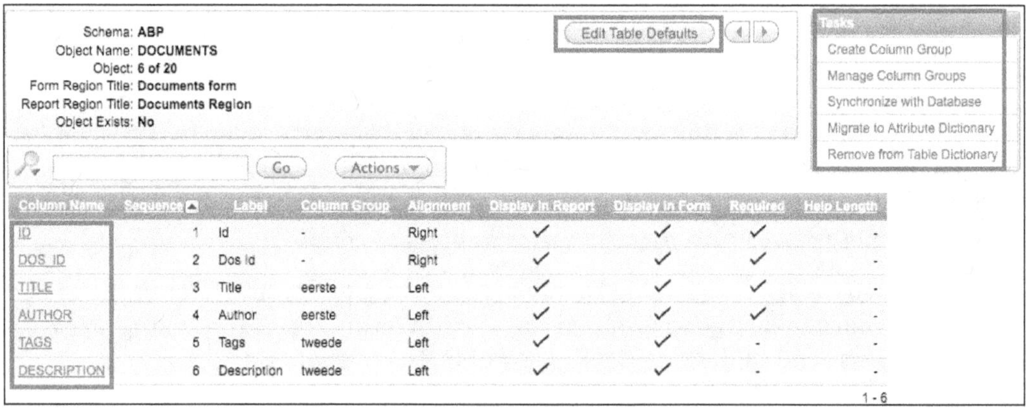

Column properties

On this screen, you can select a column to define the default properties or select **Edit Table Defaults** to define the region titles for this table. You will also see a list of tasks that you can perform. After selecting a column, we see the following screen. This is where the actual work will be done. You can see, for instance, the different sections for **Form Defaults** and **Report and Tabular Form Defaults**.

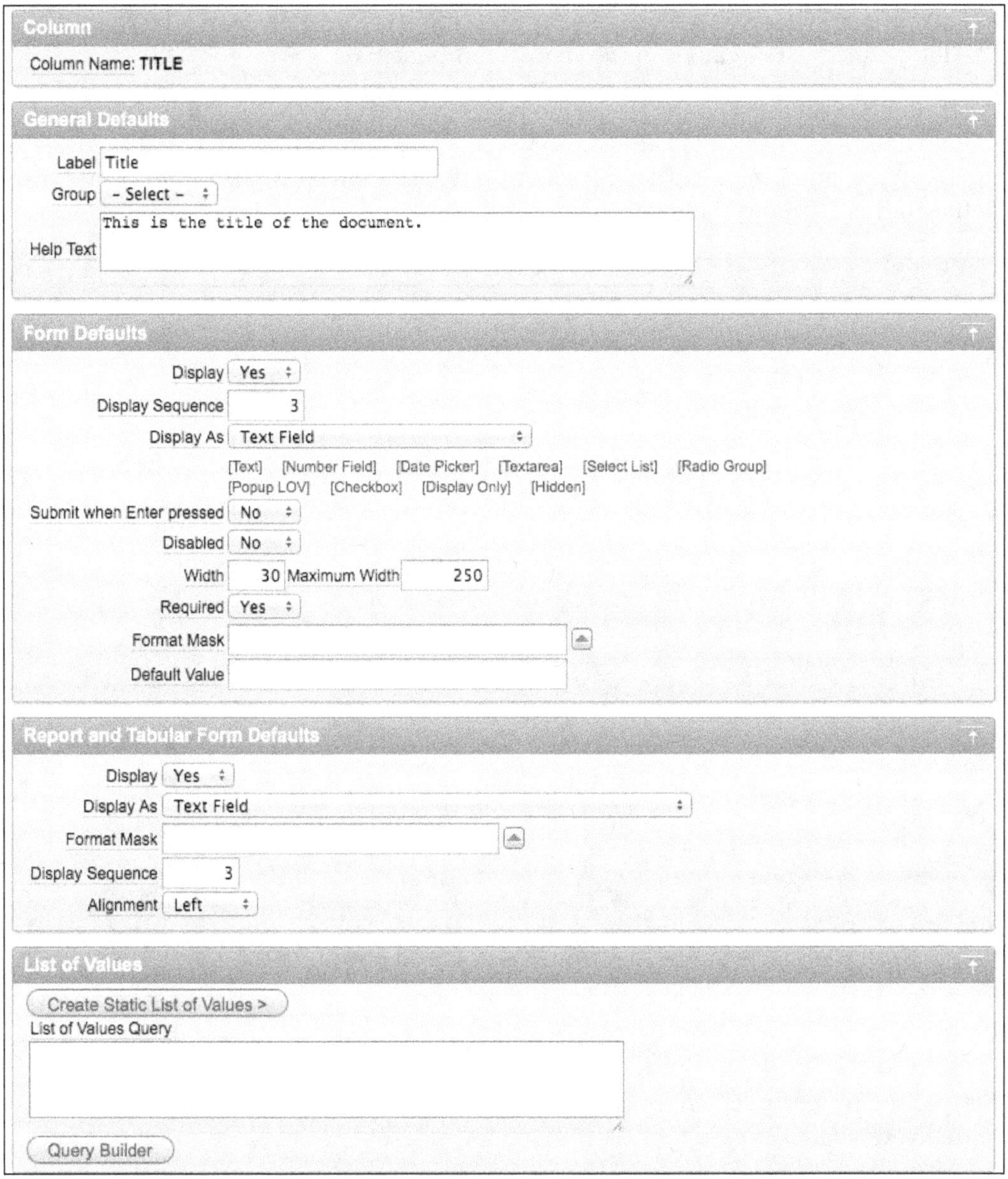

Defaults for the Table Dictionary

> It's good practice to use the plural name of the table for the region name of reports. For the name of the region of a form, we can use the singular name of the table.

A disadvantage of the defined list of values information is the fact that they are defined at workspace level and not at application level, so they cannot be shared like the defined list of values in the shared components.

After filling in all the defaults for all the tables and columns in the Table Dictionary, we can define the Attribute Dictionary by migrating some Table Dictionary entries or defining new ones. In the following screen, you can see the properties that you can define in the Attribute Dictionary:

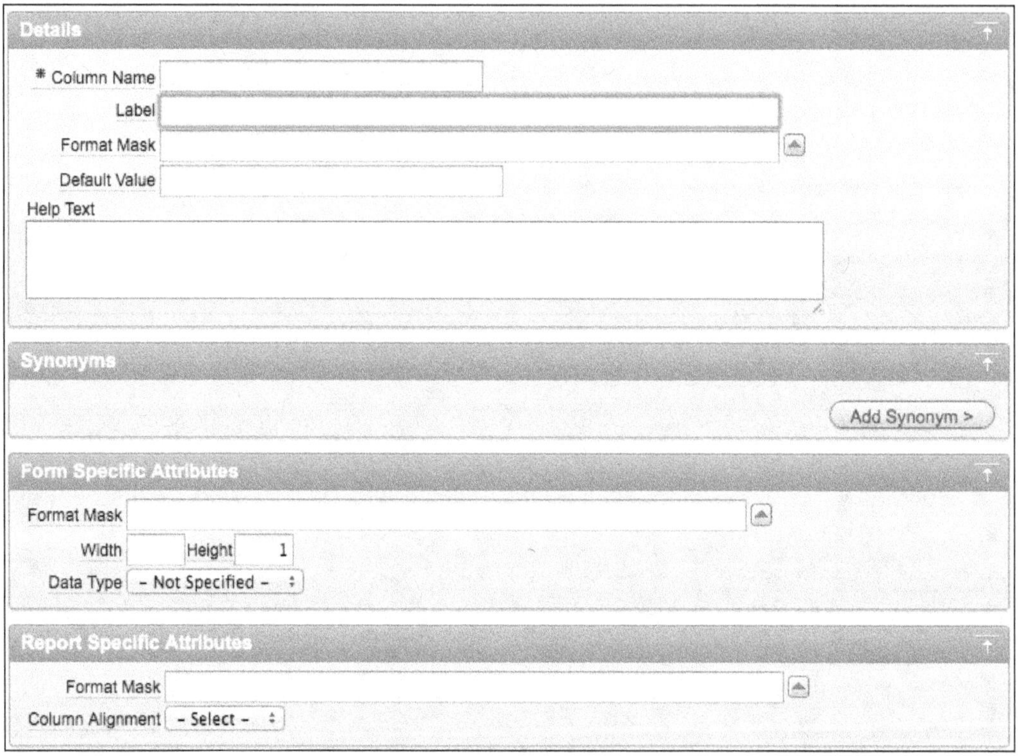

Defaults for the Attribute Dictionary

Besides the property screen for the Attribute Dictionary, we can also use a grid edit to define the defaults easily.

Page Zero

Page Zero acts as a template page for the application. All components of Page Zero will be rendered on all the pages in the application. Compared to a normal page, it consists of only the page rendering part. The following components can be used on Page Zero:

- Computations
- Branches
- Regions, for example, forms, reports, lists, and HTML
- Items
- Dynamic actions

In combination with the use of conditions for the components that determine on which specific pages the components will be rendered, is a flexible place for reusable components. Think, for example, of a menu made up of a list region, centralized help functionality, personal information, task list, and so on.

Page Zero has no processing part. The pages themselves—where the components of Page Zero will be rendered when running the application—will take care of this.

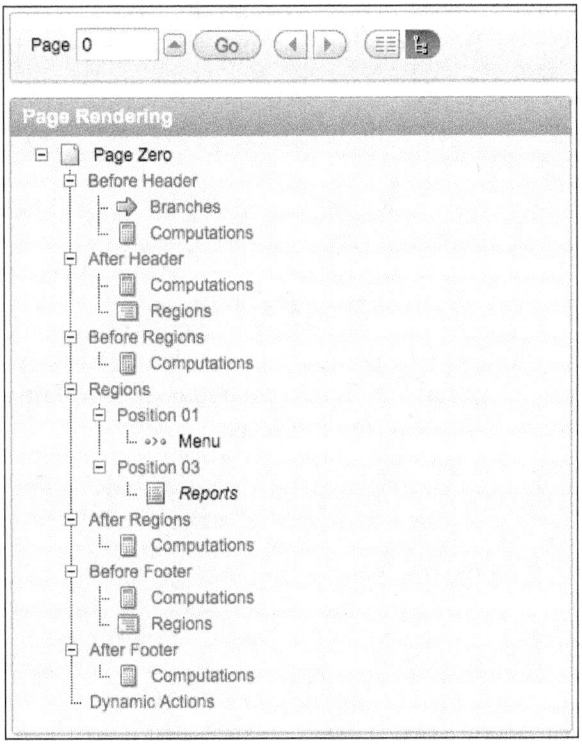

Page Zero

Structure of multiple applications

When creating applications, the less repeating work is done, the better. Within an application you can use shared components for this purpose. If our application (or better said, system) consists of more application modules than one big application, we need another approach. Between multiple applications in the same workspace, we can use the less known subscribe feature of APEX.

By using the subscribe and publish mechanism of APEX, we can create a structure of multiple applications that can serve as a good starting point. Some benefits:

- Better maintainable look and feel across multiple applications
- The use of shared components across applications
- Modular structure
- Reusable centralized functionality, such as authorization, authentication, auditing, and logging

Subscribe and publish

The subscribe and publish mechanism is very straightforward. In the following screenshot, we can see the **Subscription** part of a template definition:

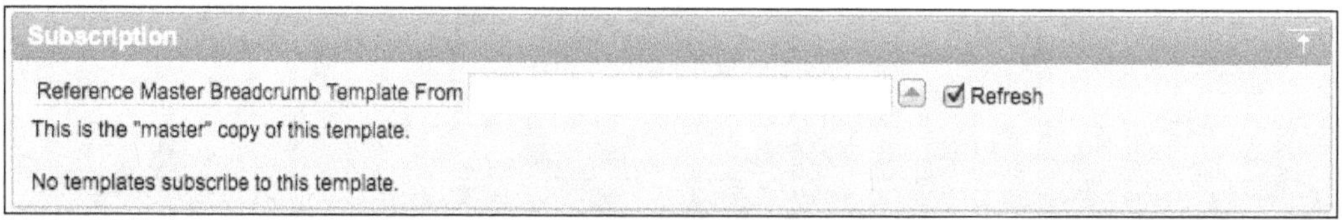

Subscription part of a template

Subscribing and publishing can be compared to pull and push. When defining a template, for instance, it's possible to reference a master template from another application. This is shown in the following screenshot:

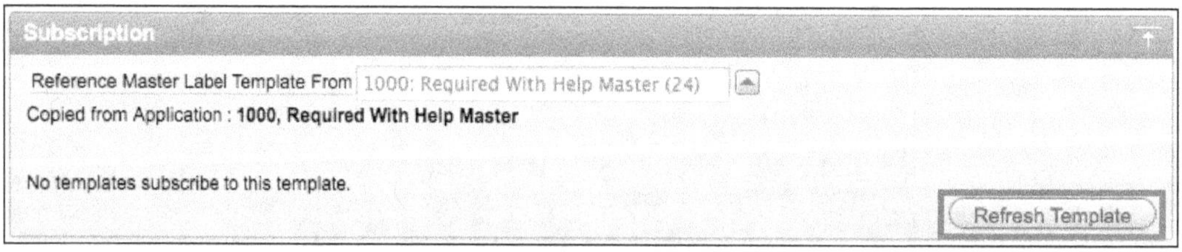

Subscribed to a master template

As we can see, there's a button for refreshing the template. After clicking on the button, the definition of the master template is loaded and copied over the current template. This is the **pulling method**. On the template overview screen, there's also a column **Subscribed** that shows which templates subscribe to a master template. Multiple template refreshing can be accomplished by clicking on the **Subscription** tab on the **Templates overview** screen.

The **pushing method** is done via the master template and it is shown in the following screenshot:

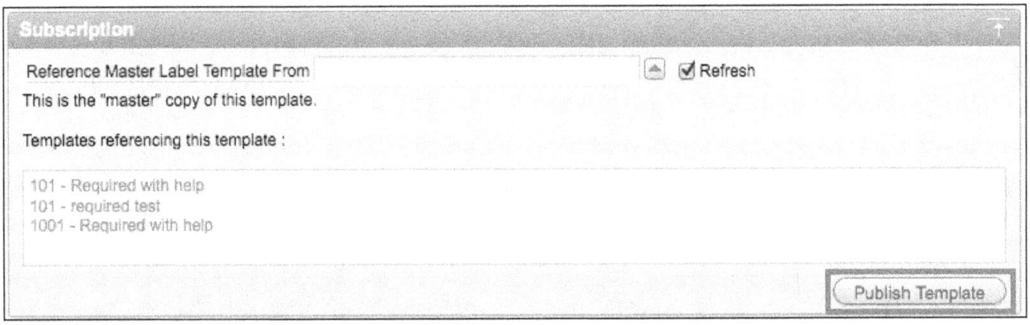

Subscribed from a master template

When we click on the **Publish Template** button, APEX published this master template to all subscribed templates from other applications. Multiple template publishing can be accomplished by clicking on the **Publish** tab on the **Templates overview** screen.

The shared components that can be subject for the subscribe and publish mechanism of APEX are as follows:

- Templates (themes)
- List of values
- Navigation bar entries
- Shortcuts
- Plug-ins
- Authentication schemes
- Authorization schemes

Notes:

- Subscribed objects are updatable, but refreshing them will overwrite these changes.
- Subscribing and publishing only works within a single workspace. It's not possible to reference, for instance, a template from an application in another workspace.

Creating a framework

A well thought out structure of applications can serve as a framework for all our future development. To create such a framework, we need a number of applications, depending on the complexity of the system and our specific needs. The applications to build are a master application, template application, and optionally a login application and/or a system application. The template application serves as a basis for the actual applications to build (application 1 to n), as we can see in the following diagram:

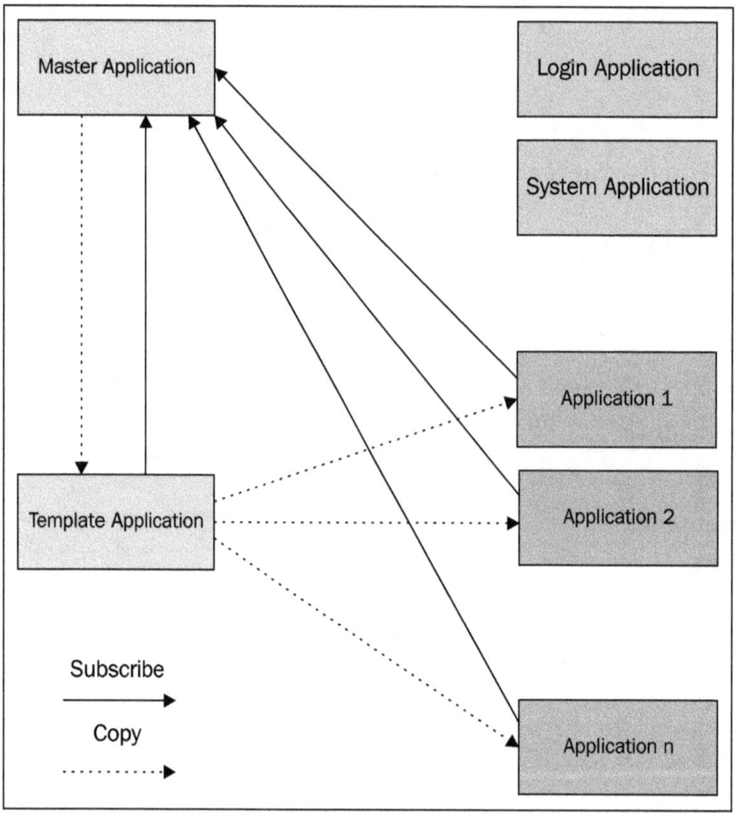

Application framework

Master and template application

Create a master application that contains publishable shared components such as authentication schemes, authorization schemes, lists of values, and templates. Changes can be pushed from the master application to all subscribing applications. Other applications will reference the standard templates by subscribing to the master application.

To make newly created applications subscribe to the master application, we need to create a template application. Create the template application as a copy of the master application and change the subscription of all the shared components to reference the master application. To change the subscription of multiple templates, you can replace templates in this application with templates from another application. This can only be done for currently used templates. Another option is to delete templates and recreate them as a copy (and subscribe) from the master application. The remaining templates and shared components can be modified manually.

The template application is also the place where Page Zero is added.

In more complex situations, the master can have more than one theme or more variants of shared components. We can then create more than one template—which serve as a starting point for the applications.

To create a new application, we simply need to make a copy of the template application. Because the new application is a copy, all the subscriptions to the master application are also copied. For the shared components, it's always possible to unsubscribe. To unsubscribe from multiple templates, the **Unsubscribe Templates** option from the **Task** menu can be selected.

Login application—optional

When more than one application in the workspace share the same authentication, we can extend the framework with an application dedicated to the authentication process. This application will handle the login and can serve as a starting menu for the other applications.

We can create this login application as a copy of the template application. The authentication of this application is different than the other applications. Here we create the actual authentication schema, which we want to use in all our applications.

When switching between applications without having to log in again, we need to share the session state between the applications. To do so we have to give the session cookie the same name. We do that in the authentication schema of the master application.

We also need to get redirected to this application when a user tries to log in directly to one of the applications. We can accomplish this by redirecting to this application by setting the **Session Not Valid** property of the authentication schema in the master application to redirect to the login application. In APEX 4.1.1, you are automatically redirected to the calling application after successful login.

Optionally, we can also set the logout URL to point to a specific page in the login application.

In the following screenshot, we can see the relevant authentication scheme settings for the master application:

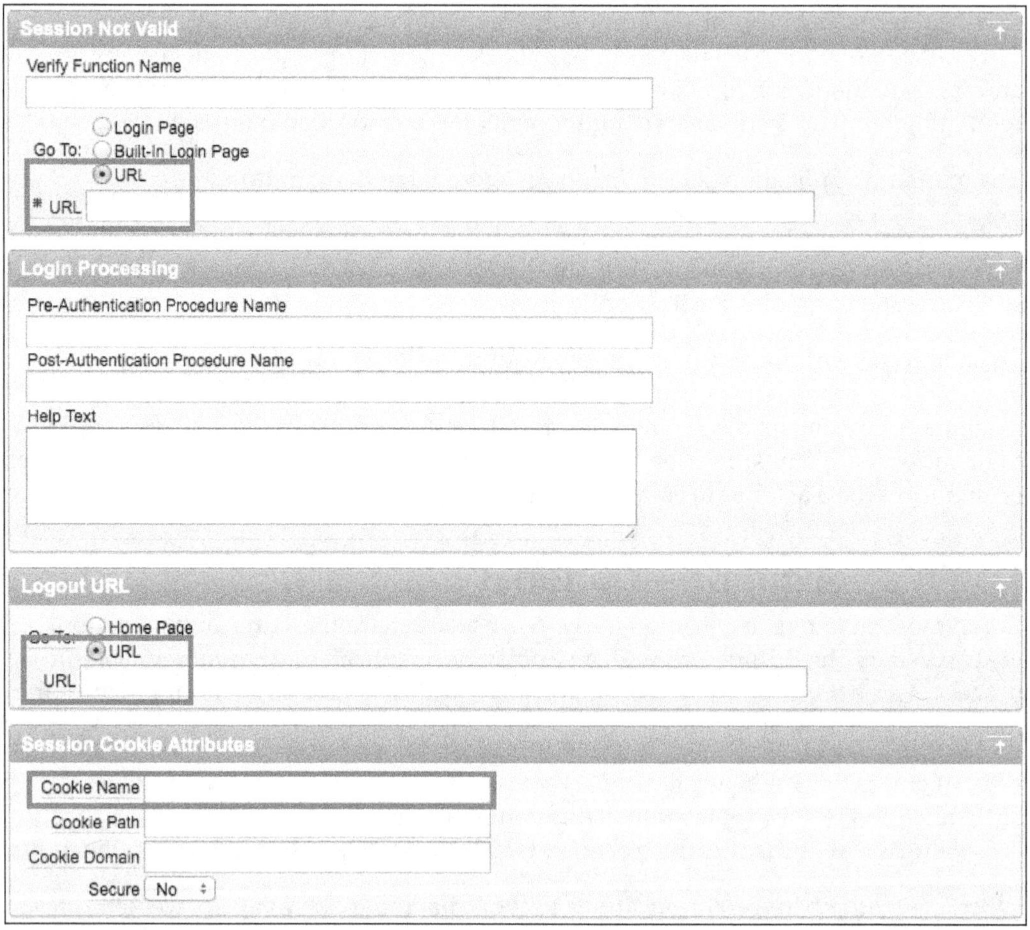

Authentication scheme settings

Other examples of pages that can be included in this application are as follows:

- User registration page for self-service applications: It can also have the functionality to send a confirmation e-mail with a link in it, which leads to an activation page.
- Application start page.
- Personal account settings page.
- Password forgotten page to reset an old password: An email with the new password is sent to the user. The e-mail can also contain a link to a landing page to change it immediately.
- Change the password page to let passwords expire after a given period of time.
- Help pages for the application(s).

System application—optional

Besides a login application, we can also create a system application for the more technically oriented system administrator or DBA. This application will offer control and maintenance functionality for all other applications and/or the whole system.

Possible functionality includes:

- Controlling e-mail queues.
- Performance reports of the pages and applications: This is also possible in APEX itself, but it could be useful to be able to access it in a convenient way within the application.
- Reading the APEX Feedback.
- Dealing with user approval of a self-service application.
- Inspecting (error) logs.
- Setting system parameters such as mail host address, mail host port, colors, and so on.
- Inspecting jobs.
- A structure for maintaining user and access roles: On this structure we can build some functionality that can be incorporated into the authorization scheme of the master application.
- Maintaining system parameters.

Depending on the situation, a part of this functionality can be part of the normal application administrator tasks of the system as well.

Deploying

To deploy these applications, we just need to export them and then do an import in the target environment, just as a single application. If it applies to the situation, also deploy the login and system application. It's not necessary to deploy the master or template application.

Template workspace

If you develop many projects for different companies with different needs, we need to create a framework for every new customer/system. What we need is in fact a template workspace as the starting point for creating the actual workspace, with a master template and login/system applications in it with the minimal used common functionality.

When we start a new project, we need to create a new workspace and place all the applications in it with export and import. If we want to use the same application IDs, we have to set up such a template workspace in a separate database.

Creating applications

Now all the definitions are in place and preparation work is done, we can finally start building our applications. Go to the Application Builder in your workspace and create an application, either by making a copy of the template application or by clicking on the **Create** button.

List of values

One of the first things that we need to tackle is the creation of list of values. There are two kinds of list of values—static and dynamic. A static list of values consists of a limited number of possible values. A dynamic list of values is defined by a query that returns the possible values. For dynamic list of values, it's also possible to make them even more dynamic, by just typing in a function that returns (dynamically) a query.

Most of the list of values will be dynamic, but we can easily think of a few static list of values that will be used in almost every system and thus are a good candidate for the template application. Two examples of them are the Yes/No and the Male/Female list of values.

If for some reason we create a list of values definition for an item by typing in a query, instead of referencing a pre-created shared component list of values, we can easily create a real reusable list of values for it, by clicking on the **Convert LOV** task. This wizard will create a reusable component list of values and replace the hand-made query with a reference to the new list of values.

There are two sources to identify our first set of application-specific list of values. The first one is for short domains, used in check constraints of a column in a table. These values can be used in static list of values. The second source is to identify base tables and create dynamic list of values of them. To identify them, see the *Base Tables* section discussed later in this chapter.

When creating list of values, always use the aliases `d` and `r` or `display_value` and `return_value` for the two columns in the query, just to be clear which values are displayed and returned.

After creating our first set of list of values, we need to add more list of values as we build our system. For more performance-related information on list of values, refer to *Chapter 2, Leveraging the Database*.

Mapping the model to pages

The next step is to map our data model to APEX pages. With mapping we mean that for every table in the data model we must define pages (with respect to the desired functionality) to manipulate or query the data. There could be exceptions, such as parameter or logging tables, although pages for those tables could also be very useful, though not necessary for a properly functioning application.

We have some guidelines regarding pages:

- If we are just selecting and if we want the user to enhance and adjust the resulting (report) page, we should use interactive reports, otherwise we should use normal reports.
- Don't confuse the user with too many objects on a page. On the other hand, we don't want to create too many pages for simple tasks.
- Basic tables should be maintained on a single page.
- Forms can always be put on a separate screen and if necessary, can be called from a link in a report.
- Be sure to use User Interface Defaults for consistency.
- Use region columns where appropriate.
- Use nested region where appropriate.

Some other points to take into account are as follows:

- At the moment, it's not possible to put more than one tabular form or more than one interactive report on a single page.
- Drawback of having everything on a single page is the number of buttons with the same name, and so on. Rename some of them, but be consistent with that renaming throughout the application. Also, some kind of current record indicator is needed. This can be accomplished by manipulating the report template.

Basically we use the following regions for building or composing a page:

- SQL report
- Interactive report
- Form on a table or view
- Tabular form
- Form on table with report
- Master detail form

When we build a page, we look at the data model and along with the requirements we try to combine one or more of these regions. Also we link those regions to each other where appropriate. While building the pages we also create the processes, validations, computations, extra items, dynamic actions, and so on, which we need to achieve the desired functionality.

Base tables

We begin with base tables that we have to maintain. These base tables are often used in LOVs. A way to recognize a base table is to look at the number of foreign keys. If there are no foreign keys in the table, it's a good candidate for a base table. Another characteristic of base tables is that the data is more or less static. It's also good practice to group these pages together on a separate tab with a name such as Basic Data or System.

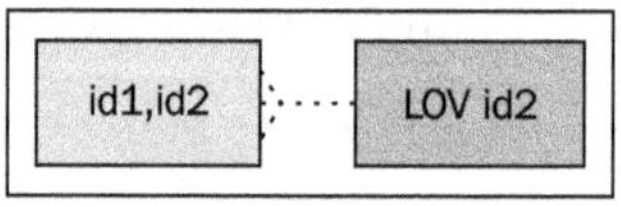

Base table with one list of values

Depending on the number of columns in the base table we have two choices regarding the layout:

- If there are a few columns in the base table, we can use a tabular form if the total width of all the columns is not too wide when placed side by side. We don't want the user to scroll horizontally.
- If we have too many columns, we can use a form on the table with a report to layout the columns neatly in the form. We could also use this approach when we have a few columns. If we do not want the user to switch between too many pages, we can generate both the form and report on one single page. We can accomplish that by filling in the same page number for the form and report in the wizard. After that we may want to place the report above the form.

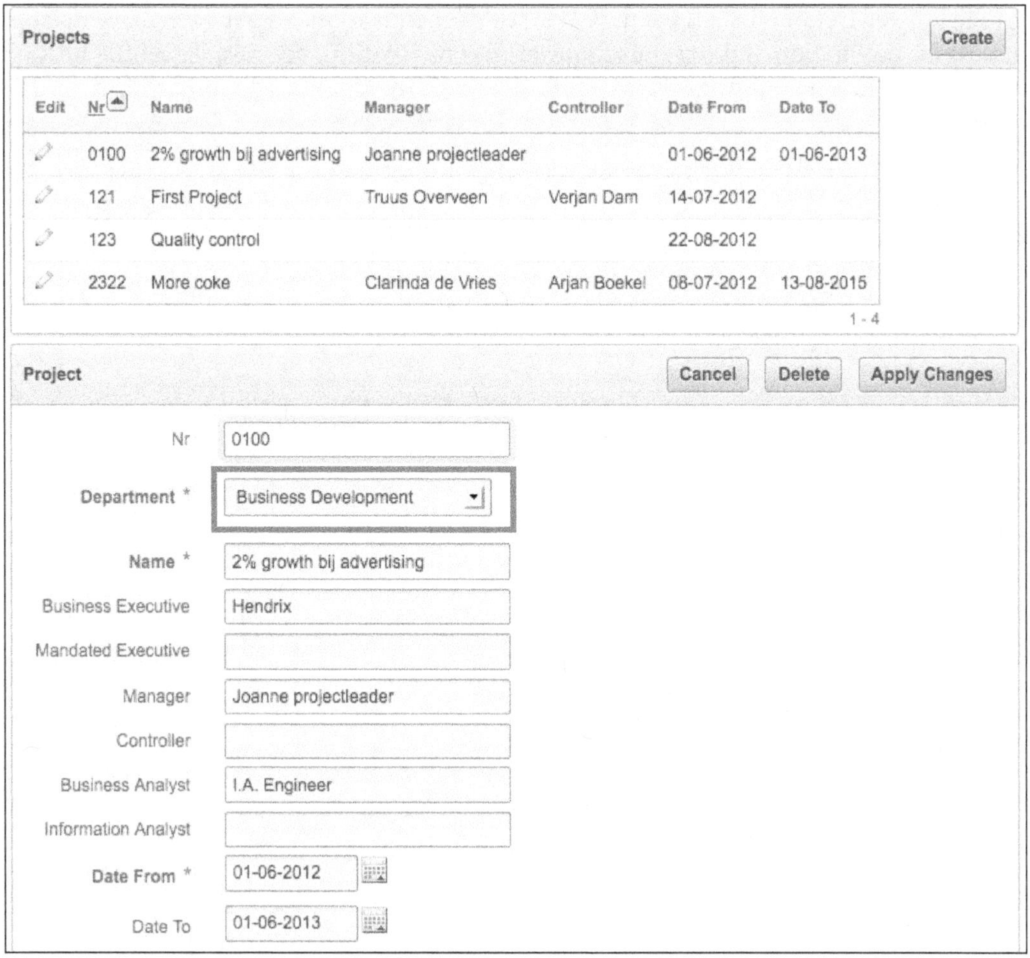

Form on a table with report

Master detail

By looking at the model, we can identify possible candidate tables for a master detail table.

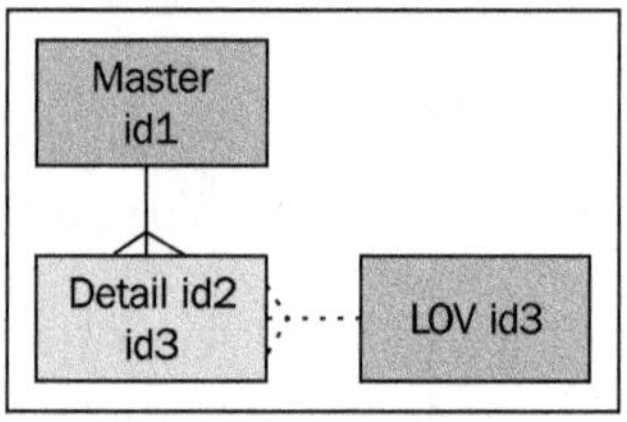

Master detail tables with one LOV

In the Master Detail wizard, we have a lot of decisions to make. Always use a master report for navigation and don't use master row navigation, because it's a little bit confusing when navigating. We can choose to edit the detail as a tabular form on the same page.

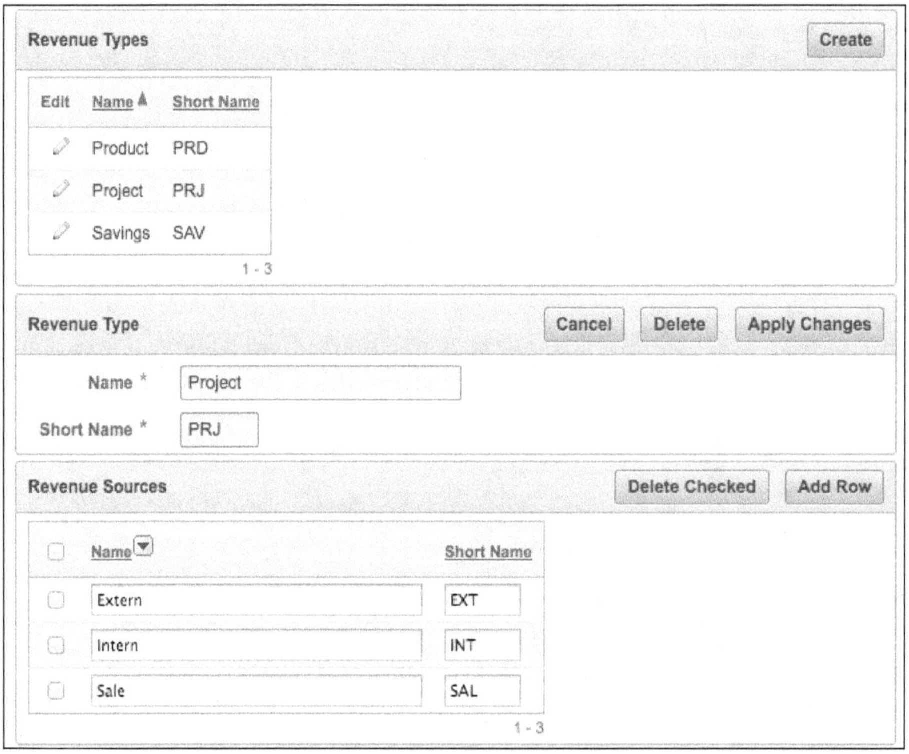

Master detail page, detail as tabular form

Another option is to generate a report as a detail region with a form on a separate page or the same page. As with base table pages, it depends on the number of columns in the detail table.

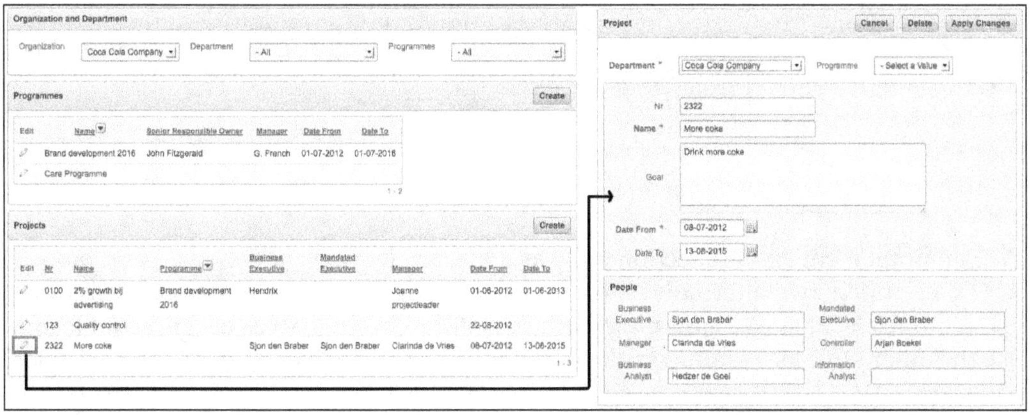

Master detail page, detail on separate page as a form

If we do not want the user to switch between too many pages, we fill in the same page number for the components that we want to appear on the same page. After that we need to place the report above the form. Beware of using breadcrumbs when we put all the regions on one page. In that case, we will get the `ORA-00001: unique constraint (APEX_040000.WWV_FLOW_UNIQUE_MENU_OPT) violated` error.

Depending on whether the master is already a base table with its own page we can maintain that table here. If we don't want to maintain it here, we can hide that generated region, so the form will never be shown. We don't have to delete it, so that we can always use it later, if necessary. After the wizard, we have to rearrange some regions to get the right page.

Another variant is master detail detail. In that case, we have to link the regions together manually.

Intersection

An intersection table can be recognized by the fact that they also have—besides their own ID—two IDs from the foreign keys. It's also possible that the intersection table contains other foreign keys or columns.

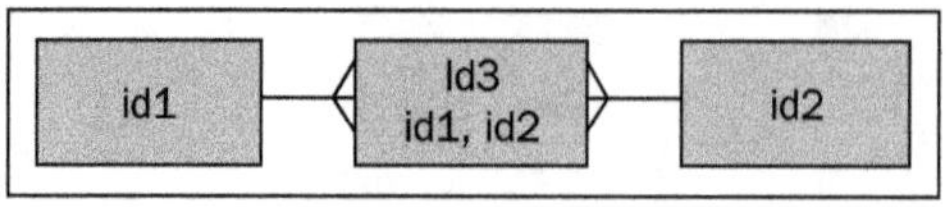

Intersection table

We can implement an intersection table as a master detail page with an LOV, but APEX also offers two alternatives to implement an intersection table—a shuttle and a multiselect list. We can implement one of the driving tables as a base table and use the other table as a lookup table. In the following screenshot we see an example of a shuttle:

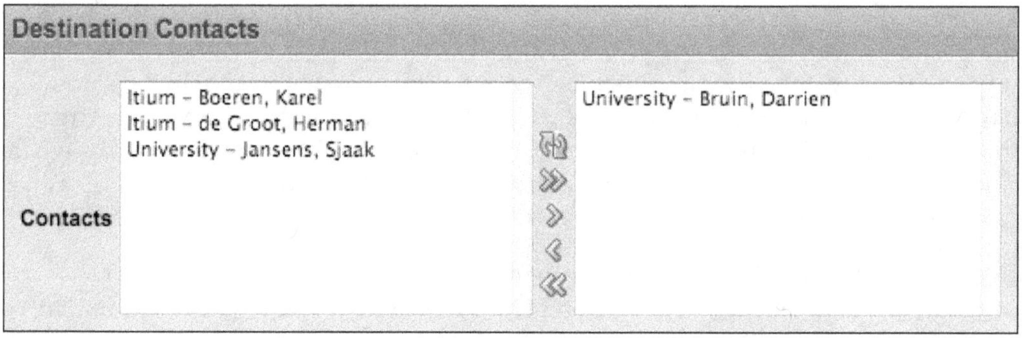

Shuttle

In the following screenshot, we can see the use of a multiselect list:

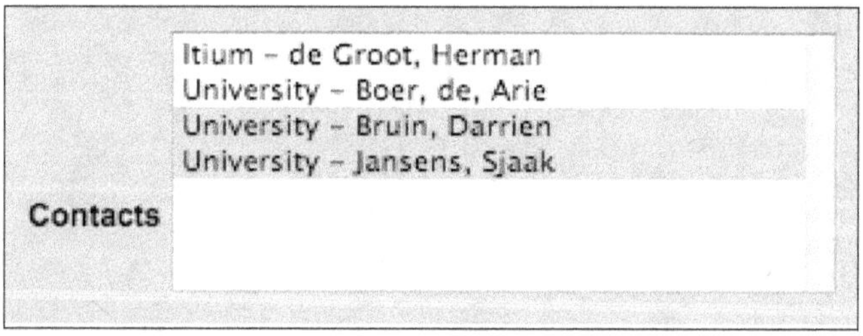

Multiselect list

Unfortunately, APEX doesn't offer standard processes for populating and maintaining shuttles or multiselect lists. The following function and procedure can be used as a generic solution for these processes. You should put them in a package and write exception handlers to log and deal with the errors that can occur (see next chapters in this book). The function `get_selectlist` can be used to populate the item. We call this function in the `On Load - After Header` process and after the `Fetch Row` process, which is generated by the wizard (if present):

```
FUNCTION GET_SELECTLIST
  (P_INTERSECTION_TABLE IN VARCHAR2
  ,P_LOOKUP_FK_NAME IN VARCHAR2
  ,P_MASTER_FK_NAME IN VARCHAR2
  ,P_MASTER_FK_VALUE IN VARCHAR2
  )
  RETURN VARCHAR2
  IS
-- Get the selectlist value as a list e.g. 1:2:4 .
-- Create the process to fire After Header and after
-- the wizard generated Fetch Row process.

  l_selected      APEX_APPLICATION_GLOBAL.VC_ARR2;
  l_sql_statement VARCHAR2(1000);
  l_dummy_number  NUMBER;


BEGIN

-- Check if master foreign key value is a number
  l_dummy_number := TO_NUMBER(p_master_fk_value);

  IF p_lookup_fk_name     IS NOT NULL AND
    p_intersection_table IS NOT NULL AND
    p_master_fk_name     IS NOT NULL AND
    p_master_fk_value    IS NOT NULL THEN

    l_sql_statement :=
      'SELECT ' || p_lookup_fk_name     || ' ' ||
      'FROM '   || p_intersection_table || ' ' ||
      'WHERE '  || p_master_fk_name     ||
      '=' || p_master_fk_value ;

    EXECUTE IMMEDIATE l_sql_statement BULK COLLECT INTO
    l_selected;

  END IF;

  -- Assign the colon separated list to l_selected
  RETURN APEX_UTIL.TABLE_TO_STRING(l_selected);
```

```
    EXCEPTION WHEN OTHERS THEN
      NULL; -- logging can be done here!

END;
```

If the intersection item `P250_shuttle` is called and the driving table ID is stored in `P250_id`, the call to this function could look as follows:

```
: P250_shuttle := get_selectlist
    ( p_intersection_table => 'dep_pages'
    , p_lookup_fk_name => 'pag_id'
    , p_master_fk_name => 'dep_id'
    , P_master_fk_value => :P250_id);
```

Beware of SQL injection and keep `P250_id` hidden and protected.

The procedure `set_selectlist` can be used to store the changes made in the shuttle or multiselect list. We call the function `On Submit - After Validations and Computations` and after that we call the DML processes generated by the wizard. Be aware of a reset process. If such a process is present, we have to call our procedure before the reset process. Otherwise, we lose all our changes and nothing is saved.

```
PROCEDURE SET_SELECTLIST
  (P_LIST IN VARCHAR2
  ,P_INTERSECTION_TABLE IN VARCHAR2
  ,P_LOOKUP_FK_NAME IN VARCHAR2
  ,P_MASTER_FK_NAME IN VARCHAR2
  ,P_MASTER_FK_VALUE IN VARCHAR2
  )
  IS
-- Insert the selectlist value (as a list e.g. 1:2:4) into
-- the intersection table. This process fires After Submit
-- and after the wizard generated process that handles
-- inserts, updates and deletes on the master table.
  l_selected      APEX_APPLICATION_GLOBAL.VC_ARR2;
  l_sql_statement VARCHAR2(1000);
  l_id            NUMBER;
  l_dummy_number  NUMBER;

BEGIN

  -- Check if master foreign key value is a number
  l_dummy_number := TO_NUMBER(p_master_fk_value);

  IF p_lookup_fk_name      IS NOT NULL AND
    p_intersection_table IS NOT NULL AND
    p_master_fk_name     IS NOT NULL AND
    p_master_fk_value    IS NOT NULL THEN
```

```
  -- Convert the colon separated string of values
  -- into a PL/SQL array
  l_selected := HTMLDB_UTIL.STRING_TO_TABLE(p_list);

  -- Clean up the intersection table first
  -- Delete necessary records only
  l_sql_statement :=
    'DELETE FROM ' || p_intersection_table || ' ' ||
    'WHERE '  || p_master_fk_name || '=' ||
    p_master_fk_value || ' ' ||
    'AND  instr('':''|| p_list ||'':'','':''||TO_CHAR('||
    p_lookup_fk_name||')||'':'' )=0'
  EXECUTE IMMEDIATE l_sql_statement;

  -- Loop over the array to insert lookup_ids and
  -- master_id into the intersection table
  FOR i IN 1..l_selected.count LOOP

    -- Check if the record already exists
    l_sql_statement :=
      'SELECT ' || l_selected(i) ||' ' ||
      'FROM ' || p_intersection_table || ' ' ||
      'WHERE '  || p_master_fk_name || '=' ||
      p_master_fk_value || ' ' ||
      'AND ' || p_lookup_fk_name ||'='|| l_selected(i);

  BEGIN
    -- when the record exists do nothing
    EXECUTE IMMEDIATE l_sql_statement INTO l_id;
    EXCEPTION WHEN OTHERS THEN
    -- In case there is no record, insert it
    l_sql_statement :=
    'INSERT INTO ' || p_intersection_table || ' ' ||
    '(' || p_master_fk_name || ',' ||
    p_lookup_fk_name || ') ' ||
    'VALUES (' || p_master_fk_value || ',' ||
    l_selected(i) || ')';
     -- no parent key exception
    BEGIN
      EXECUTE IMMEDIATE l_sql_statement;
      EXCEPTION WHEN OTHERS THEN
      NULL; -- logging can be done here!
    END;
  END;

  END LOOP;

END IF;
```

```
    EXCEPTION WHEN OTHERS THEN
      NULL; -- logging can be done here!

END;
```

If the intersection item P250_shuttle is called and the driving table ID is stored in P250_id, the call to this procedure could look as follows:

```
set_selectlist ( p_list => :P250_shuttle
                 , p_intersection_table => 'dep_pages'
                 , p_lookup_fk_name => 'pag_id'
                 , p_master_fk_name => 'dep_id'
                 , p_master_fk_value => :P250_ID );
```

Simple report

If we have only one simple read-only table or query for a page, we can use a SQL report or an interactive report. With the latter, the user has a lot of possibilities, including the presentation and filtering of the data.

Other pages

There are always certain pages that don't fall in the aforementioned categories, with special functionality—for example, parameter sections or charts with management information. These pages must be built up with separate regions and after that those must be attached together. Another example is a wizard for the end user that can be used to accomplish rather complex input tasks with validations between the sub-screens.

Summary

With every new version of APEX, new features and capabilities are being added to the tool and it's constantly evolving. It's almost impossible to describe all the possibilities of APEX in this chapter, but with the information in this chapter you will be able to kick start and structure your development.

In this chapter, we got an overview of the installation and preparation tasks before actually building the application. We discussed User Interface Defaults and the application structure. We saw techniques to transform the data model into initial screen designs. We also discussed a lot of best practices and guidelines during the building phase.

In the next chapter, we will be using some advanced database features to enhance our application.

2
Leveraging the Database

Even with basic SQL and PL/SQL skills, it is possible to create applications with APEX that are both fast and secure. You probably know that the APEX engine is built by using SQL and PL/SQL. This means that all the features available in SQL and PL/SQL are available to you when you create an application with APEX. When you leverage the functionality that the database has to offer, you will get functionality developed and supported by Oracle. By utilizing the built-in functionality, you will not only save time, but also money to be spent on development. The key thing is to leverage what is available to you instead of trying to reinvent the wheel.

In this chapter we will cover the following subjects:

- Instrumentation
- Efficient lookup tables
- Analytic and aggregate functions
- Offloading long running programs
- Pipelined table functions
- Resizing images
- Oracle text

Instrumentation

Have you ever found yourself in a situation where a user contacts you and reports a problem, which you can't reproduce on your own environment? What would really be helpful is knowing how your code was being used, with which values your stored procedures were called, and which code path the user took to get to the situation they found themselves in before they contacted you.

There is a way to know all this information, and the way to get it is by properly instrumenting your code. Instrumenting your developed code means putting in debug statements throughout. In these debug statements, there should be the information you need to track the execution of the developed code. Also, it should be complete with timestamps and other meaningful information.

Tyler Muth has written an excellent utility to help you with instrumenting your code. This package is called **Logger** and can be used to instrument your code—not only your APEX code, but also your database stored procedures. One of the functions that you can use specifically for APEX is to capture all items and values from session state.

> The Logger package, which was written by Tyler Muth and is presently available with release 1.4, can be downloaded for free from `http://sn.im/logger1.4`.
>
> Please note that this is a temporary location; at the time of writing the package was moved to different locations.
>
> When all other approaches fail, you can always search on the Internet for "Muth and Logger"; undoubtedly you will find the current site where this package can be downloaded from.

Inside each of the package bodies that contains the database code, we declare a global constant as follows:

```
g_package constant varchar2(31) := $$plsql_unit||'.';
```

Because we declare it inside the package body, it is available for all procedures and functions inside the package body. `$$plsql_unit` is a predefined inquiry directive that indicates the current program unit. Unfortunately, it only returns the top-level program unit, in this case the name of the package—not the individual procedure inside the package.

Because of this limitation, we use a local constant to identify the procedure name, using the global constant that we have declared previously:

```
l_proc constant varchar2(61) := g_package||'test';
```

In this example, the name of the procedure is concatenated to the global `g_package` and called as `test`. This declaration of the variable should be placed in each procedure and function in the package. The reason we use the global constant concatenated with the name of the procedure is to support the case when the procedure needs to be transferred to a different package. When the procedure moves to a different package, the procedure name remains the same and `g_package` should be available in the other package as well. This way we can easily instrument our code with a template such as the following:

```
begin
    logger.log (p_text  => 'start'
               ,p_scope => l_proc
               );
    logger.log_information
          (p_text  => 'p_parameter: '||p_parameter
          ,p_scope => l_proc
          );
    ...
    logger.log (p_text  => 'end'
               ,p_scope => l_proc
               );
end;
```

The first statement in the code is to signal the beginning of the stored procedure—note the use of the local constant as being passed in the `p_scope` parameter, followed by recording the names, and values of the parameters with which this procedure was being called. The actual code is to be filled in on the three dots. The last line of code should be a line signaling the end of the procedure. If you are using a function instead of a procedure, the returned value should be logged prior to the final return statement. The last part of the template will look as follows, in the case of a function:

```
    logger.log_information
         (p_text  => 'Return Value: '||l_retval
         ,p_scope => l_proc
         );
    logger.log (p_text  => 'End'
               ,p_scope => l_proc
               );
    return l_retval;
end;
```

Using the Logger facility from your APEX application, the usage is slightly different. It is not advisable to use elaborate PL/SQL code in the APEX application itself use calls to stored database code instead. This centralizes the source code, which facilitates re-use.

```
begin
    logger.log (' ** Call the Stored Procedure');
    package.procedure (p_parameter => 'Hello');
end;
```

If needed, you can also store the items and values in the Logger tables:

```
logger.log_apex_items('Debug the called Stored Procedure');
```

A very handy view to query the Logger tables, is `logger_logs_5_min`. This view shows you all the logging statements that happened in the last five minutes. When you run into something you can't explain yet, this view will help in identifying which code path was taken and where it went wrong. There is also a similar view that shows the last 60 minutes worth of logger data. To query the APEX items and values, you need to query `logger_logs_apex_items`.

There is a lot more functionality in the Logger package, and it is certainly worth trying out by yourself. Adding timing information is just one example. Maybe it feels like overkill when you begin with instrumenting your code, but when you instrument your code for the first time you will need it to track down a bug. The information you will get from instrumenting your code is invaluable.

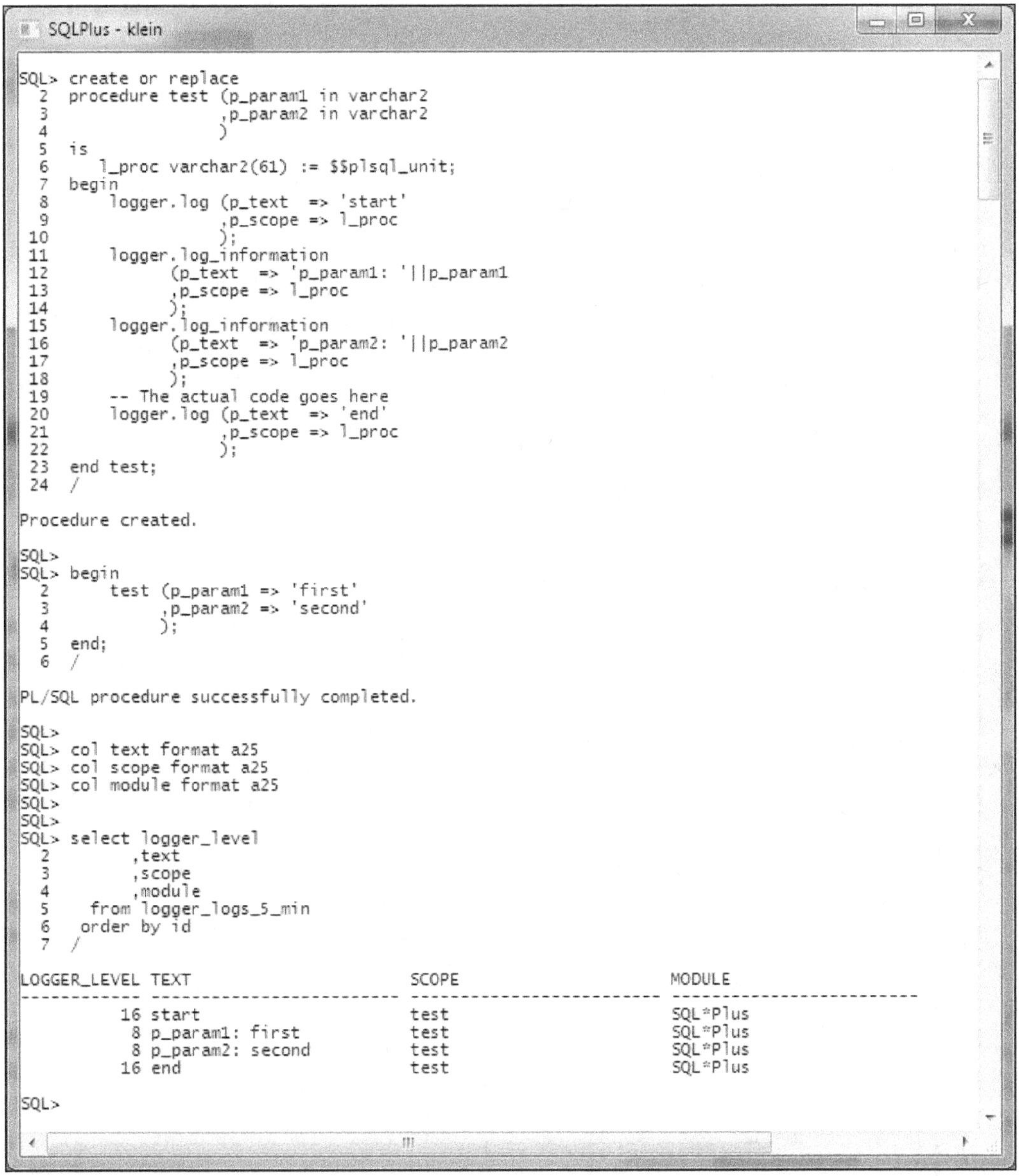
SQLPlus - klein
SQL> create or replace
2 procedure test (p_param1 in varchar2
3 ,p_param2 in varchar2
4)
5 is
6 l_proc varchar2(61) := $$plsql_unit;
7 begin
8 logger.log (p_text => 'start'
9 ,p_scope => l_proc
10);
11 logger.log_information
12 (p_text => 'p_param1: '||p_param1
13 ,p_scope => l_proc
14);
15 logger.log_information
16 (p_text => 'p_param2: '||p_param2
17 ,p_scope => l_proc
18);
19 -- The actual code goes here
20 logger.log (p_text => 'end'
21 ,p_scope => l_proc
22);
23 end test;
24 /
Procedure created.
SQL>
SQL> begin
2 test (p_param1 => 'first'
3 ,p_param2 => 'second'
4);
5 end;
6 /
PL/SQL procedure successfully completed.
SQL>
SQL> col text format a25
SQL> col scope format a25
SQL> col module format a25
SQL>
SQL>
SQL> select logger_level
2 ,text
3 ,scope
4 ,module
5 from logger_logs_5_min
6 order by id
7 /
LOGGER_LEVEL TEXT SCOPE MODULE
16 start test SQL*Plus
8 p_param1: first test SQL*Plus
8 p_param2: second test SQL*Plus
16 end test SQL*Plus
SQL>

Comprehensive example of using the logger package

In the preceding screenshot, you can see a small example of how you can use the Logger package to instrument your code.

The steps that are performed are as follows:

1. A procedure is created with the name `test`. This procedure takes two arguments and the only thing that the procedure does is make calls to the Logger package.
2. The procedure is being executed in an anonymous block where the arguments are being passed by using the named notation.
3. Lastly the `logger_logs_5_min` view is queried to see what is being recorded. There are many more columns available, including the complete callstack.

There are different opinions regarding logging in a production environment. Should you have logging turned on all the time? I believe it should be turned on always. The moment you need logging most is when something goes wrong. This moment is impossible to predict, so keeping logging on is the only option. When you feel really strongly about turning off logging in a production environment, the Logger package also accommodates this. It is possible to install the `logger_no_op` (no operation) version of the package. This is simply a shell that does not log anything in tables; it does not even create the tables.

Efficient lookup tables

Properly designing the data model plays a crucial part in the success of your application. An application can have a really good-looking interface, but when the performance is very poor the users still won't be happy with the application. To ensure your user has an overall positive experience, the application needs to be visually attractive and responsive to the actions that the user carries out.

> Designing the application begins with designing a logical and physical data model. There are many types of database objects, that can be used in an Oracle database, such as heap tables, index organized tables, clusters, b-tree indexes, or bitmap indexes. Each of these objects has its own usage. Before implementing the physical data model, you should know each of these object types and when to use them properly. You will not be able to know which object type to choose, if you don't know how the application is going to be used. Knowing how the application is going to be used, in combination with the available data objects, is key to the success of the application. Your DBA should be able to help you in implementing the proper database objects for your application.

In this section, we will take a closer look at one of the most common types of structure in almost every data model—the lookup table.

Lookup tables are tables where the data change is slow, meaning that the data hardly (if ever after the initial load) changes. The data is inserted once, but is queried very frequently. These tables are often used as **List of Values** (**LOV**) in your application. Because these tables are queried so frequently, it is important to make the actual query as efficient as possible. Tables like these are excellent candidates to be implemented as single-table hash clusters, provided that the size of the table is primarily static and the lookup is done with an equality query. Another option is to use an index-organized table; think of it as a combination of an index and table in one structure. This will be discussed later in this chapter.

Single-table hash clusters

Detailed explanation about single-table hash clusters can be found in the Oracle documentation—*Oracle database concepts, 11g Release 2 (11.2)*—at `http://docs.oracle.com/cd/E11882_01/server.112/e25789/tablecls.htm#CNCPT88831`.

> *"A single-table hash cluster is an optimized version of a hash cluster that supports only one table at a time. A one-to-one mapping exists between hash keys and rows. A single-table hash cluster can be beneficial when users require rapid access to a table by primary key. For example, users often look up an employee record in the employees table by employee_id."*

A lookup table fits this description like a glove.

Normally a database block stores data for exactly one table. A cluster allows you to store data from more than one table on a block. However this is not the case with a single-table hash cluster. As you might have guessed from the name, only the data of a single table is stored in the cluster. The first thing we need before we can create a single-table hash cluster, is the cluster itself:

```
SQL> create cluster lookup_c
  2  (id number)
  3  single table
  4  hashkeys 50000
  5  size 50
  6  /

Cluster created.
```

It is not a regular cluster, but a special type. Line 3 indicates that this cluster is going to be used only for a single table.

When we create the table definition, we need to specify the cluster that we just created and named as `lookup_c`. For this example, we are going to create a table, based on a query, with 50,000 records in it:

```
SQL> create table lookup_hash
  2  (id
  3  ,description
  4  )
  5  cluster lookup_c (id)
  6  as
  7  select rownum
  8       , object_name
  9    from (select * from dba_objects
 10          union all
 11          select * from dba_objects
 12          )
 13   where rownum <= 50000
 14  /

Table created.
```

To generate enough records for this example, `DBA_OBJECTS` is used twice with `UNION ALL` to accommodate the required number of records.

On line 5, we indicate the cluster to be used. The final step for this table is to create a primary key.

```
SQL> alter table lookup_hash
  2  add constraint hspk primary key (id)
  3  /

Table altered.
```

To get a feel of the efficiency of a single-table hash cluster, we need another type of table to compare it with. The content and structure of the comparison table will be identical to the single-table hash cluster. For the comparison, we will create a default table type called a **heap table**.

The following statements will create the heap table with a primary key constraint for the comparison:

```
SQL> create table lookup_heap_t
  2  as
  3  select rownum      id
  4       , object_name description
  5    from (select * from dba_objects
  6          union all
  7          select * from dba_objects
  8          )
  9   where rownum <= 50000
 10  /

Table created.

SQL> alter table lookup_heap_t
  2  add constraint hpk primary key (id)
  3  /

Table altered.
```

Now that both tables are in place, statistics are gathered on both tables. Consider the following query:

```
SQL> begin
  2     dbms_stats.gather_table_stats (user
  3                                    ,'LOOKUP_HASH'
  4                                    ,cascade => true
  5                                    );
  6     dbms_stats.gather_table_stats (user
  7                                    ,'LOOKUP_HEAP_T'
  8                                    ,cascade => true
  9                                    );
 10  end;
 11  /

PL/SQL procedure successfully completed.
```

The following is just a quick test to verify whether there is data in the table or not, and to get the same amount of caching for a single row lookup:

```
SQL> select *
  2    from lookup_hash
  3   where id = 4325
  4  /

        ID DESCRIPTION
---------- ------------------------------
      4325 DBMS_STAT_FUNCS_AUX_LIB

SQL> select *
  2    from lookup_heap_t
  3   where id = 4325
  4  /

        ID    DESCRIPTION
---------- ------------------------------
      4325    DBMS_STAT_FUNCS_AUX_LIB
```

Both queries return the same data from the table; let's have a look at the explain plan for both statements.

> Before you can examine the explain plan and use the autotrace facility as described in the examples, you need to set up `PLAN_TABLE` and create the `PLUSTRACE` role. This role should be granted to the user that is running the examples. `PLAN_TABLE` can be created by using the `utlxplan.sql` file. The `PLUSTRACE` role can be created by using the `plustrce.sql` file.
>
> The location of these files depends on your operating system. You might need to get your DBA involved, as the `PLUSTRACE` role needs to be set up by `SYS`.

```
SQLPlus - klein
SQL> set autot trace expl stat
SQL>
SQL> select *
  2    from lookup_hash
  3   where id = 4325
  4  /

Execution Plan
----------------------------------------------------------
Plan hash value: 1545516788

---------------------------------------------------------------------------------
| Id  | Operation          | Name         | Rows  | Bytes | Cost (%CPU)| Time     |
---------------------------------------------------------------------------------
|   0 | SELECT STATEMENT   |              |     1 |    30 |     1   (0)| 00:00:01 |
|*  1 |  TABLE ACCESS HASH| LOOKUP_HASH  |     1 |    30 |     1   (0)| 00:00:01 |
---------------------------------------------------------------------------------

Predicate Information (identified by operation id):
---------------------------------------------------

   1 - access("ID"=4325)

Statistics
----------------------------------------------------------
          0  recursive calls
          0  db block gets
          1  consistent gets
          0  physical reads
          0  redo size
        412  bytes sent via SQL*Net to client
        411  bytes received via SQL*Net from client
          2  SQL*Net roundtrips to/from client
          0  sorts (memory)
          0  sorts (disk)
          1  rows processed

SQL>
```

Execution plan for a single table hash cluster

For the single-table hash cluster, you can see the effect of the cluster in **Execution Plan**. It shows **TABLE ACCESS HASH**, which is a very efficient way to look up the value that we are searching for. Also, in the **Statistics** part of the preceding screenshot, note the number of **db block gets** and **consistent gets**. These numbers give an indication of the amount of I/O that takes place to return the results to you. The less I/O that needs to be done, the query tends to be more scalable. This means that more requests can be handled without affecting response time and throughput.

From the preceding screenshot, note that the value with **consistent gets** is only **1**.

Let's do the same exercise with the heap table.

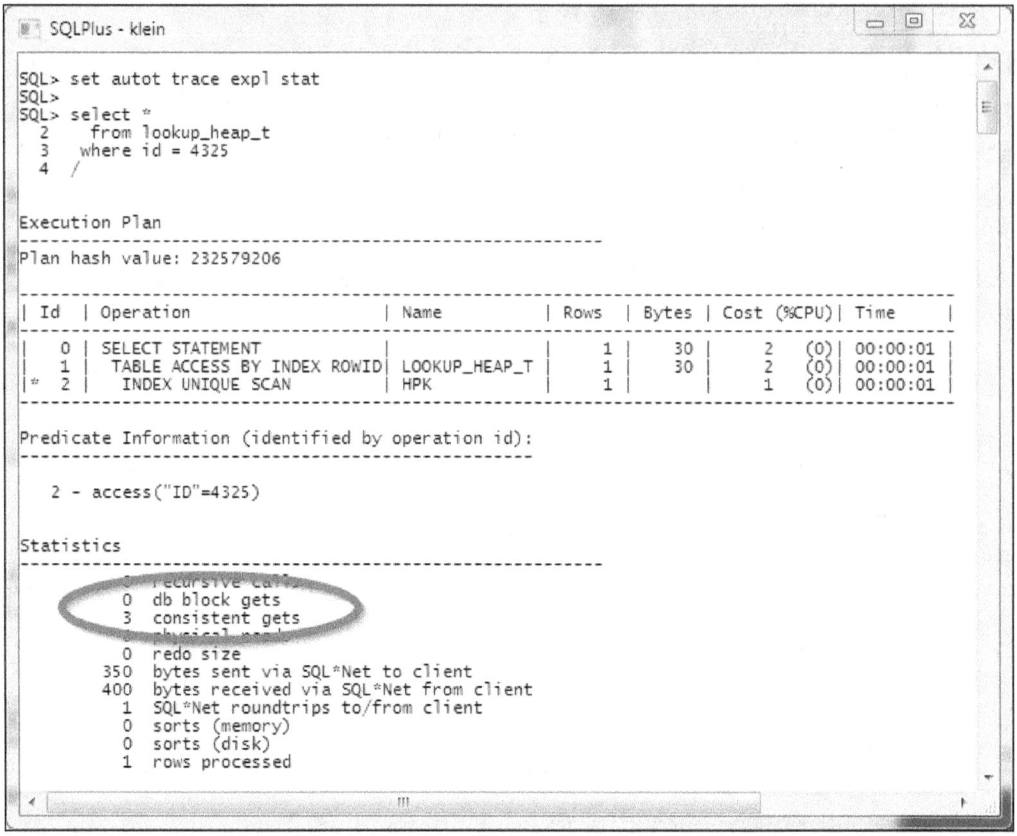

Execution plan for a heap table

The heap table query uses **INDEX UNIQUE SCAN**, the index of the primary key, to look up the values that we are looking for. It is also a very efficient way to look up the values. As you can see in the **Statistics** part, the number of **consistent gets** is slightly higher (**3**) than the number of **consistent gets** of the single-table hash cluster query. This is the first indication that the single-table hash cluster query is slightly more efficient compared to using a regular heap table to do a lookup.

Index-organized tables

The characteristic feature of an index-organized table is the way in which it stores the data. Instead of storing the data where it fits, like with a heap table, the data is stored in a structure similar to a b-tree index. This means that not only the key is stored in the index structure, but also the other data resides there as well. Because you traverse the index structure and immediately find the data that you are looking for, this type of table is very efficient for lookup purposes.

Because the data needs to be stored alongside the key, it can only be stored at a certain location. Hence, performing the `INSERT` or `UPDATE` operations on data in index-organized tables is not as efficient as storing data in a heap table. In the case of lookup tables, which are being discussed here, data changes slowly and is created once but queried over and over again, making the DML operations less prone to an issue. Unlike the single-table hash cluster, where you need to know the size of the table in advance and allocate this space as well, this is not necessary with an index-organized table.

To compare an index-organized table to a regular heap table, an index-organized table that resembles the previously created heap table is created.

```
SQL> create table lookup_io_t
  2   (id primary key, description)
  3   organization index
  4  as
  5  select rownum      id
  6        , object_name description
  7    from (select * from dba_objects
  8          union all
  9          select * from dba_objects
 10          )
 11   where rownum <= 50000
 12  /

Table created.
```

An index-organized table needs to have a primary key. The primary key is defined on line 2 of the preceding code sample. To indicate that an index-organized table is needed, include `organization index` on line 3.

Just like the single-table hash cluster and the heap table were populated with 50,000 records, the index-organized table is also populated with 50,000 records with the same structure.

Statistics are gathered on the index-organized table:

```
SQL> begin
  2      dbms_stats.gather_table_stats (user
  3                                    ,'LOOKUP_IO_T'
  4                                    ,cascade => true
  5                                    );
  6  end;
  7  /

PL/SQL procedure successfully completed.
```

Now everything is ready to look into the autotrace report.

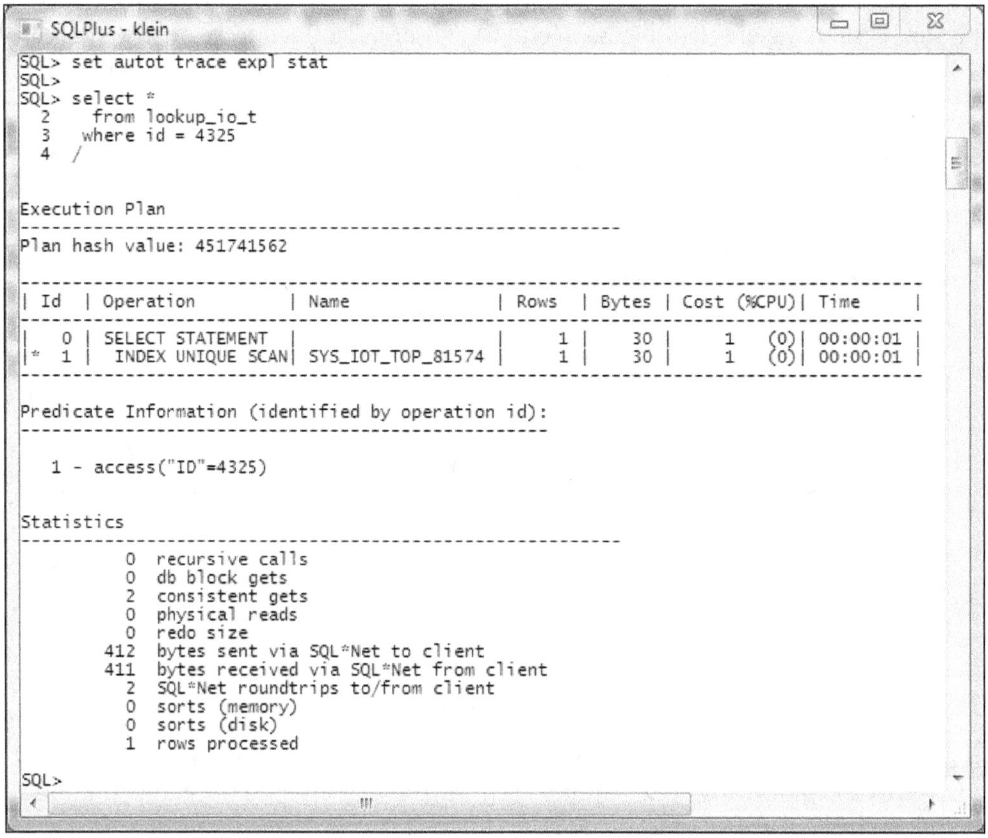

```
SQLPlus - klein
SQL> set autot trace expl stat
SQL>
SQL> select *
  2    from lookup_io_t
  3   where id = 4325
  4  /

Execution Plan
----------------------------------------------------------
Plan hash value: 451741562

-------------------------------------------------------------------------------------
| Id  | Operation          | Name               | Rows  | Bytes | Cost (%CPU)| Time     |
-------------------------------------------------------------------------------------
|   0 | SELECT STATEMENT   |                    |     1 |    30 |     1   (0)| 00:00:01 |
|*  1 |  INDEX UNIQUE SCAN| SYS_IOT_TOP_81574 |     1 |    30 |     1   (0)| 00:00:01 |
-------------------------------------------------------------------------------------

Predicate Information (identified by operation id):
---------------------------------------------------

   1 - access("ID"=4325)

Statistics
----------------------------------------------------------
          0  recursive calls
          0  db block gets
          2  consistent gets
          0  physical reads
          0  redo size
        412  bytes sent via SQL*Net to client
        411  bytes received via SQL*Net from client
          2  SQL*Net roundtrips to/from client
          0  sorts (memory)
          0  sorts (disk)
          1  rows processed

SQL>
```

Execution plan for an index-organized table

When you look at the execution plan in the preceding screenshot, notice that **INDEX UNIQUE SCAN** is done on **SYS_IOT_TOP_81574**. This is the system-generated name for the index created for the index-organized table. The number of **consistent gets** for this statement is only **2**—slightly better than the heap table, but slightly worse than the single-table hash cluster.

Depending on the nature of the lookup tables in your application, the frequency with which the data changes, and the amount of storage that may be needed, you might want to choose single-table hash clusters or index-organized tables.

Analytic functions

Analytic functions were introduced quite a long time ago—Oracle 8.1.6 Enterprise Edition in around 1999—yet they are still quite unknown to a lot of developers.

With analytic functions you can retrieve data from more than one row at the same time without the need for a self join. You can create a ranking based on a value within a group of values. They are not easy to use, but once mastered, analytic functions can make your life a lot easier. With analytic functions, you can create the overviews that the customer may want within a few lines of code.

Syntax overview

The processing order of a query with analytic functions happens in three stages. First of all the Joins, `WHERE` conditions, `GROUP BY`, and `HAVING` clauses are applied. Next, the analytic functions are applied to the resulting result set. Finally, the `ORDER BY` clause is processed. This order of processing is important to know, because after getting comfortable with analytic functions, it is quite easy to get carried away. Use traditional aggregates before you decide on analytic functions.

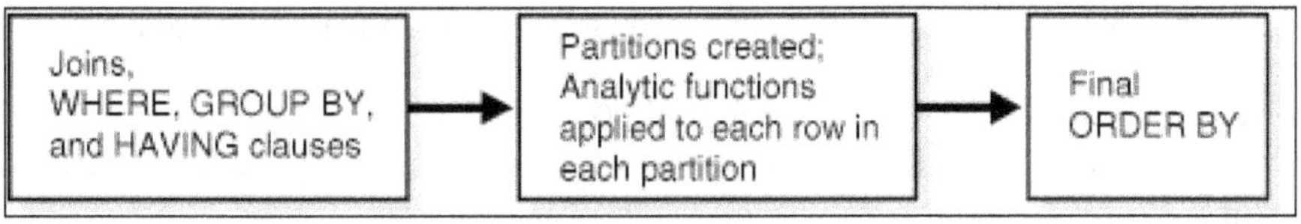

Processing order of a query

The first part of the analytic function that you need to identify is the "what". There are a lot of regular aggregate functions, which also have an analytic counterpart. Some examples of these are `SUM`, `AVG`, and `COUNT`. The easiest way to know that you are dealing with the analytic counterpart is by checking that the reserved word `OVER` is present after the function name:

```
avg(sal) over ()
```

The preceding sample shows the analytic counterpart of the `AVG` function. The parentheses after `OVER` are mandatory. Even though it looks like an aggregate, an analytic function is not an aggregate. Aggregate functions will reduce the number of rows while analytic functions will not. The preceding example will return as many records as there are in the table that you are querying and each record will have the average of the column in the final result set.

There are also a number of functions that you will use rarely if at all; just to name a few—`COVAR_SAMP`, `VAR_POP`, or `STDDEV_SAMP`. These functions serve a statistical purpose. It may be advisable to have a statistical analyst sitting beside you while using these esoteric functions to interpret the results that they produce. Functions such as `ROW_NUMBER`, `RANK`, `LEAD`, and `LAG` are quite useful on a day-to-day basis.

After you decide which analytic function you need, the next step is to determine those parts of the result set to which the function should be applied. In this case, we will talk about partitions. **Partitions** break up the result set into smaller groups.

> Partitions in the context of analytic functions are not related to table partitioning. Analytic partitions are a logical grouping of data.

A partition can be as small as a single row, or as large as the whole result set.

```
avg(sal) over (partition by deptno, job)
```

The partition clause breaks up the result set into groups. Each group has the analytic function applied to it. The criteria in the partition clause determines how many different groups you'll have—never more than one per record, and never less than one per result set. If you don't specify any partition clause, the whole result set is considered as a single partition or group. The results for the function are only applied to a single partition; it cannot cross partitions. If you have, say a running total for salaries per department, the counter is set at zero for each department.

Within each partition, it's possible to specify a window. The window determines the range of rows in the current partition for which you want to perform calculations for the current row.

Analytic functions are always performed from the perspective of the current row. You can consider the current row as the reference point for the window. Windows come in two flavors. The first one is an anchored window, and the second is a sliding window.

The default windows clause is `RANGE UNBOUNDED PRECEDING`. This means that the window is expanding from the first row in the partition to the current row. Because the first row in the result set is the starting point for the window, and therefore has a fixed point, this is called an **anchored window**.

In a sliding window this is different. A **sliding window** moves along with the current row. The sliding window comes in two varieties. There is a **range window**, determined by a numeric offset. This window includes all rows where the specified column has a value that falls within the range starting from the current row. For example, all rows where the sal is between 200 less than the current sal and 350 more than the current sal:

```
over (order by sal range between 200 preceding
                             and 350 following
     )
```

This type of window can only be used as a numeric offset on number types and dates. With dates, the offset is the number of days.

The second type of sliding window is the **row window**. Here, you can specify how many rows you want to look back or look forward into the result set. For example, calculate the analytic function for the current record over (no more than) two records prior to the current record and (no more than) two records following the current record—with all records sorted by salary:

```
over (order by sal rows between 2 preceding and 2 following)
```

These preceding examples don't have a partition by clause—which is optional—meaning that the partition is as large as the result set over which the analytic function is performed.

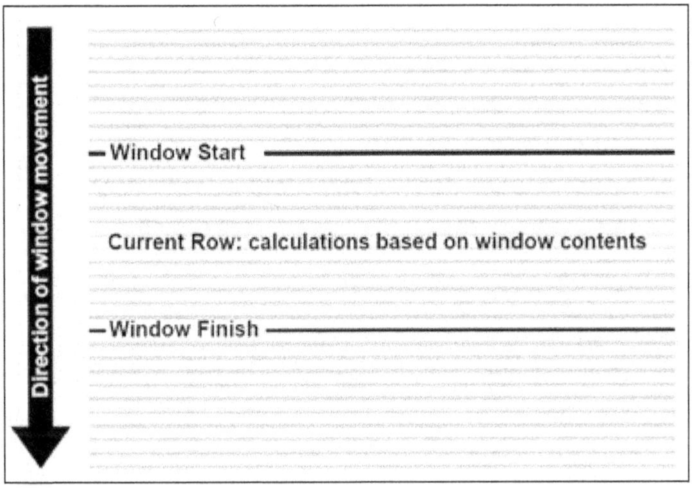

Movement of the window with the current row

Examples

Let's look at some of the most common usages of analytic functions. Of course, there are many more possibilities. These merely serve as examples to get you going. It is possible to reproduce these result sets with plain old SQL, but the analytic way is so much more attractive and elegant, and often better in terms of performance. A lot of questions on the SQL and PL/SQL forum on Oracle Technology Network can be answered by using analytic functions. The most common questions are used as examples in this section.

Running totals

Running totals are easy to create, using analytic functions. To accomplish something similar the traditional way can be quite challenging. Let's see an example of a running totals query:

```
SQL> select empno
          , ename
          , sal
          , sum (sal) over (order by empno) overall_total
       from emp
      order by empno
     /

     EMPNO ENAME             SAL OVERALL_TOTAL
---------- ---------- ---------- -------------
      7369 SMITH             800           800
      7499 ALLEN            1600          2400
      7521 WARD             1250          3650
      7566 JONES            2975          6625
      7654 MARTIN           1250          7875
      7698 BLAKE            2850         10725
      7782 CLARK            2450         13175
      7788 SCOTT            3000         16175
      7839 KING             5000         21175
      7844 TURNER           1500         22675
      7876 ADAMS            1100         23775
      7900 JAMES             950         24725
      7902 FORD             3000         27725
      7934 MILLER           1300         29025
```

In this example, you can see that the `partition` keyword is omitted; therefore there's only one single group. There is, however, a window that is expanding with each row. The window is determined by the `order by` clause in line 4. The (implicit) window clause in this example is `RANGE UNBOUNDED PRECEDING`, which is the default for the `Window` clause. This means that all preceding salaries are added to the current row's salary, thereby creating a running total.

If we look at `EMPNO 7521` (`WARD`), we can see that the `OVERALL_TOTAL` column shows `3650`. This is a summary of all preceding salaries, including Ward's (800 + 1600 + 1250). To make this a running total per department, simply add a `partition` clause as done in the following example:

```
SQL> select empno
          , ename
          , sal
          , deptno
          , sum (sal) over (partition by deptno
                                order by empno
                           ) department_total
       from emp
      order by deptno, empno
   /

     EMPNO ENAME             SAL     DEPTNO DEPARTMENT_TOTAL
---------- ---------- ---------- ---------- ----------------
      7782 CLARK            2450         10             2450
      7839 KING             5000         10             7450
      7934 MILLER           1300         10             8750
      7369 SMITH             800         20              800
      7566 JONES            2975         20             3775
      7788 SCOTT            3000         20             6775
      7876 ADAMS            1100         20             7875
      7902 FORD             3000         20            10875
      7499 ALLEN            1600         30             1600
      7521 WARD             1250         30             2850
      7654 MARTIN           1250         30             4100
      7698 BLAKE            2850         30             6950
      7844 TURNER           1500         30             8450
      7900 JAMES             950         30             9400
```

When we look at `EMPNO 7521` (`WARD`) again, we see that the `DEPARTMENT_TOTAL` column shows `2850`. This is a summary of all preceding salaries within his department (1600 + 1250). Just to show the effect of a running total more clearly, I adjusted the final `order by` predicate to match the window's sort condition. It should be noted that there's no need to do this. When the final `order by` is different from the sort order in the partition, the final result can be rather confusing. The final `order by` has no impact on the values determined by the analytic functions.

Visualizing the window

To help you visualize where a window starts and where it ends, you can use the analytic functions `FIRST_VALUE` and `LAST_VALUE`, which return the specified column value for the first or last record in the window:

```
SQL> select ename
          , sum (sal) over (partition by deptno
                                order by empno
                           ) dept_total
          , first_value (ename) over (partition by deptno
                                          order by empno
                                     ) fv
          , last_value (ename) over (partition by deptno
                                         order by empno
                                    ) lv
       from emp
      where deptno = 20
      order by deptno
             , empno
  /

ENAME      DEPT_TOTAL FV         LV
---------- ---------- ---------- ----------
SMITH             800 SMITH      SMITH
JONES            3775 SMITH      JONES
SCOTT            6775 SMITH      SCOTT
ADAMS            7875 SMITH      ADAMS
FORD            10875 SMITH      FORD
```

Here you can see that the window is expanding per row. When we look at `SCOTT`, the window starts with the employee named `SMITH` and ends with the current row (`SCOTT`).

But how do the `FIRST_VALUE` and `LAST_VALUE` functions handle NULL? It's nothing special really; when the first or last value is a NULL then a NULL is shown. If you want to get the last NOT NULL value then you can use the `IGNORE NULLS` clause. This clause was added in Oracle 10*g* for `FIRST_VALUE` and `LAST_VALUE`. In Oracle 11*g* Release 2 a lot of other analytic functions can use the `IGNORE NULLS` clause, such as `LEAD` and `LAG`.

```
SQL> select ename
  2        , comm
  3        , last_value (comm) over (partition by deptno
  4                                  order by comm
  5                             ) lv
  6        , last_value (comm ignore nulls) over
  7                       (partition by deptno
  8                           order by comm
  9                       ) lv_ignore
 10     from emp
 11    where deptno = 30
 12   ;

ENAME            COMM         LV  LV_IGNORE
---------- ---------- ---------- ----------
TURNER              0          0          0
ALLEN             300        300        300
WARD              500        500        500
MARTIN           1400       1400       1400
JAMES                                  1400
BLAKE                                  1400
```

In the preceding example, the effect of `ignore nulls` (line 6) is shown. Because `MARTIN` is the last employee with a commission, his amount is shown in the last column for `JAMES` and `BLAKE`.

Accessing values from other records

There are three different functions that allow you to access values from elsewhere in the result set, namely `FIRST_VALUE`, `LAST_VALUE`, and `NTH_VALUE`. The `FIRST_VALUE` function retrieves a value from the first row in the window, and `LAST_VALUE` retrieves a value from the last row in the window. `NTH_VALUE` allows you to access a value from any row in the window.

With these functions, you can do a comparison between different rows in your result set. For example, determining the difference between the highest earning employee and the second highest earning employee:

```
SQL> select deptno
  2       , ename
  3       , first_value(sal) over (partition by deptno
  4                                          order by sal desc
  5                                     )
  6         - nth_value(sal,2) from first
  7              over (partition by deptno
  8                        order by sal desc
  9                  )
 10         top2_difference
 11     from emp
 12  /

    DEPTNO    ENAME       TOP2_DIFFERENCE
---------- ---------- ---------------
        10    KING
        10    CLARK                  2550
        10    MILLER                 2550
        20    SCOTT                     0
        20    FORD                      0
        20    JONES                     0
        20    ADAMS                     0
        20    SMITH                     0
        30    BLAKE
        30    ALLEN                  1250
        30    TURNER                 1250
        30    MARTIN                 1250
        30    WARD                   1250
        30    JAMES                  1250
```

The second argument with `NTH_VALUE` (line 6) identifies the nth value in the window. As you may notice on line 6 in the preceding code, there is a `from first` clause. This clause determines where to start counting from in the result set. There is also a `from last` clause. `FIRST_VALUE` can also be retrieved with the following statement:

```
nth_value (sal, 1) from first over ()
```

`LAST_VALUE` can be retrieved as follows:

```
nth_value (sal, 1) from last over ()
```

Another way of accessing other rows in the result set

Occasionally, it's necessary to access values from different rows in the result set. The `LAG` and `LEAD` functions do just that. `LAG` looks at values from previous rows, and `LEAD` looks to the following records in the result set. The current row is always the starting point for the number of rows you want to look forward or back into the result set. The need for a self-join has vanished in many cases.

Let's take a look at another example. For each employee, we want to show the next employee to be hired in the same job:

```
SQL> select ename, job
  2         , hiredate
  3         , lead (ename) over (partition by job
  4                                    order by hiredate
  5                               ) next_hiree_in_job
  6     from emp
  7    order by job
  8            , hiredate;

ENAME      JOB       HIREDATE  NEXT_HIREE
---------- --------- --------- ----------
FORD       ANALYST   03-DEC-81 SCOTT
SCOTT      ANALYST   19-APR-87
SMITH      CLERK     17-DEC-80 JAMES
JAMES      CLERK     03-DEC-81 MILLER
MILLER     CLERK     23-JAN-82 ADAMS
ADAMS      CLERK     23-MAY-87
JONES      MANAGER   02-APR-81 BLAKE
BLAKE      MANAGER   01-MAY-81 CLARK
CLARK      MANAGER   09-JUN-81
KING       PRESIDENT 17-NOV-81
ALLEN      SALESMAN  20-FEB-81 WARD
WARD       SALESMAN  22-FEB-81 TURNER
TURNER     SALESMAN  08-SEP-81 MARTIN
MARTIN     SALESMAN  28-SEP-81
```

In this example, we used the `LEAD` function to look to the next records. We divided the results in partitions based on the job and sorted them by hiredate. When we look at the managers, you can see that the next hiree from Blake's perspective is Clark. From Clark's perspective there were no new managers hired; that's why this row's value for the `NEXT_HIREE` column is null.

It's also possible to look further ahead or back in the result set. `LAG` and `LEAD` have two additional optional parameters. One parameter is for the offset of number of records. The third parameter provides a default value in case `LAG` or `LEAD` points outside the window.

As stated before, the `LAG` and `LEAD` function can also include the `IGNORE NULLS` clause, allowing you to skip over the `NULL` values and return the last `NOT NULL` value.

Ranking—top N

Showing the top 3 of each department is a breeze with analytic functions. What we need to do is create partitions and assign a rank to each row within the partition. There are three variants to the ranking function—`RANK`, `DENSE_RANK`, and `ROW_NUMBER`. These functions assign numbers based on the `ORDER BY` clause within each partition. They all do it a little bit differently.

The difference lies in the way equality is resolved. `RANK` allows ranking numbers to be skipped. `DENSE_RANK` uses a different kind of ranking, which doesn't skip any number. `ROW_NUMBER` assigns an arbitrary number to each row when it is not possible to resolve `ORDER BY` of the windows clause, comparable to the way `ROWNUM` assigns a value to a row.

Take a look at the following example. You can see the differences between types of ranking. When we look at department `20` more closely, you can see that there is a tie for first place: both have `3000` under the `SAL` column. The second highest salary (`2975`) has the `RANK` value of `3`, while for `DENSE_RANK`, the value is `2`. `RANK` skipped second place altogether—we do not award a silver medal if we already have two gold medalists. In the last column, where `ROW_NUMBER` is used, a value is assigned arbitrarily to the highest paid employees.

```
SQL> select ename
          , deptno
          , sal
          , rank() over (partition by deptno
                              order by sal desc
                         ) rk
          , dense_rank() over (partition by deptno
                                    order by sal desc
                               ) dr
          , row_number() over (partition by deptno
                                    order by sal desc
                               ) rn
      from emp
     where deptno = 20
     order by deptno
```

```
 16          , sal desc;
ENAME        DEPTNO        SAL         RK         DR         RN
---------- ------- ---------- ---------- ---------- ----------
SCOTT            20       3000          1          1          1
FORD             20       3000          1          1          2
JONES            20       2975          3          2          3
ADAMS            20       1100          4          3          4
SMITH            20        800          5          4          5
```

Because analytic functions cannot be used in the `WHERE` clause (the final predicate) of a query, it's necessary to push the analytic function into an inline view to restrict the final result set to a regular top N, in this case a top 3 of the highest salaries.

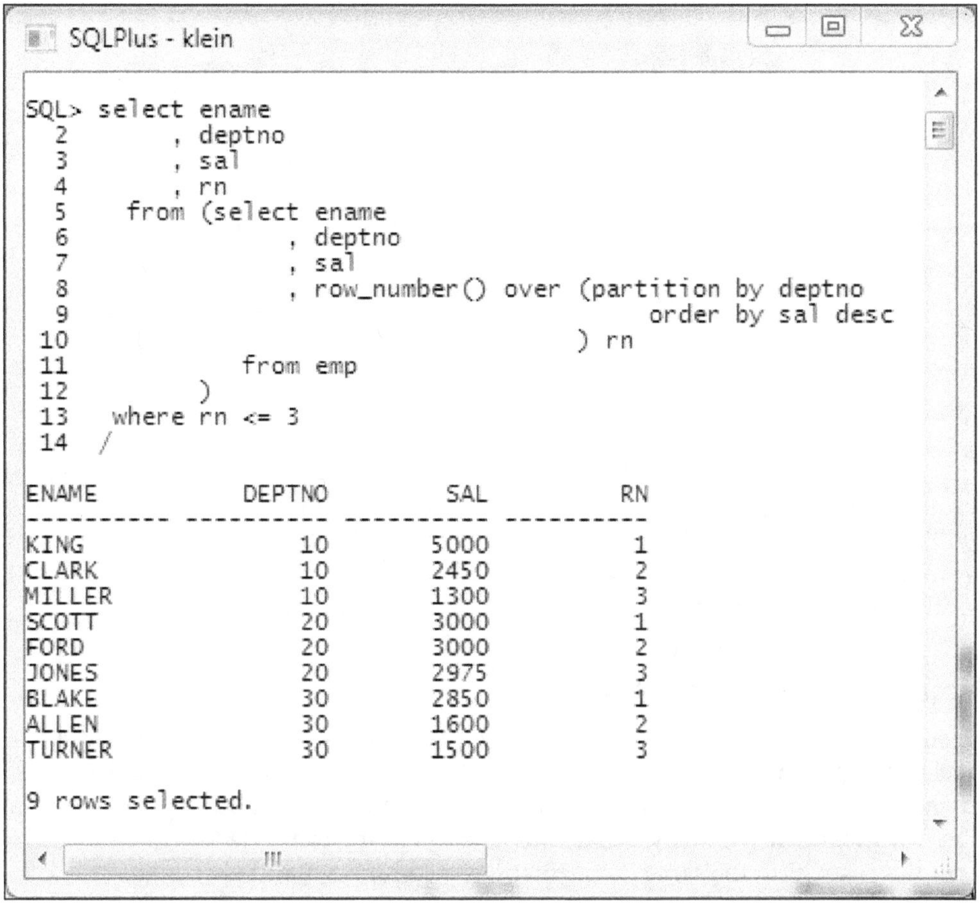

One very neat trick with the ranking functions is to pivot the result set. Instead of showing the rows of the result set down the page, have the results go across the page. In the following example, the ranking function `ROW_NUMBER` is combined with the `PIVOT` function:

```
SQL> select *
  2    from (select ename
  3                , deptno
  4                , rn
  5             from (select ename
  6                , deptno
  7                , row_number() over (partition by deptno
  8                                         order by sal desc
  9                                    ) rn
 10              from emp
 11           )
 12           where rn <= 3
 13     )
 14     pivot (max (ename)
 15              for rn in (1,2,3) )
 16  /

    DEPTNO 1          2          3
---------- ---------- ---------- ----------
        10 KING       CLARK      MILLER
        20 SCOTT      FORD       JONES
        30 BLAKE      ALLEN      TURNER
```

At first, the ranking numbers are assigned in lines 7 to 9 in an inline view. Next the result set is filtered in line 12. The final step is to use the `PIVOT` function in line 14. In case you are wondering if you need to hardcode which rankings you want to pivot, the answer is yes; currently there is no way to do this declaratively.

Stringing it all together

A frequent requirement is for a way to aggregate strings. In older versions of the Oracle database this could be implemented, but it was less than trivial to do so. Nowadays the `LISTAGG` function has relieved this burden. Although not strictly an analytic function, it can be used like one. The following example shows all the names of employees within the same department as a comma-separated string:

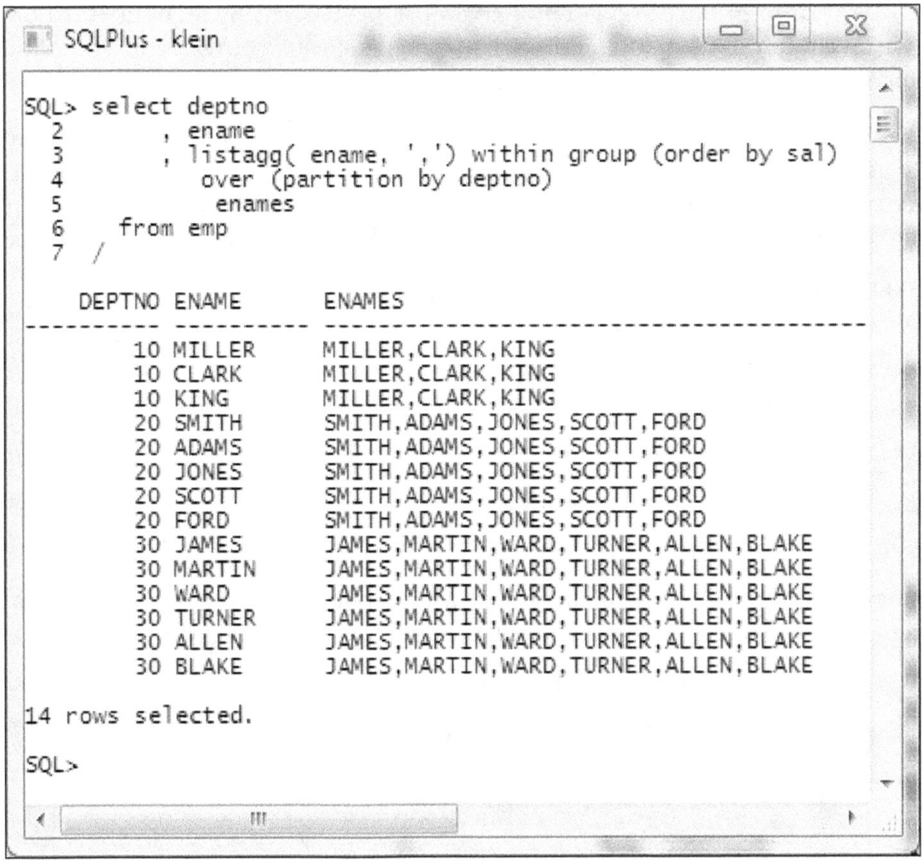

```
SQLPlus - klein

SQL> select deptno
  2         , ename
  3         , listagg( ename, ',') within group (order by sal)
  4           over (partition by deptno)
  5             enames
  6     from emp
  7  /

    DEPTNO ENAME      ENAMES
---------- ---------- ----------------------------------------
        10 MILLER     MILLER,CLARK,KING
        10 CLARK      MILLER,CLARK,KING
        10 KING       MILLER,CLARK,KING
        20 SMITH      SMITH,ADAMS,JONES,SCOTT,FORD
        20 ADAMS      SMITH,ADAMS,JONES,SCOTT,FORD
        20 JONES      SMITH,ADAMS,JONES,SCOTT,FORD
        20 SCOTT      SMITH,ADAMS,JONES,SCOTT,FORD
        20 FORD       SMITH,ADAMS,JONES,SCOTT,FORD
        30 JAMES      JAMES,MARTIN,WARD,TURNER,ALLEN,BLAKE
        30 MARTIN     JAMES,MARTIN,WARD,TURNER,ALLEN,BLAKE
        30 WARD       JAMES,MARTIN,WARD,TURNER,ALLEN,BLAKE
        30 TURNER     JAMES,MARTIN,WARD,TURNER,ALLEN,BLAKE
        30 ALLEN      JAMES,MARTIN,WARD,TURNER,ALLEN,BLAKE
        30 BLAKE      JAMES,MARTIN,WARD,TURNER,ALLEN,BLAKE

14 rows selected.

SQL>
```

Caveats

As with all features, it's not always gold. Once you master the syntax of these analytic functions, then the sky is the limit, but there are some things to be wary of.

Analytic functions cannot be used in the `WHERE` clause or the final `ORDER BY` clause. To circumvent this limitation, you can push the analytic function into an inline view. Another way of circumventing the limitation with `ORDER BY` is to use a column alias in the `ORDER BY` clause.

You also need to look out for the ordering of the `NULL` values and how this will affect the `ORDER BY` clause of the analytic window. Yet another thing to look out for is the performance impact. Analytic functions may look like the best thing that ever happened, especially regarding performance. Using different windows and sort orders may use a considerable amount of sorting and shifting. This might influence the overall performance of the query. As with all features that you use, you should test with a representative set of data before you move to production.

Finally , a warning—once you get more comfortable with using analytic functions, you will want to use them all the time. It's easy to get carried away and you might produce some code that is hard, if not impossible to maintain.

Just to illustrate, here is a quick demonstration of how you might get carried away. Using an analytic function with the `DISTINCT` keyword in the same statement is a telltale sign that you are getting carried away. Say we have a table that contains the contents of the EMP table multiple times and we want to identify the duplicate names.

The table used for this example contains around 900,000 records:

```
SQL> select count(*)
  2    from big_emp
  3  /

  COUNT(*)
----------
    917504
```

One method might be to create partitions based on the name in the table—assign a ranking number to each of them and filter out the names which rank higher than one.

```
SQLPlus - klein

SQL> select distinct
  2            ename
  3       from (select ename
  4                  , row_number() over (partition by ename
  5                                           order by null
  6                                      ) rn
  7               from big_emp
  8            )
  9      where rn > 1;

ENAME
----------
ADAMS
ALLEN
BLAKE
CLARK
FORD
JAMES
JONES
KING
MARTIN
MILLER
SCOTT
SMITH
TURNER
WARD

14 rows selected.

SQL>
```

The reason that the `distinct` keyword is needed in the code snippet shown in the preceding screenshot, is that the inline view (lines 3 through 7) will yield the names multiple times—around 65,535 times per name in the `big_emp` table.

A more traditional way to fulfill the same requirement is shown in the following query:

```
SQL> select ename
  2    from big_emp
  3   group by ename
  4  having count(*) > 1;

ENAME
----------
ADAMS
ALLEN
BLAKE
```

(Complete data is not shown here for brevity)

Besides having to write less code, the performance of the second option is also better.

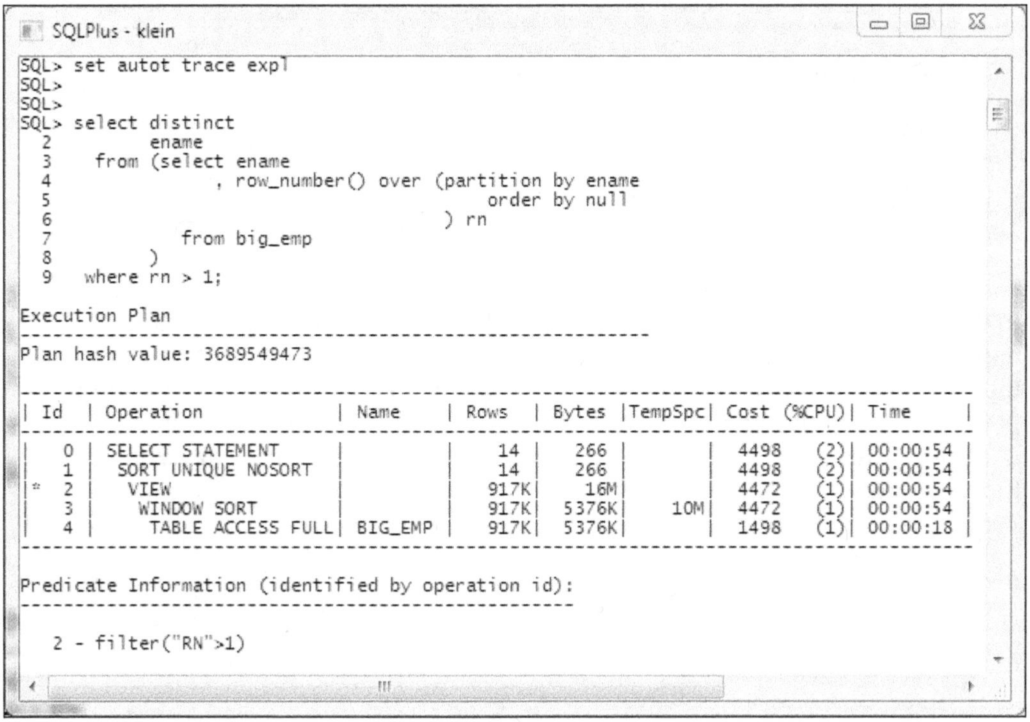

```
SQLPlus - klein
SQL> set autot trace expl
SQL>
SQL>
SQL> select distinct
  2         ename
  3    from (select ename
  4               , row_number() over (partition by ename
  5                                        order by null
  6                                   ) rn
  7            from big_emp
  8         )
  9   where rn > 1;

Execution Plan
----------------------------------------------------------
Plan hash value: 3689549473

-----------------------------------------------------------------------------------------------
| Id  | Operation              | Name    | Rows  | Bytes |TempSpc| Cost (%CPU)| Time     |
-----------------------------------------------------------------------------------------------
|   0 | SELECT STATEMENT       |         |    14 |   266 |       |  4498   (2)| 00:00:54 |
|   1 |  SORT UNIQUE NOSORT    |         |    14 |   266 |       |  4498   (2)| 00:00:54 |
|*  2 |   VIEW                 |         |  917K|    16M|       |  4472   (1)| 00:00:54 |
|   3 |    WINDOW SORT         |         |  917K|  5376K|    10M|  4472   (1)| 00:00:54 |
|   4 |     TABLE ACCESS FULL| BIG_EMP |  917K|  5376K|       |  1498   (1)| 00:00:18 |
-----------------------------------------------------------------------------------------------

Predicate Information (identified by operation id):
---------------------------------------------------

   2 - filter("RN">1)
```

Execution plan for the analytic function query

The execution plan in the preceding screenshot, with the analytic function and the `DISTINCT` keyword, clearly shows the steps that are performed to answer the query. The late filtering, reducing the number of rows from `917K` to `14`, is done after the table has been accessed and the window sort is done.

Let's compare the execution plan for the more traditional way to answer the question.

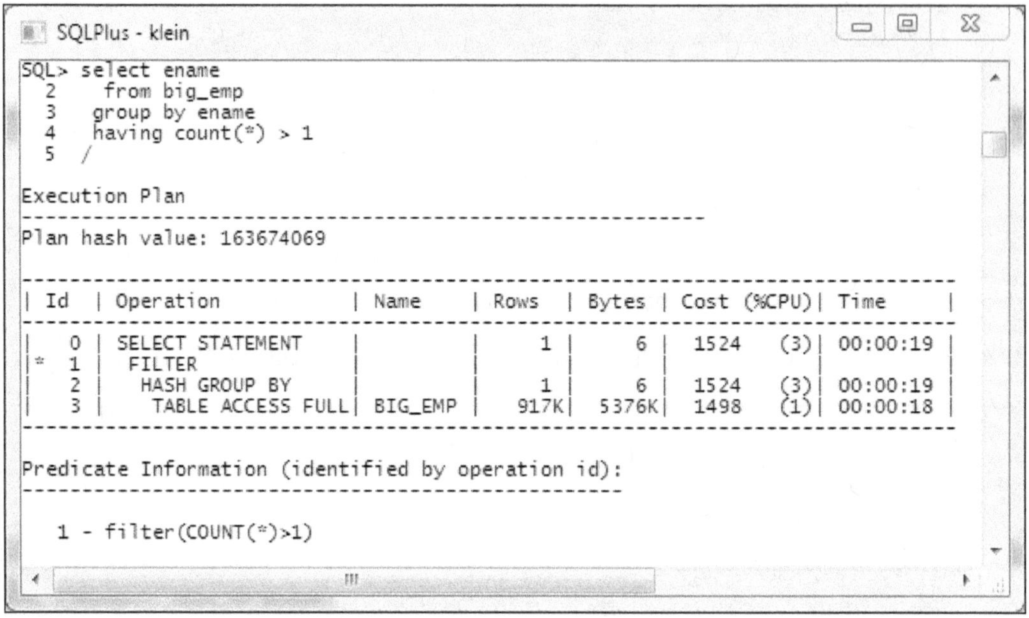

```
SQLPlus - klein
SQL> select ename
  2     from big_emp
  3   group by ename
  4   having count(*) > 1
  5  /

Execution Plan
----------------------------------------------------------
Plan hash value: 163674069

-------------------------------------------------------------------------------
| Id  | Operation           | Name    | Rows  | Bytes | Cost (%CPU)| Time     |
-------------------------------------------------------------------------------
|   0 | SELECT STATEMENT    |         |     1 |     6 |  1524   (3)| 00:00:19 |
|*  1 |  FILTER             |         |       |       |            |          |
|   2 |   HASH GROUP BY     |         |     1 |     6 |  1524   (3)| 00:00:19 |
|   3 |    TABLE ACCESS FULL| BIG_EMP |  917K|  5376K|  1498   (1)| 00:00:18 |
-------------------------------------------------------------------------------

Predicate Information (identified by operation id):
---------------------------------------------------

   1 - filter(COUNT(*)>1)
```

Execution plan for the traditional query

In the execution plan shown in the preceding screenshot, you can see that the number of rows has decreased rapidly. After executing the `HASH GROUP BY` step, the number of rows has reduced to `1`. Also note the last column of the execution plan—the `Time` column. For the last statement the value in the `Time` column is significantly lower than the timing for the execution plan for the analytic function query.

Aggregate functions

Creating multilevel totals with aggregate functions might not be the first thing you think about. This has been a capability of the aggregate functionality for quite some time.

The purpose of the GROUP BY clause is to group rows together, based on the columns specified. But with aggregates, you don't always need to specify columns. When you want a grand total, you can omit the GROUP BY clause altogether:

```
SQL> select sum (sal)
  2     from emp
  3  /

  SUM(SAL)
----------
     29025
```

Omitting the GROUP BY clause leads to a grand total, but you can also use an empty set in the GROUP BY clause:

```
SQL> select sum (sal)
  2     from emp
  3    group by ()
  4  /

  SUM(SAL)
----------
     29025
```

On line 3 the empty set is used, denoted by the opening and closing braces ().

There is a lot more about aggregates, such as GROUPING SETS, ROLLUP, and CUBE.

Grouping sets

In the preceding example, we created a grand total by using an empty set in the `GROUP BY` clause. The `GROUPING SETS` clause lets you create multiple sets, to use them in the `GROUP BY` clause. Let's take a look at an example:

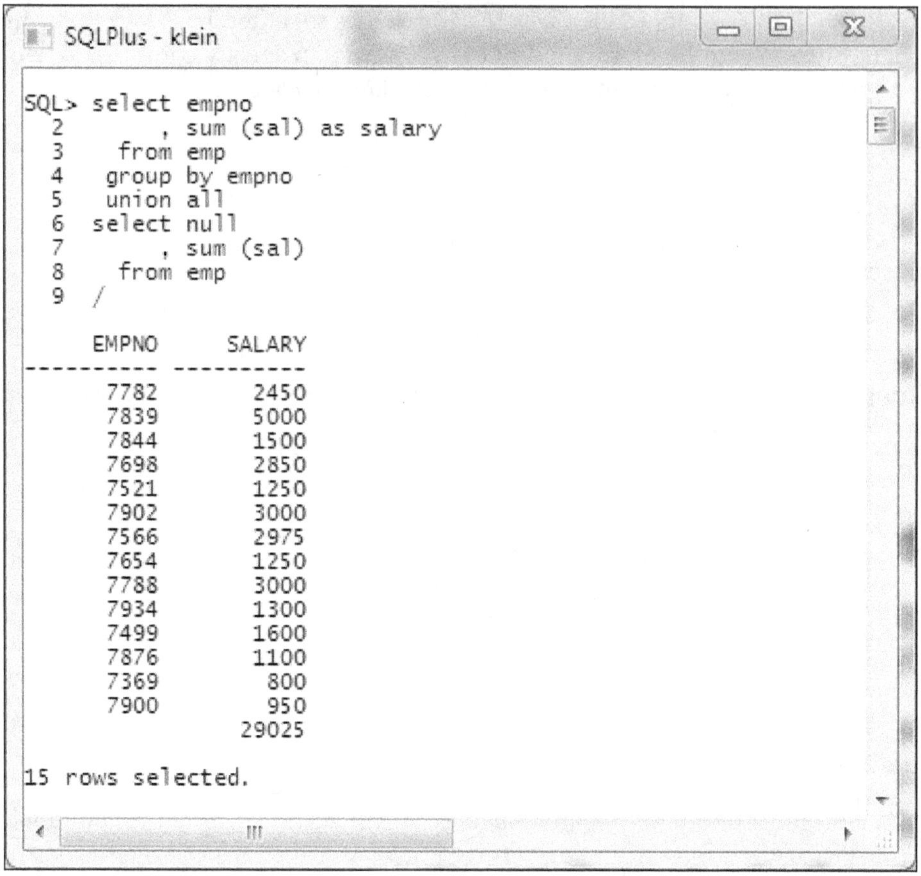

The query shown in the preceding screenshot is a combination of two separate queries to create `empno` with the value in the `SALARY` column for each employee as well as a grand total of values in the `SALARY` column. The `emp` table has only 14 employees, but because of the grand total the total number of records in the `SALARY` column is 15.

In this query, the first part—lines 1 through 4—the `GROUP BY` set consists of `empno`. The second part of the query—lines 6 through 8—consists of groups on an empty set.

To get the same results, you can combine these two separate statements by using a single `GROUP BY` clause with the `GROUPING SETS` keyword.

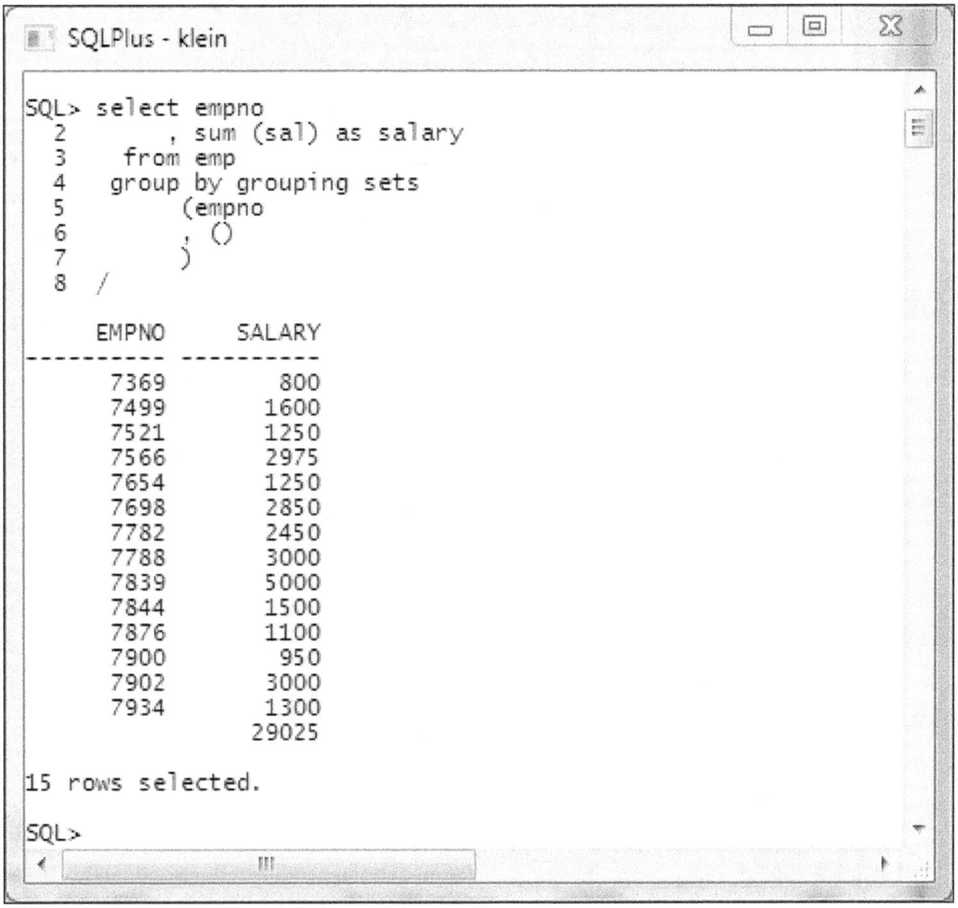


```
SQL> select empno
  2       , sum (sal) as salary
  3    from emp
  4   group by grouping sets
  5         (empno
  6         , ()
  7         )
  8  /

     EMPNO     SALARY
---------- ----------
      7369        800
      7499       1600
      7521       1250
      7566       2975
      7654       1250
      7698       2850
      7782       2450
      7788       3000
      7839       5000
      7844       1500
      7876       1100
      7900        950
      7902       3000
      7934       1300
                29025

15 rows selected.

SQL>
```

In the preceding screenshot, on line 5 in the `GROUP BY` clause, the keyword `GROUPING SETS` indicates a list of expressions indicating the sets. The two grouping sets used in this query are on line 5—one is `empno` and other is an empty set indicated by empty braces.

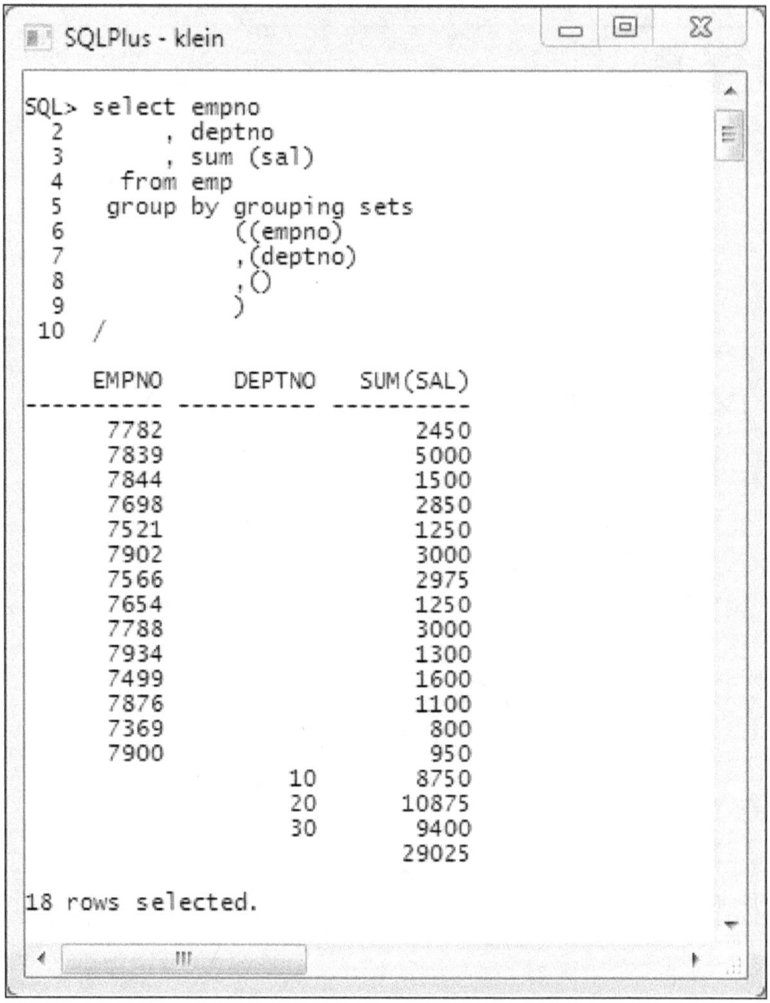

As you can see in the result set shown in the preceding screenshot, `GROUPING SETS` allow you to create multiple sets to group results. There are output records for each `empno` (the first set—line 6), per `deptno` (the second set—line 7), and a grand total (the empty third set—line 8).

Which grouping sets you need to include in the query depends on the requirements that you are trying to fulfill. If you don't want a grand total, just leave out the empty set. This is shown in the query in the following screenshot:

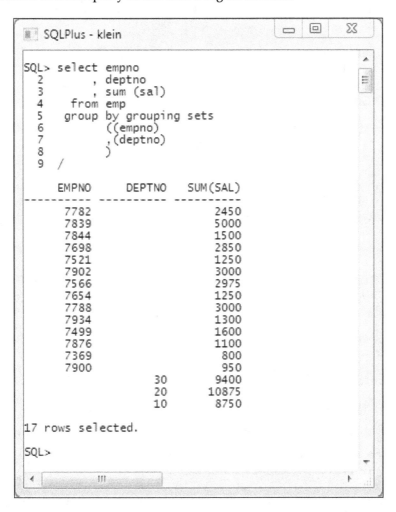

```
SQLPlus - klein

SQL> select empno
  2       , deptno
  3       , sum (sal)
  4    from emp
  5   group by grouping sets
  6         ((empno)
  7         ,(deptno)
  8         )
  9  /

     EMPNO     DEPTNO   SUM(SAL)
---------- ---------- ----------
      7782                  2450
      7839                  5000
      7844                  1500
      7698                  2850
      7521                  1250
      7902                  3000
      7566                  2975
      7654                  1250
      7788                  3000
      7934                  1300
      7499                  1600
      7876                  1100
      7369                   800
      7900                   950
                   30       9400
                   20      10875
                   10       8750

17 rows selected.

SQL>
```

Now the result set will not show the grand total. The `GROUPING SETS` functionality is very powerful.

Rollup

Rollups is a specialized type of grouping functions. Even though we have discussed rollups before discussing grouping sets, when you understand the grouping sets the `Rollup` clause becomes very easy to grasp.

Rollups generates a subtotal line for every set in the `Rollup` clause. The sets in this case might not be as straightforward as with the grouping sets (they were between parenthesis). With the `Rollup` clause, the grouping sets are a combination of the arguments, but not in a random order. Let's take a look at an example to identify the sets.

```
SQL> select deptno
  2         , sum (sal)
  3     from emp
  4    group by rollup
  5          (deptno)
  6  /

    DEPTNO   SUM(SAL)
---------- ----------
        10       8750
        20      10875
        30       9400
                29025
```

There are two grouping sets in the above example, one for `deptno` and another for the empty set. The `Rollup` expression in the preceding example can be written as follows:

```
group by grouping sets
       ((),deptno)
```

The method to determine the grouping sets with the `Rollup` clause is as follows:

- First all the arguments in the `Rollup` clause are one grouping set
- Then all the arguments minus the last one comprise the next grouping set
- All the arguments minus the last two comprise the following grouping set, and so on.

Until there are no more arguments left, the empty set is added as the final grouping set—the empty set being the grand total. Rollup is really a shorthand notation for combining multiple grouping sets to create multiple subtotals as well as the grand total. Rollups come in very handy for management reports where this information is often required.

Cube

The `Cube` clause is typically used in online analytic processing. When you want to provide aggregated results along with every possible dimension, the `Cube` clause fits the bill. The `Cube` clause consists of all possible combinations of the arguments. To illustrate this, let's take a look at the following example:

```
SQLPlus - klein

SQL> select deptno
  2       , job
  3       , sum (sal)
  4    from emp
  5   group by cube
  6          (deptno, job)
  7  /

    DEPTNO JOB         SUM(SAL)
---------- --------- ----------
                          29025
           CLERK           4150
           ANALYST         6000
           MANAGER         8275
           SALESMAN        5600
           PRESIDENT       5000
        10                 8750
        10 CLERK           1300
        10 MANAGER         2450
        10 PRESIDENT       5000
        20                10875
        20 CLERK           1900
        20 ANALYST         6000
        20 MANAGER         2975
        30                 9400
        30 CLERK            950
        30 MANAGER         2850
        30 SALESMAN        5600

18 rows selected.
```

The query in the preceding screenshot shows a summation of the salary:

- Per department and job
- Per department
- Per job
- Grand total

This query can be written with the `GROUPING SETS` clause as follows:

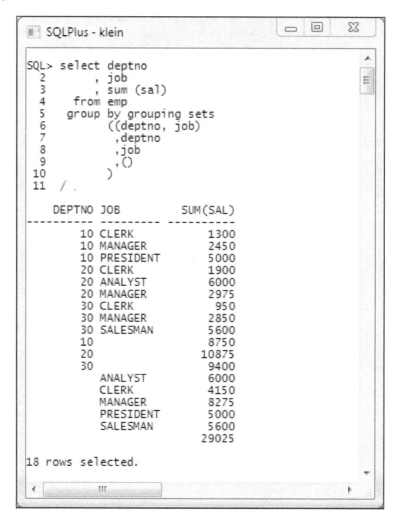

```
SQLPlus - klein

SQL> select deptno
  2         , job
  3         , sum (sal)
  4     from emp
  5    group by grouping sets
  6         ((deptno, job)
  7           ,deptno
  8           ,job
  9           ,()
 10         )
 11  /

    DEPTNO JOB         SUM(SAL)
---------- --------- ----------
        10 CLERK           1300
        10 MANAGER         2450
        10 PRESIDENT       5000
        20 CLERK           1900
        20 ANALYST         6000
        20 MANAGER         2975
        30 CLERK            950
        30 MANAGER         2850
        30 SALESMAN        5600
        10                 8750
        20                10875
        30                 9400
           ANALYST         6000
           CLERK           4150
           MANAGER         8275
           PRESIDENT       5000
           SALESMAN        5600
                          29025

18 rows selected.
```

As you can see in lines 6 through 11, with the `GROUPING SETS` clause you have more granular control, but it can be quite verbose. The `Cube` clause is compacter and processes equivalent results.

Identifying the totals and subtotals with grouping

In the result sets you might notice that it can be confusing to detect which rows in the result set are the aggregated records and which are not. Oracle did recognize the need to identify the aggregated records and created some support functions to do so. These functions are `Grouping`, `Grouping_id`, and `Group_id`.

Each of these functions returns an integer indicating whether or not the record is an aggregate. In this section we will see how to use `Grouping`. In this case, `1` signals an aggregate, and `0` indicates a regular output record. To illustrate this, let's take a look at an example:

```
SQL> select deptno
  2        , sum (sal) as sum_salary
  3        , grouping (deptno)as grp
  4     from emp
  5    group by rollup
  6          (deptno)
  7  /

    DEPTNO SUM_SALARY        GRP
---------- ---------- ----------
        10       8750          0
        20      10875          0
        30       9400          0
                29025          1
```

The preceding query uses the `Rollup` clause to generate a grand total record in the result set. This record can be identified by using the `Grouping` function (line 3)—the last column in the result set. In the preceding result set, this record is in the last row and has a value 1 in the last column.

You can use this information to further enhance the output, such as in the following example, where we use a simple `CASE` expression in combination with the `GROUPING` function:

```
SQL> select case grouping (deptno)
            when 1
            then 'Total: '
            else
                to_char (deptno)
            end department
          , sum (emp.sal) as sum_salary
       from emp
      group by rollup
            (deptno)
    /

DEPARTMENT      SUM_SALARY
--------------- ----------
10                    8750
20                   10875
30                    9400
Total:               29025
```

On lines 1 through 6, the simple `CASE` expression determines whether to show the text `Total` or `deptno`. You may notice that `TO_CHAR` has to be executed on `deptno` in order to have the datatypes match up.

Offloading your frontend and scheduling a job

The built-in package `DBMS_JOB` has been around for a very long time. With this package you could schedule jobs in the database but the possibilities of scheduling the job were pretty limited. Oracle 10*g* introduced `DBMS_SCHEDULER`, the new and improved way of scheduling jobs in the database. This built-in package adds more functionality to scheduling the jobs—like a more sophisticated way to determine the set times when a job is supposed to run.

But there are more things—such as offloading a process from your application to a background process—that you can do with jobs. Instead of having your end user wait for the process to complete, let the process take place in the background. This way your user can carry on with the tasks at hand, while the process is being done elsewhere. The user experience will be enhanced drastically. The application will react more responsively to user actions.

One-off job

A **one-off job** is a job that only runs once, at most. In order to offload the process to the background, the job only needs to run once. After the job is completed it is no longer needed and can therefore be removed. Because the requirements are simple, we can use `DBMS_JOB` for this task.

A job is run as a background process; this means that the actions are initiated by your user but are carried out in the background. Your user's session will continue with whatever he/she pleases.

Say you have a long running program that you want to be initiated by the user of your application when he/she presses a button. To simulate a long running program, we will use the following procedure:

```
SQL> create or replace
procedure long_running
is
begin
   sys.dbms_lock.sleep (seconds => 3);
end long_running;
/

Procedure created.
```

This procedure waits for three seconds before giving control back to the caller of the procedure. When you call this procedure from SQL*Plus, you will have to wait for three seconds.

When the following program is called from your application, your user would have to wait for three seconds, which may seem like forever to a user. This is simply not acceptable.

```
SQL> set timing on
SQL> begin
  2      long_running;
  3  end;
  4  /

PL/SQL procedure successfully completed.

Elapsed: 00:00:03.00
```

The trick is to schedule a job, which would call the long running program for you. Then you won't have to wait for three seconds for the program to complete. What you need to do is create a process that will submit the job, instead of calling the `long_running` program. Now, we will see how it is done in SQL*Plus:

```
SQL> declare
  2      j pls_integer;
  3  begin
  4      dbms_job.submit (job => j
  5                      ,what => 'long_running;'
  6                      );
  7      dbms_output.put_line ('The job has number: '
  8                           || to_char (j)
  9                           );
 10  end;
 11  /
The job has number: 68

PL/SQL procedure successfully completed.

Elapsed: 00:00:00.00
```

As you can see in the preceding code, it takes hardly any time to submit the job (none in my environment). Results may vary, but it will never be as long as your long running process.

In order for the job to start, you will need to issue a `COMMIT` clause:

```
SQL> commit
  2  /

Commit complete.

Elapsed: 00:00:00.00
```

As you can see, this also takes hardly any time. To make sure that the job is scheduled to run in the background, you can query `DBA_JOBS` (or `USER_JOBS` in case you do not have access to `DBA_JOBS`) to see the job in action.

In the following results, you may notice that the `WHAT` column shows what the job is doing. It also shows whether next time this job will be run again or not. This is shown in the `INTERVAL` column, which is `NULL`, meaning that it will not reschedule itself anymore. The last column is the `Broken` indicator. If this column has a value `Y`, the job will not attempt to run again. This only happens when a job fails 16 times.

```
SQL> select j.job
  2       , j.what
  3       , j.interval
  4       , j.broken
  5    from dba_jobs j
  6   where j.job = 68
  7  /

       JOB WHAT           INTERVAL                            B
---------- -------------- ----------------------------------- -
        68 long_running;  null                                N

SQL> /

no rows selected
```

If you wait a little bit—three seconds or more—and rerun our query against `DBA_JOBS` once more, you will notice that the job has been completed successfully and has been removed.

If, for whatever reason, the job cannot be completed in one go, the job reschedules itself to run after some time. If the job still can't be completed successfully, the job reschedules itself again but with an increasing interval. This mechanism will try to run the job up to 16 times. If the job still can't complete, the job is marked as `Broken`. This means that the job will not be tried again.

In the following example, there is a long running program, which can only be called by pressing the button in the APEX application:

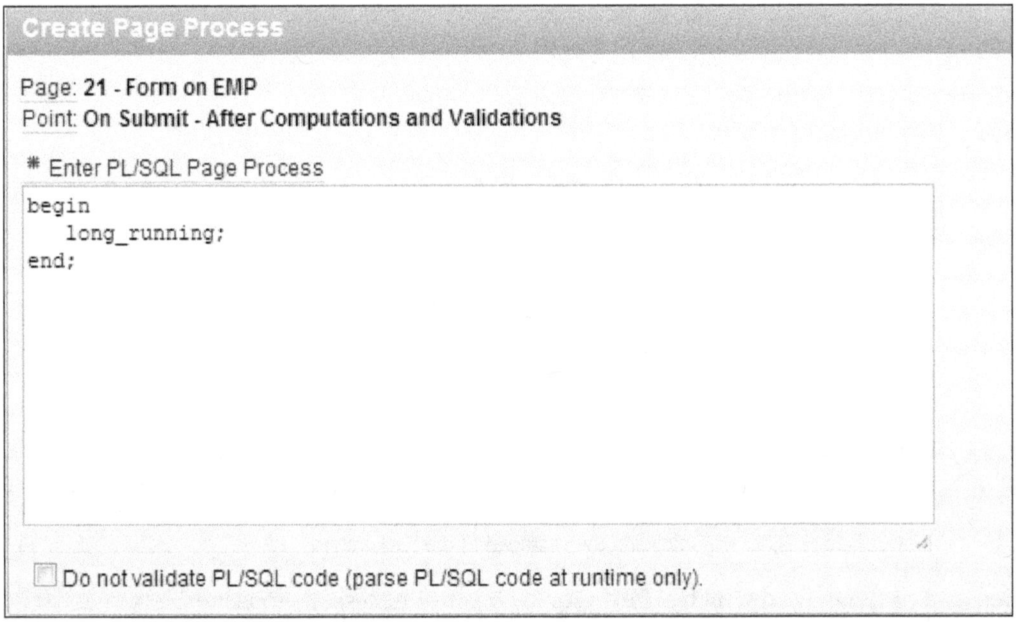

Calling the long_running process directly

In the preceding screenshot, a `page` process is created. This process calls the long running program directly in an anonymous PL/SQL block. Because we want to call this program when a button is pressed, the condition **When Button Pressed** for the `page` process is set to the button (called **LONG_RUNNING**), as shown in the following screenshot:

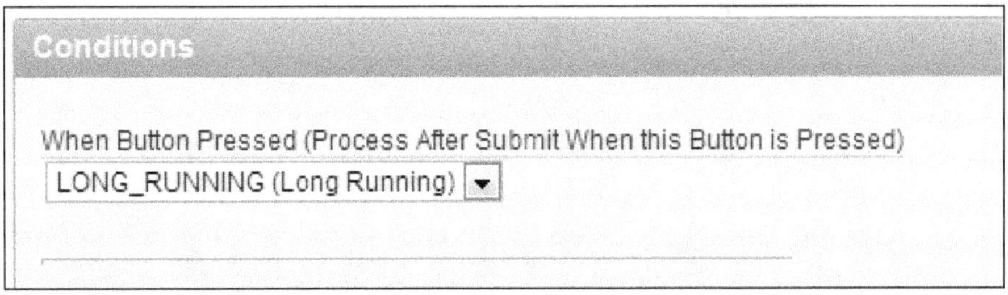

Instead of making the user to wait for the process to finish, we can change the code to schedule the job:

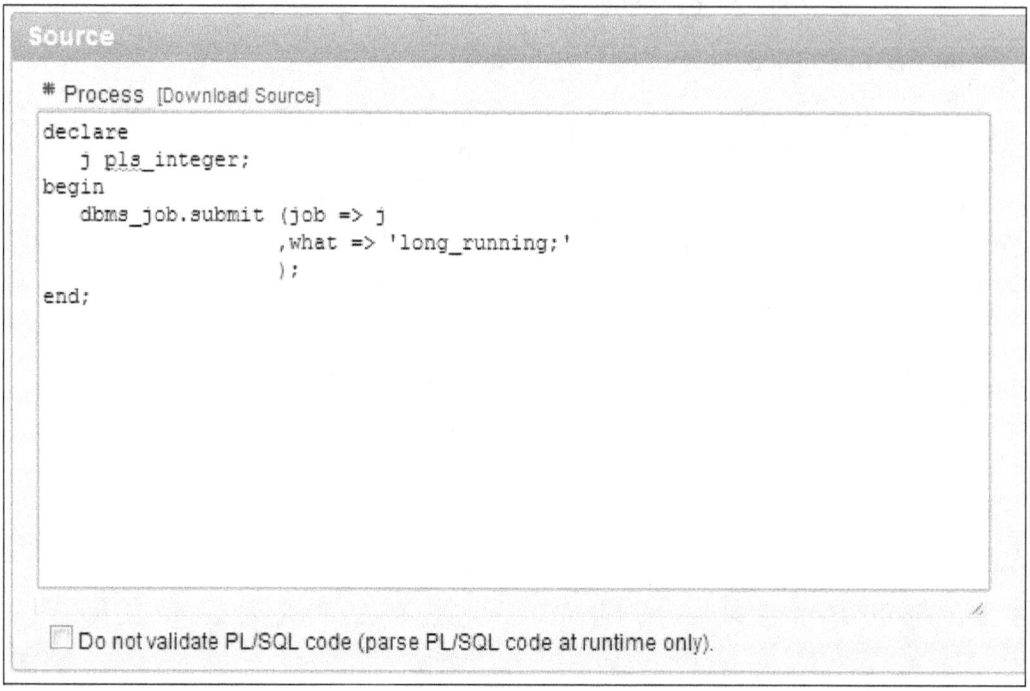
Source
* Process [Download Source]
declare
j pls_integer;
begin
dbms_job.submit (job => j
,what => 'long_running;'
);
end;
Do not validate PL/SQL code (parse PL/SQL code at runtime only).

Offloading the workload to the background

Because of the way in which APEX works, it is not necessary to issue `COMMIT` explicitly; this is done automatically.

After pressing the button, the job can be seen in `DBA_JOBS`, but only for about three seconds—that's the time we used to simulate a long running process. After this period, the job will be carried out and will automatically disappear into oblivion.

```
SQL> select j.job
  2         , j.what
  3         , j.interval
  4         , j.broken
  5     from dba_jobs j
  6   /

       JOB WHAT             INTERVAL                         B
---------- --------------- --------------------------------- -
        22 long_running;    null                             N
```

The process is not going any faster; it is still taking three seconds to complete, but the user experience is better. The page will respond immediately after clicking on the button. The only action that needs to be completed on the APEX page, before giving control back to the user, is submitting the job. When the `page` process is done with submitting the job, the user gets control back and can continue working with the application.

Pipelined table functions

One of the key features of functions is that they return a value. This value can be either a scalar value of a composite value such as a record or an object, or even a set of values such as an associative array, a nested table, or a varray. A regular function returns its value after the function is completely finished and the `RETURN` statement is encountered. The program that calls a function will have to wait until the function is finished with its task, before the caller can continue with processing.

A pipelined table function is slightly different. This type of function can return values before the final `RETURN` statement is encountered. This means that it can return values for multiple times. This feature allows you to use a pipelined table function in the `FROM` clause of a query.

First we will take a look at a small example, then we will look at how you can apply this function in your APEX application.

A pipelined table function needs to return a collection type, such as a nested table of varrays. This can be a collection of objects—if this is what you need. For this example, we will keep things simple and create a collection of `Varchar2`:

```
SQL> create or replace type time_list is
     table of varchar2(10)
     /

Type created.
```

Now, we need to create the function that returns the previously created collection `pipelined`:

```
SQL> create or replace
     function show_time
        return time_list pipelined
     is
     begin
        for i in 1..5
        loop
```

```
  8         dbms_lock.sleep (1);
  9         pipe row (to_char (sysdate, 'hh24:mi:ss'));
 10      end loop;
 11      return;
 12   end show_time;
 13   /

Function created.
```

This function is returning a list of five time information outputs, each with a second inbetween. Line 8 takes care of the one-second pause, using `DBMS_LOCK.SLEEP`. In the `Return` clause of the function signature, is the `PIPELINED` keyword (line 3). On line 9, the values are returned from the function. `PIPE ROW` is the key to return the values, in our case the time component of `SYSDATE`.

Finally, `RETURN` on line 11 signals the end of the function and returns control to the calling function.

Now we can see the power of the pipelined table function in action, used in the `from` clause of the following query:

```
SQL> select to_char (sysdate, 'hh24:mi:ss')
  2         , column_value
  3     from table (show_time)
  4   /

TO_CHAR( COLUMN_VAL
-------- ----------
21:49:13 21:49:14
21:49:13 21:49:15
21:49:13 21:49:16
21:49:13 21:49:17
21:49:13 21:49:18
```

In this query, we have shown the current time, as well as the results from the pipelined table function that we created earlier. On line 3, the pipelined table function is called, inside the `table` operator, in the `from` clause. As you can see from the output, the value for the current time is determined at the start of the query (read consistency in action) and is fixed at `21:49:13`. The pipelined table function returns its values with one second pause in between. So, the rows are returned—not all at the same time, but one after the other—until the function is completely finished.

When you run this example on your own database—such as SQL*Plus, you need to change your `arraysize` setting to observe this. The default setting for the `arraysize` in SQL*Plus is `15`. As there are fewer than 15 records returned from the query, the `one record at a time` clause is not observed. One little oddity—even if you set the `arraysize` to `1`, first you will see one record, then the following records are returned in pairs (two at a time).

```
SQL> set arraysize 1
```

Pipelined table functions in APEX

After this brief introduction to pipelined table functions, we will take a look at how to use pipelined table functions in APEX.

The goal that we want to achieve is to create a comma-delimited list of employee names for a given department number. This is a very contrived example as Oracle 11*g* R2 already has a built-in function that can do this for you—`LISTAGG`.

What we first need is a collection type. For this example, we will use a nested table of the `varchar2` objects:

```
SQL> create type string_tt is table of varchar2(250)
     /

Type created.
```

And of course we will need a pipelined table function as well—one that takes in a department number and returns the list of employee names in comma-delimited form:

```
SQL> create function enames (p_deptno in number)
        return string_tt pipelined
     is
        l_str varchar2(32767);
     begin
        for rec in (select ename
                      from emp
                     where deptno = p_deptno
                   )
        loop
           l_str := l_str ||rec.ename||',';
        end loop;
        pipe row (
           case
            when length (l_str) > 250
            then substr (l_str, 1, 247)||'...'
            else rtrim (l_str, ',')
```

```
18          end
19       );
20       return;
21    end enames;
22    /

Function created.
```

This function takes up the department number and looks for the employees who work for that department (lines 6 to 8). The results are concatenated together, separated by a comma (line 11). The resulting string is returned by the function, after dealing with strings which are too long (lines 13 to 19).

When all these things are in place, we can turn our focus to creating a report in APEX. For this report, we will use the query shown in the following screenshot:

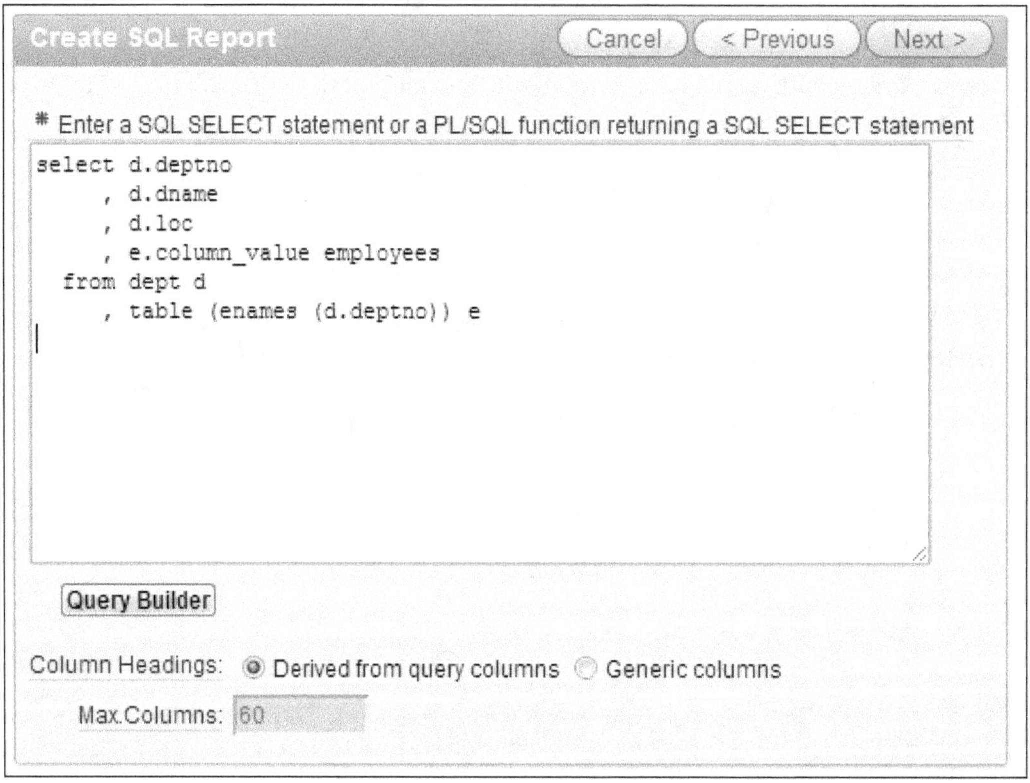

Query where pipelined table function is used

When you run the report, the results will show the employees per department as a comma-delimited string:

DEPTNO	DNAME	LOC	EMPLOYEES
10	ACCOUNTING	NEW YORK	KING,CLARK,MILLER,ALEX
20	RESEARCH	DALLAS	JONES,SCOTT,FORD,SMITH,ADAMS
30	SALES	CHICAGO	BLAKE,ALLEN,WARD,MARTIN,TURNER,JAMES
40	OPERATIONS	BOSTON	

1 - 4

Using a pipelined table function to base a report upon

This example just showed you what is possible with pipelined table functions, to spark your imagination.

Using images

A picture is worth a thousand words, the old adage goes. Including an image in your application can really make your application more appealing for your users. Maybe because of the rise of the smartphone, people are taking more and more photos nowadays—the fact is, photos have become an important part of many applications. Users want to be able to upload photos and view them from within the application. In this section, we will take a closer look at how to store photos in the database.

The Oracle database has a special datatype for dealing with photos—`OrdImage`. This datatype can be found in the `OrdSys` schema. `OrdSys` is part of Oracle Multimedia (formerly known as InterMedia). Oracle APEX doesn't know how to deal with the `OrdImage` datatype directly, but it knows how to deal with images stored in a BLOB column.

When you create your table to store the photo in a BLOB column, you should also include columns to store the following information:

- File name
- Mime type
- Last updated date

APEX uses this information to handle the photo properly. This information is needed for forms as well as reports.

In one of the sample applications that come with APEX, images are used to display products. The current version of this sample application only uses very small images throughout. If you only store small images, and you want to show a larger size on some pages, you would need to resize the image in order to get the enlarged version. By doing this, the quality will deteriorate dramatically. When you store the large version of the image, the quality will be much better. The downside is that if you use these large images as thumbnails by resizing them to a small image, they are still actually large—just sized to appear smaller. The loading time of your pages will increase because of the size of the image (say multiple MB instead of a few KB).

The solution to this problem is quite easy. Store a large and a small version of the image. Resizing an image can easily be done by using the `OrdImage` functionality, and this also works on BLOBs. It should be noted that the reduction in size only happens when the user has already uploaded the photo to the database.

```
SQL> create or replace
     procedure thumbnail (p_id in number)
     is
        l_photo  blob;
        l_thumb  blob;
     begin
        select p.photo
             , p.photo
          into l_photo
             , l_thumb
          from products p
         where p.id = p_id
           for update
         ;
         -- Scale the images down
         ordsys.OrdImage.process (l_thumb, 'maxScale=75 75');
         ordsys.OrdImage.process (l_photo, 'maxScale=2000 2000');
         -- Store the resized images back into the table
         update products p
            set p.thumbnail = l_thumb
              , p.photo     = l_photo
          where p.id        = p_id
         ;
     end thumbnail;
     /
```

This procedure takes the primary key and resizes the original photo to a more manageable size and also creates a real thumbnail. The first thing we need to do is declare two BLOB variables (lines 4 and 5). These BLOB variables will be filled with the original photo from the table. Note that you need to use `FOR UPDATE` to lock the record (line 13). Now you can resize both images, using the `ordsys.OrdImage.process` procedure (lines 16 and 17). The second argument determines the size of the final image. Lastly, write the resized images back to the table (lines 19 through 22).

This procedure can be called right after you upload a photo in the APEX application, but the `ordsys.OrdImage.process` procedure takes quite a long time to complete. The time it takes increases when the size of the uploaded photo increases. A procedure such as this one is an excellent candidate to be called asynchronously, using the technique described earlier in the section called *Offload your frontend, schedule a job*. This way the application becomes more responsive to the end user.

Because the job will run in the background, it takes some time for the thumbnail to show up in the application. As long as you can explain this to your end user, this shouldn't be a problem.

Depending on what we need in the page, we either use the larger photo or the smaller thumbnail.

Searching the contents of documents

Because we are creating a document management system, there are going to be documents stored inside the database, obviously. Searching through these documents is a must-have feature. Oracle supports this kind of functionality in the form of Oracle Text functionality.

In order to work with the Oracle Text feature, we need a special type of index—a context index—on our `documents` tables, more specifically on the column that stores the document:

```
SQL> create index doc_index on documents (document)
  2  indextype is ctxsys.context
  3  parameters ('SYNC (ON COMMIT) TRANSACTIONAL')
  4  /

Index created.
```

The index type that is needed for Oracle Text is `CTXSYS.CONTEXT` (line 2). On line 3, we specify that we want this index to be refreshed when a commit is issued.

> There are many more options that can be used with Oracle Text, such as searching for alternative spelling, searching for words in a certain context, or searching independent diacritic characters. More suggestions on using Oracle Text are listed in *Chapter 1, Prepare and Build.* All these features are outside the scope of this chapter.

When you create the index, you will notice that a number of tables are created to support the index. These tables have the prefix `DR$DOC`, which Oracle uses to support Oracle Text searches. This index will allow you to search through large amounts of text such as Word, PDF, XML, HTML, or plain text documents.

For the following example, I have uploaded the document containing this chapter into our Documents table, so we might find some text that the reviewer told me to remove. Because the Oracle Text index is in place, we can use the functions available to us to search for certain keywords.

```
SQL> col mimetype format a22
SQL> col snippet format a38 word wrapped
SQL> select doc.mimetype
  2       , ctx_doc.snippet ('doc_index'
  3                         ,id
  4                         ,'express'
  5                         ) snippet
  6    from documents doc
  7   where contains(doc.document, 'express') > 0
  8  /

MIMETYPE               SNIPPET
---------------------- --------------------------------------
application/msword     Application <b>Express</b>. And that i
                       s true up to a certain point. You prob
                       ably know that the Oracle Application
                       <b>Express</b> engine is

1 row selected.
```

In the preceding query, we have used the `contains` query operator to search for `express` (line 7). The `contains` operator returns a relevant score for every selected row. Because when we want all rows where the word "express" is in the text of the `documents` column, we use the greater than zero comparison. You may notice that we have put `express` in lowercase and we still get results back even though we didn't use "express" in lowercase in this chapter (until this part of it at least). `contains` can search through texts in a case-insensitive manner.

When we want to see a part of the text where our search keyword is located, we can use a function from the `ctx_doc` package to do this. On lines 2 through 5, we have used this function. The first argument for this function is the name of the Oracle Text Index that we created earlier. The second argument is the primary key column of the `documents` table. The third argument is the search criteria used to extract a part of the text. As you can see in the output (in the column `SNIPPET`), the word we were looking for is in html tags (`<b>Express</b>`). If you don't like these tags, you can overrule them in the `snippet` function.

```
SQL> select doc.mimetype
  2       , ctx_doc.snippet ('doc_index'
  3                        ,id
  4                        ,'express'
  5                        ,'<span style="color:blue">'
  6                        ,'</span>'
  7                        ) snippet
  8    from documents doc
  9   where contains(doc.document, 'express') > 0
 10  /

MIMETYPE               SNIPPET
---------------------- --------------------------------------
application/msword     Application <span style="color:blue">E
                       xpress</span>. And that is true up to
                       a certain point. You probably know tha
                       t the Oracle Application <span style="
                       color:blue">Express</span> engine is
```

When you use the preceding query in a report, make sure to change the `Column` attribute of the `snippet` column to `Standard Report Column`, so that you can see the HTML markup in the way it is supposed to be.

For this example, we hard coded the `search` keyword, which you wouldn't do in a real world application, of course. There you would use bind variables to support this functionality. If you happen to get `ORA-0600` errors when using `ctx_doc.snippet` along with bind variables, you may encounter a bug—`number 5476507`. When this bug is solved, you may have to patch your database or upgrade to a newer version.

This was just a quick introduction to the wonderful functionality of Oracle Text, and there is a lot more to explore. The Oracle documentation on Oracle Text is the best place to start your investigation.

Summary

In this chapter, we looked at some of the lesser-known features of SQL and PL/SQL, but there are many, many more. Thorough knowledge of SQL and PL/SQL is essential to an APEX developer.

We started by examining a method to instrument your database code. This enables you to keep track of the code path and the arguments that are passed down.

Next different options were investigated to have efficient lookup tables for your application. Creating a proper physical data model by using the right types of database object where appropriate will also contribute to a successful application and a better user experience.

Analytic and aggregate functions leverage the functionality that SQL has to offer out of the box. Using these functions, you can create statements that are both elegant and perform well.

When you have programs that take a long time, and you don't want to have the user wait for the response, you can offload these programs to the background. We saw an example on using `DBMS_JOB` to do just that.

With pipelined table functions, you are not depended on standard SQL functionality alone—you can leverage all your PL/SQL skills to accommodate your needs. Using a user-defined PL/SQL function as the source to query from is an extremely powerful process—pipelined table functions enable you to do just that.

Using images in your application can make the application more attractive. When you have to deal with images that are being uploaded to the database, make sure that you keep a close eye on the size of the images.

Lastly we saw a small example that showed how you can use Oracle Text to search through documents with more features than just the standard `LIKE` syntax.

The more you know, the more you can release the power of the Oracle database, and the better your application will be.

The next chapter will explore different methods of creating printed reports.

3
Printing

This chapter deals with different aspects of printing in Oracle Application Express. We will start with the two most used architectures in Application Express printing, Apache FOP and Business Intelligence Publisher. Then, we will see how to install and configure both Apache FOP and Business Intelligence Publisher. After the installation we will discuss how to investigate printing problems.

The main part of this chapter deals with layout of your report and describes how to include things such as charts and images.

Finally, we will look at some alternatives that can be used for PDF printing, plug-ins.

In this chapter, we will cover the following topics:

- Different printing architectures such as Apache FOP and Business Intelligence Publisher
- Installation and configuration of the Apache FOP report server and Business Intelligence Publisher
- Debugging printing problems
- Creating a simple report against the Business Intelligence Publisher
- Creating a report that can output in different formats
- Adding charts to reports
- Adding dynamic images to reports
- Description of the Print API
- Alternatives for printing reports

Printing architecture

PDF printing in Oracle Application Express requires an externally defined print or report server. An external report server can be the Apache FOP reports server from Apache, the reports server from Business Intelligence Publisher, or server from a third-party such as Jasper reports. Different flavors of an external report server are possible. When the user clicks on a print link in Application Express, the Application Express engine generates the corresponding report data in XML format and a report template in XSL-FO or RTF format.

All of this architectural complexity is transparent to the end users and developers. Here, transparent means that the end user only sees the print link and the end result, and not the architecture behind. So end users just click on the print links, and developers just declaratively set regions to support PDF printing.

Your report server can be Oracle BI Publisher, Oracle Application Server Containers for J2EE (OC4J) with Apache FOP, or another processing engine.

If you choose BI Publisher as your report server, you will enjoy a higher level of functionality. Oracle Application Express provides two levels of functionality—External (Apache FOP) and BI Publisher (Advanced). With Apache FOP, you are limited to XSL-FO report templates only.

What is planned for the future version of APEX Listener?

The idea is that instead of having to configure a separate print rendering engine, this engine would be enabled automatically when using the APEX Listener. And rather than sending XML and XSL out from the database and retrieving the PDF back into the database, we would just send the XML and XSL to the APEX Listener, which would process the PDF and send that straightaway to the client.

Of course, this might be considered forward looking and there is a need to point here as well to the Safe Harbor Statement of Oracle Corporation. Hopefully this feature will make it, but who knows.

The following diagram shows the printing architecture using Business Intelligence Publisher:

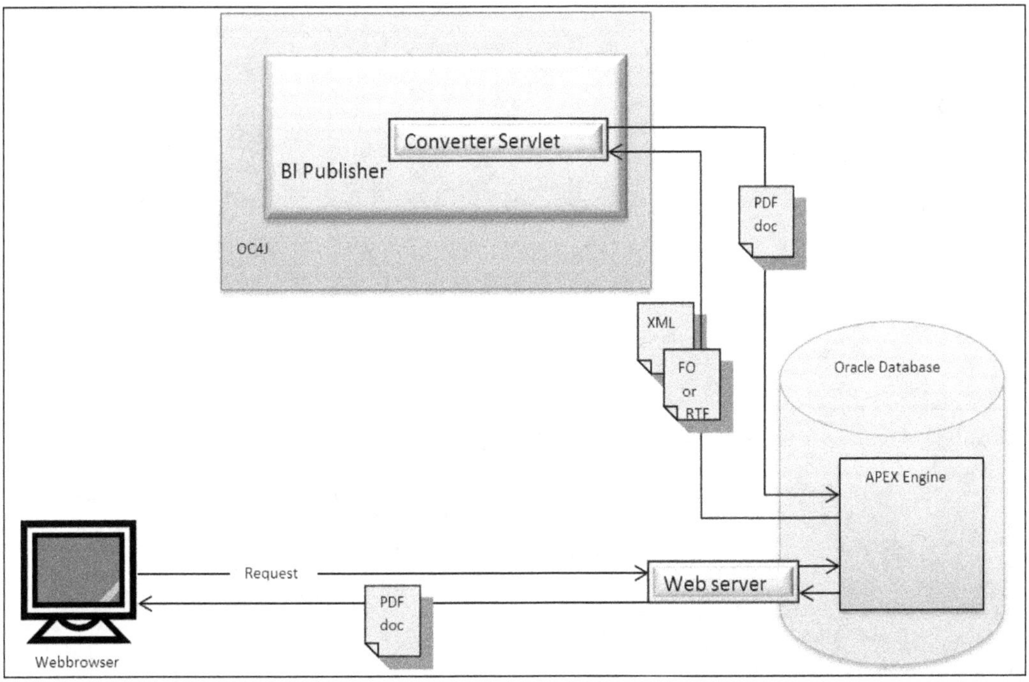

Installation and configuration of the Apache FOP report server

Apache FOP enables you to print report regions and report queries by using either the built-in templates (provided with a standard XSL-FO processing engine) or other formats created by you. The output formats include PDF and XML. This setting does not support **Rich Text Format** (**RTF**).

Application Express calls `apex_fop.jsp` through the `UTL_HTTP RDBMS` package.

The following diagram shows the printing architecture against the Apache FOP report server:

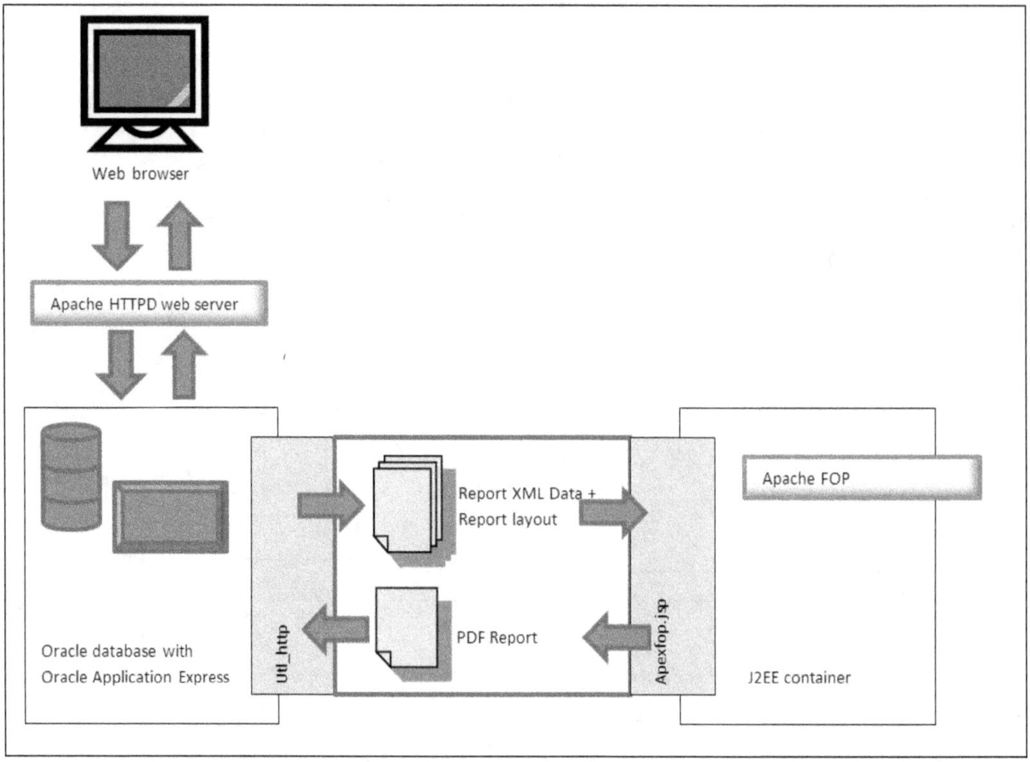

Remark

The Apache FOP is only supported against the OC4J web server, due to the XML parser being used. Currently, it is not supported with the GlassFish and/or WebLogic Servers. Support for WebLogic Server and GlassFish with the Apache FOP solution is planned, especially when running the APEX Listener on one of those servers. However, it is not yet decided when this will be implemented (official statement from Oracle Support Services).

The Apache FOP installation is included in the Application Express distribution under `apex_install_directory/utilities/fop/fop.war`. You need to realize that `fop.war` delivered by Application Express is not the latest version of `fop.war` available. The latest version can be downloaded from `http://xmlgraphics.apache.org/fop/download.html`.

How to configure Apache FOP

Oracle Containers for J2EE (10.1.3.2 or above) needs to be configured for using Application Express. **Oracle Containers for Java** will be abbreviated to **OC4J** in the rest of this chapter. OC4J is delivered in a ZIP file and can be downloaded at Oracle Technology Network:

```
http://www.oracle.com/technetwork/middleware/ias/downloads/
utilsoft-090603.html
```

Creating a batch file or shell script is the most handy way to start OC4J. For example:

```
set ORACLE_HOME=d:\oc4j (Location from OC4j Installation)

set JAVA_HOME=D:\Program Files\Java\jdk1.6.0_version_of_JDK
(Location of JDK)

oc4j -start
```

OC4J is dependent on the **Java Runtime Environment (JRE)**—this is officially supported against JRE version 1.5 and higher, but it is strongly recommended to run against JRE version 1.6.0_33 or higher, or version 1.7. To verify which version of JRE is installed run the following command:

```
java -version
```

The output of this command will look as follows:

```
java version "1.6.0_33"
Java(TM) SE Runtime Environment (build 1.6.0_33-rev-b07)
Java HotSpot(TM) Client VM (build 16.3-b05, mixed mode, sharing)
```

When starting OC4J for the first time, you will be prompted for the password—`oc4jadmin`. The entered password is used as password for the oc4jadmin website. The next step is the deployment of the `fop.war` (web archive) file. Deployment can be performed in the Enterprise Manager from OC4J.

Steps for the deployment from the `fop.war` file are as follows:

1. Click on the **Applications** tab in the Enterprise Manager.
2. Click on the **Deploy** button.
3. Choose **Archive is present on local host. Upload the archive to the server where application server control is running.**. Browse to the **fop.war** file (in the `utilities/fop` directory) and click on **Next**.
4. Make **application name** equal to **FOP**, clear the content in **Context Root**, and click on the **Next** button.
5. Click on the **Deploy** button.

After a successful deployment, you will see an application named **FOP** in the OC4J Enterprise Manager website (`http://hostname:port/em/applications/deploy/fop`).

The following screenshot shows the deployment of `fop.war` in the Enterprise Manager:

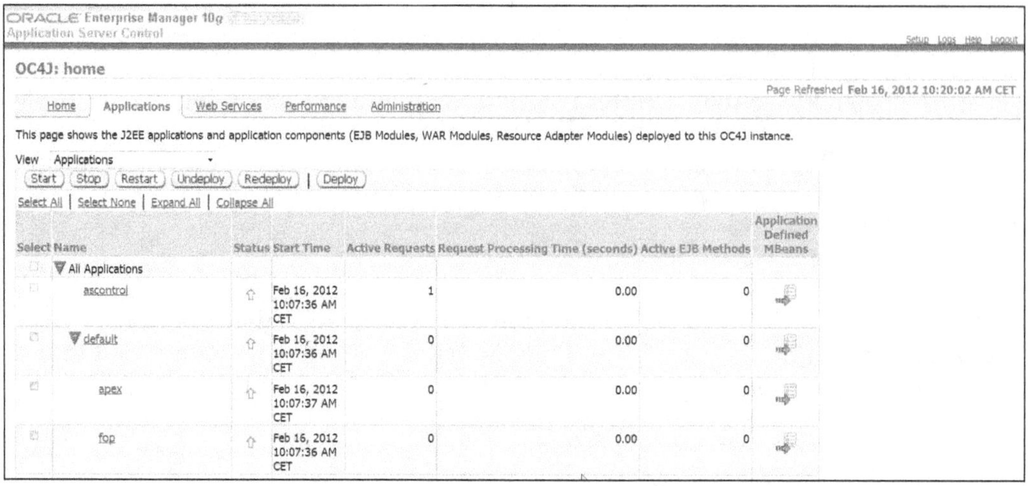

To use the Apache FOP as your report server, you need to configure the Report Printing parameters. A login to the administration site of application express is required (`http://hostname:port/apex(DAD)/apex_admin`).

Navigate to instance settings and enter the required data.

The following screenshot shows the administration website of Application Express and the **Instance Settings** option:

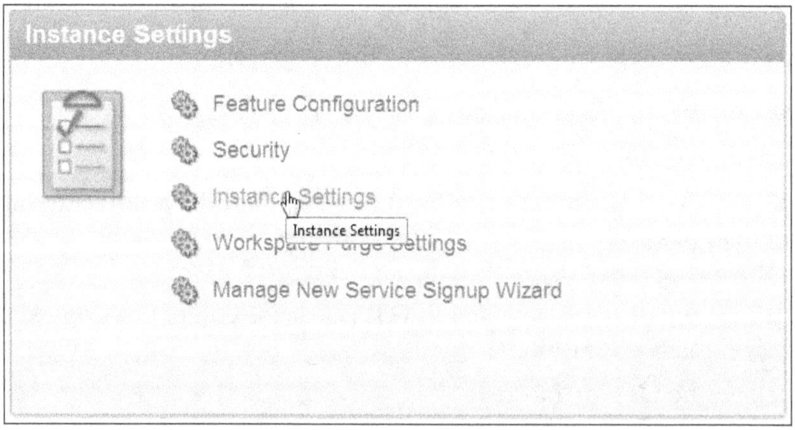

The following data is required to be entered:

- **Print Server**: Select **External (Apache FOP)** from the dropdown list
- **Print Server Protocol**: Choose either **HTTP** or **HTTPS** (depends on your configuration)
- **Print Server Host Address**: The hostname for the machine where you installed `fop.war`
- **Print Server Port**: The port given at the end of the Apache FOP
- **Print Server Script**: `/fop/apex_fop.jsp`

The following screenshot shows the data that needs to be entered for the Apache FOP configuration:

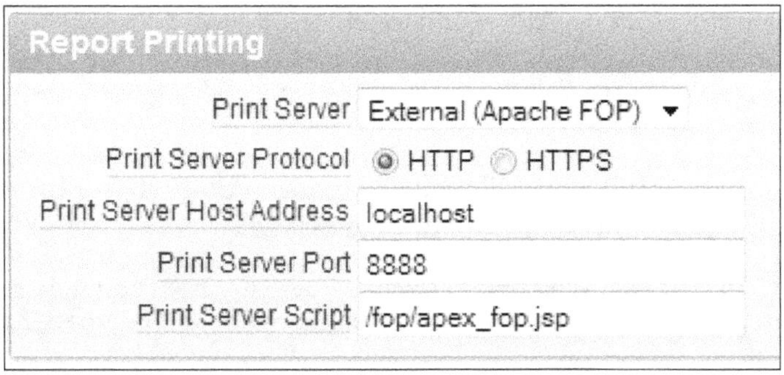

In RDBMS version 11, the next step is enabling network services. By default, the ability to interact with network services is disabled in Oracle Database 11*g* releases 1 and 2. Therefore, if you are running Oracle Application Express with Oracle Database 11*g* release 1 or 2, you must use the new `DBMS_NETWORK_ACL_ADMIN` package to grant connect privileges to any host for `APEX_version` (depending on the Application Express version).

```
DBMS_NETWORK_ACL_ADMIN -

BEGIN
  DBMS_NETWORK_ACL_ADMIN.CREATE_ACL(
  acl => 'print_service.xml',
  description => 'PRINTER ACL',
  principal => 'APEX_040100',
  is_grant => true,
  privilege => 'connect');
```

```
DBMS_NETWORK_ACL_ADMIN.ADD_PRIVILEGE(
  acl => 'print_service.xml',
  principal => 'APEX_040100',
  is_grant => true,
  privilege => 'resolve');

  DBMS_NETWORK_ACL_ADMIN.ASSIGN_ACL(
  acl => 'print_service.xml',
  host => 'localhost',
  lower_port => 8888,
  upper_port => 8888);

COMMIT;
END;
/
```

(The preceding script is using APEX version 4.1.1.)

You can read more at `http://docs.oracle.com/cd/B28359_01/appdev.111/b28419/d_networkacl_adm.htm`.

Failing to grant these privileges will result in issues with PDF/report printing. Specifically, you will get the following error message:

```
ORA-20001: The printing engine could not be reached because either the
URL specified is incorrect or a proxy URL needs to be specified
```

To test a simple report against the Apache FOP report server, perform the following steps:

1. Create a simple report and enable report printing.
2. For the **Report** region under the **Print** tab, select **Yes** for **Print enabled** and create a link label name.
3. Run the report and test the printing.

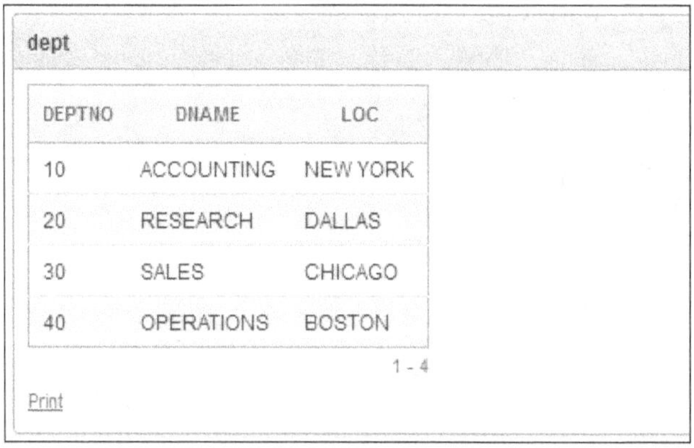

Business Intelligence Publisher

To use Oracle Business Intelligence Publisher as your report server, you need to install Oracle Business Intelligence Publisher version 10.1.3.2.1 or above. Business Intelligence Publisher can be downloaded from the Oracle Technology network (`http://www.oracle.com/technetwork/middleware/bi-publisher/downloads/index.html`).

Business Intelligence Publisher version 11 runs against WebLogic Server.

Installation of Business Intelligence Publisher Version 11

BI Publisher 11.x is installed by using the Oracle Business Intelligence 11*g* Installer. For the integration with Application Express, you only need to install and configure Business Intelligence Publisher. In the **Configure Components** page of the installation, you only need to check the **Business Intelligence Publisher** component. The following screenshot shows the **Components Configuration** screen:

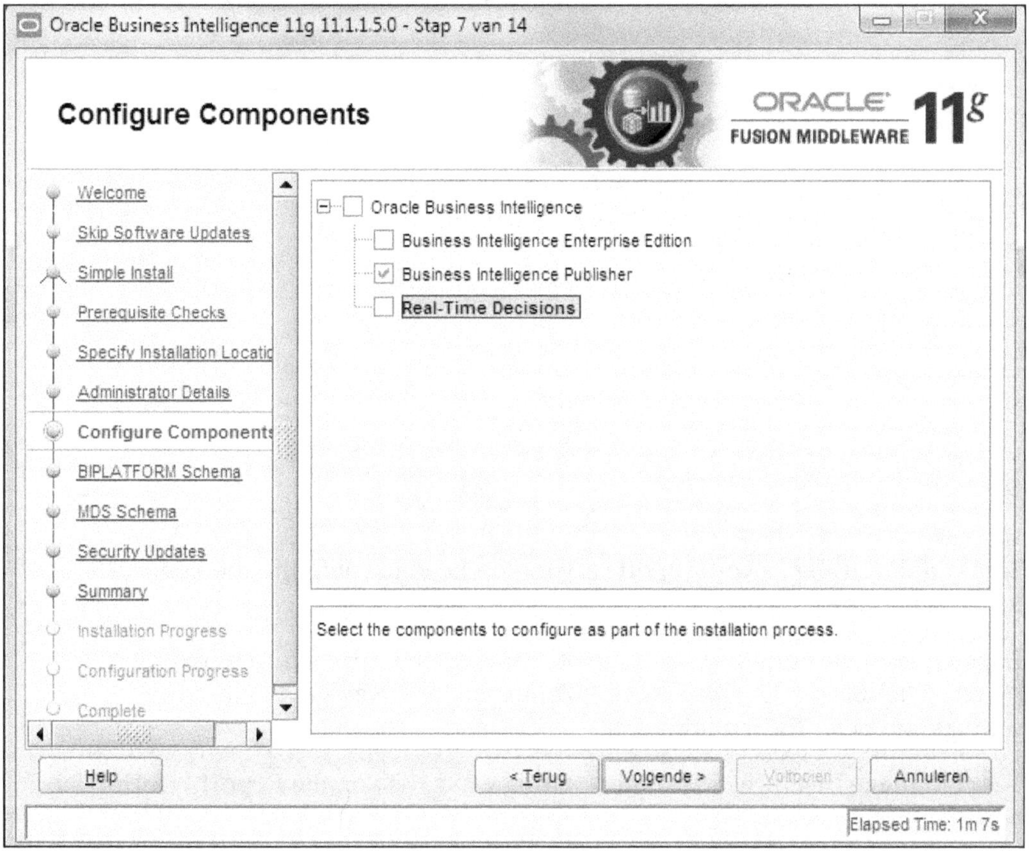

Only BI Publisher needs to be checked in the **Configure Components** screen.

Before installing Business Intelligence Publisher, you must run the **Repository Creation Utility** (**RCU**). RCU creates the `BIPLATFORM` schema to support **Oracle Business Intelligence Enterprise Edition Plus** (**OBIEE Plus**). In RCU, specify the prefix for this schema; the default value is `DEV` for development, but you can change it. This is a pre-requisite from Business Intelligence Publisher version 11. At the end of a successful installation, the BI Publisher Server should be up and running.

The following screenshot shows the main screen from BI Publisher; this screen is used to create your report layout:

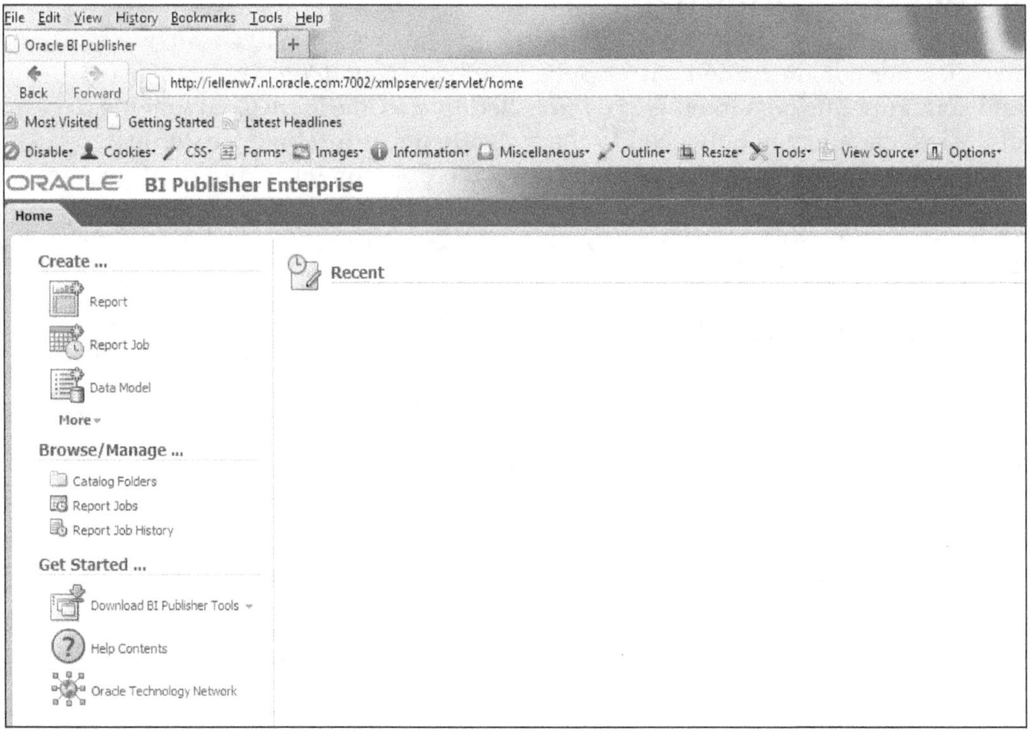

To use BI Publisher as your report server, you need to configure the Report Printing parameters.

Logging in to the administration site of Application Express is required (`http://hostname:port/apex(DAD)/apex_admin`). Navigate to instance settings and enter the required data.

Select **Manage Instance** or **Instance Settings** and click on the **Report Printing** tab.

The following attributes need to be specified:

- **Print Server**: Select **Oracle BI Publisher** from the dropdown list
- **Print Server Protocol**: Choose either **HTTP** or **HTTPS** (depends on your configuration)
- **Print Server Host Address**: The hostname for the machine where you installed Business Intelligence Publisher
- **Print Server Port**: The port given at the end of the BI Publisher installation (port from the managed server)
- **Print Server Script**: `/xmlpserver/convert`

The following screenshot shows the configuration from BI Publisher in the administration website from Application Express:

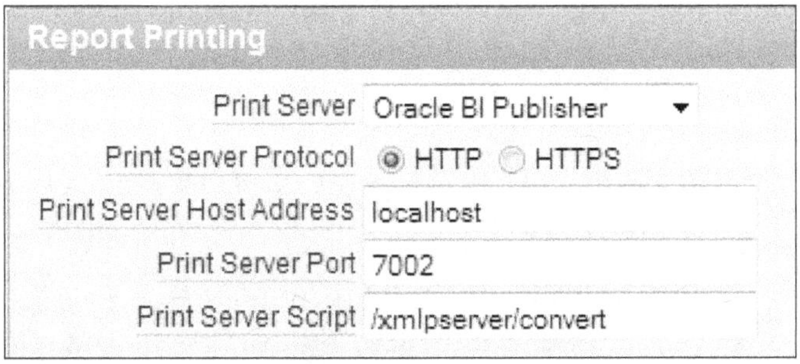

Simple print test using BI Publisher

Printing can be tested by using the sample application from Application Express. The name of the sample application is product portal, database application. **Enable Report Printing** needs to be configured in the **Printing** attributes page. In the same page, give the link a name. The following screenshot shows the **Print** tab for the **Report** region:

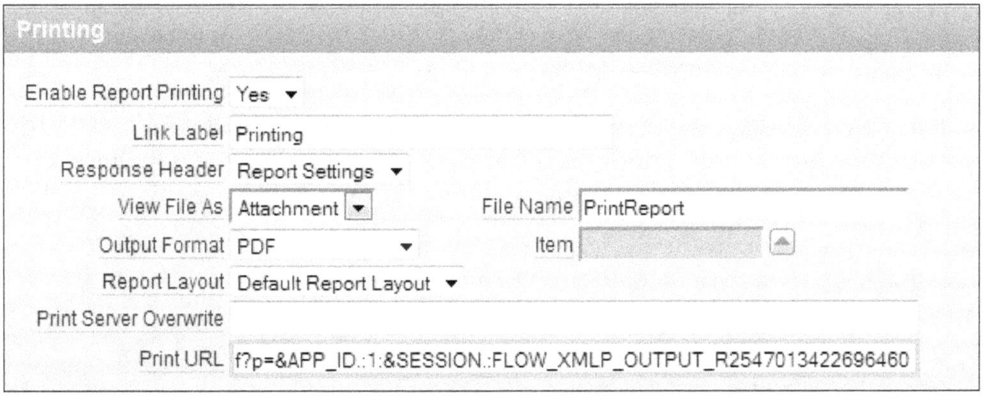

When running the print page, you will see **Print link** somewhere near the report and clicking on that link will give you a report in the format selected in the **Printing** attributes page.

How to debug or troubleshoot printing issues

My statement is, "Keep it as simple as possible." So when you face issues with testing the report server, start by taking Application Express out of scope.

One way to make sure that your print server is up, running, and configured properly is to set up a static HTML form that simulates what Application Express is doing internally, that is, posting some XML data along with an XSL-FO stylesheet to a print server via HTTP and receiving back a PDF document as the response. If this works properly, you can at least be sure that your print server is working.

Example

The example file, *How To Debug APEX and PDF Printing Integration Issues: BI Publisher / Apache FOP (Doc ID 454701.1)*, can be downloaded from My Oracle Support:

- Download the attached ZIP file (`testpdf.html`).
- Open the `testpdf.html` file in a browser and enter one of the following URLs for your print server installation:

  `http://servername.domain.com:9704/xmlpserver/convert (BI Publisher)`

  `http://servername.domain.com:8888/fop/apex_fop.jsp`
- Click on the **Submit** button.

If this is successful and the report server can be contacted, you should see a PDF file document. If not, there is something wrong in contacting the report server. Check the URL entered for the test to make sure you have not entered the instance details incorrectly.

Another way to check if the report server can be reached without taking Application Express in the picture, is to check the outcome of the following PL/SQL block. Of course, you need to replace the hostname with your own hostname and the port with your printer server port.

```
DECLARE
    req   utl_http.req;
    resp  utl_http.resp;
    value VARCHAR2(1024);
```

```
BEGIN
  req := utl_http.begin_request('http://hostname:printer server
  port/xmlpserver');
  utl_http.set_header(req, 'User-Agent', 'Mozilla/4.0');
  resp := utl_http.get_response(req);
  LOOP
    utl_http.read_line(resp, value, TRUE);
    dbms_output.put_line(value);
  END LOOP;
  utl_http.end_response(resp);
EXCEPTION
  WHEN utl_http.end_of_body THEN
    utl_http.end_response(resp);
END;
```

How to check if network services are enabled

Network services need to be enabled for Oracle RDBMS version 11 and higher. When an error occurs in the printing, the network services need to be checked.

```
select acl, principal, privilege, is_grant
from dba_network_acl_privileges;
```

The outcome is as follows:

```
ACL                                Principal            Privilege
Is_Grant

/sys/acls/power_users.xml  APEX_040100   Connect              True
```

The preceding query will check the necessary privileges that are needed for the printing feature in Application Express. These rows need to be present for enabling printing. If the necessary privileges are not granted when you are printing, the following error will be generated:

```
ORA-20001: The printing engine could not be reached because either the
URL specified is incorrect or a proxy URL needs to be specified
```

When there are no rows, ACL needs to be added. The code needed to fix this problem is available in the Installation Guide from Application Express, under the header *3.3.7 Enable Network Services in Oracle Database 11g* (`http://docs.oracle.com/cd/E23903_01/doc/doc.41/e21673/pre_require.htm#i1009513`).

A second check is done to ensure the remote hosts are assigned to the ACLs:

```
connect / as sysdba

column host       format a30
column acl        format a30
column principal  format a20

column start_date format a20
column end_date   format a20
column lport      format 9999
column uport      format 99999
column R          format a1

set pagesize 999
set echo on

spool support_acl.txt

select *
from   v$version;

show parameter smtp

select host
     , acl
     , lower_port lport
     , upper_port uport
From   dba_network_acls;

select acl
     , principal
     , decode(u.type#,0,'*',1,' ') "R"
     , privilege
     , is_grant
     , to_char(start_date,'YYYY-MON-DD') start_date
     , to_char(end_date,'YYYY-MON-DD') end_date
from   dba_network_acl_privileges p
     , user$ u
where  u.name=p.principal;

spool off
-- end list ACL setup
```

Creating a report with BI Publisher

There are four steps for creating your APEX application report with BI Publisher:

1. Create the report query.
2. Design the report layout.
3. Upload the layout.
4. Link the report to your application.

You can print a report region by defining a report query as a shared component. Unlike SQL statements contained in regions, report queries are not validated to ensure they are formatted correctly and the objects they reference exist. With report queries, the query is used to generate the file that we create to build a template.

Creating the report query

The first step is to create the report query. Click on **Shared Components** and then click on **Report Queries** under the **Reports** section to create a query:

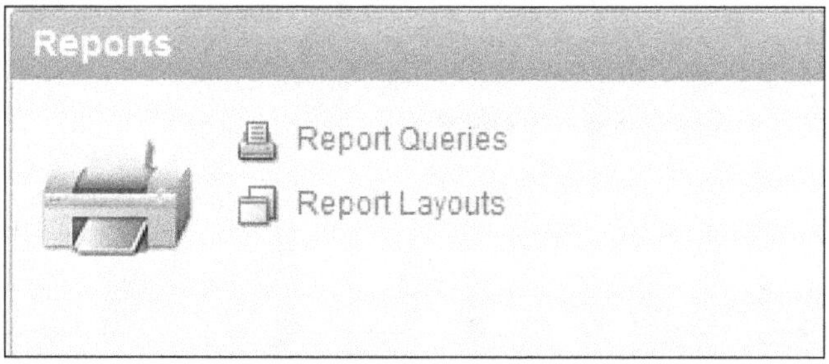

Enter a name for the query in **Report Query Name** (anything is fine), then select **Output Format** from the list, and click on **Next** as shown in the following screenshot:

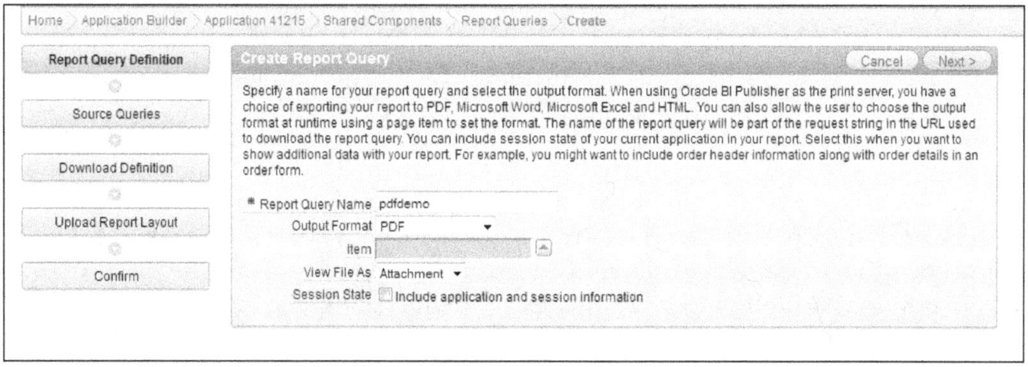

Enter the query and click on the **Next** button. See the following screenshot:

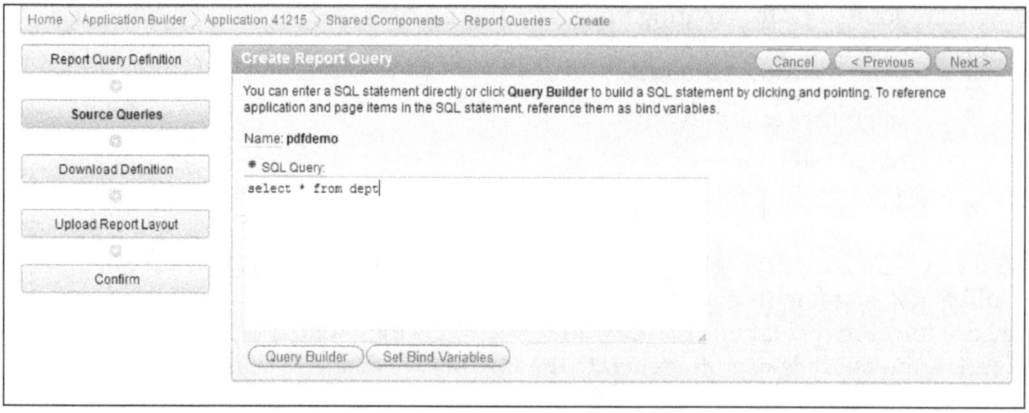

To end the report query, click on the **Finish** button. See the following screenshot:

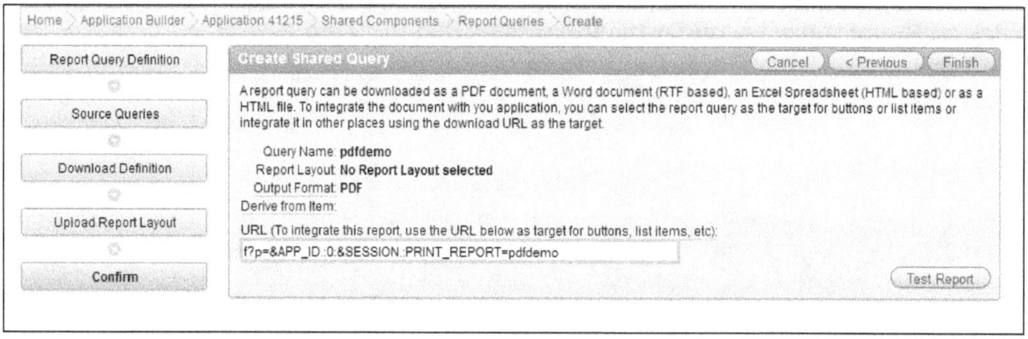

Designing the report layout

The second step is to design the report layout. Now that you have created a report query, you can design the report output with MS Word, but before doing so you need to download the XML data onto your local machine. BI Publisher provides you an MS Word add-in called **Template Builder**, which helps you to design the reports and preview the result easily and quickly (`http://www.oracle.com/technetwork/middleware/bi-publisher/downloads/index.html`).

You can associate a report query with a report layout and download it as a formatted document. If no report layout is selected, a generic layout is used. The generic layout is intended to be used to test and verify a report query. When using the generic layout option and multiple source queries are defined, only the first result set is included in the document.

Downloading XML data

Open the report query that has just been created and click on the **Download** button under the **Source Queries** section:

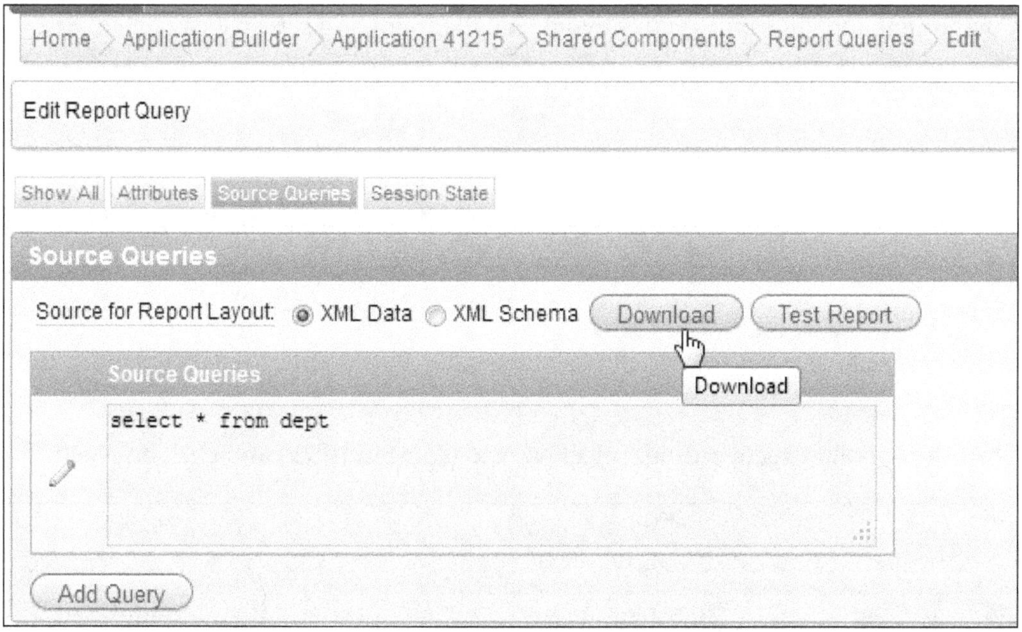

You can save the generated XML data on your local machine.

Designing with the RTF template (MS Word)

This would be a regular step for BI Publisher users. The RTF template is one of the report layout options that BI Publisher provides in addition to other options such as the BI Publisher template, Excel template, Flex template (for Flash), PDF template, and so on. You can use MS Word to design report layouts from simple reports to very complex, pixel-perfect, and high fidelity reports. You can take a look at the *BI Publisher Report Designer's guide* for details (`http://docs.oracle.com/cd/E14571_01/bi.1111/e13881/toc.htm`).

Uploading the report layout

The third step is to upload the layout. Once you finish designing the report layout with the RTF template, you can upload it to Oracle APEX and associate it to the report query. Log in to Oracle APEX and go to your application. Go to **Shared Component** and click on **Report Layout**. See the following screenshot:

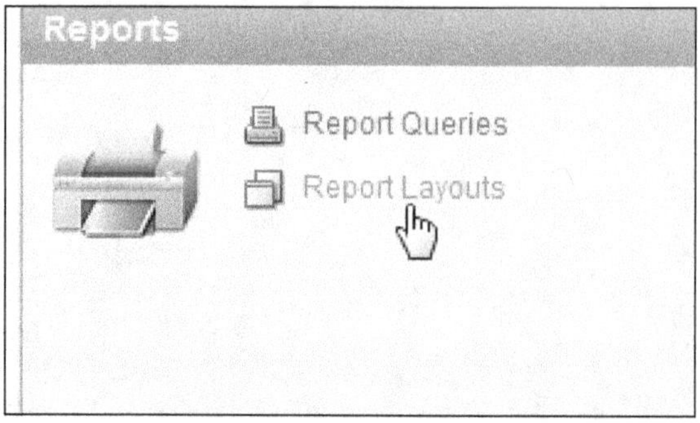

Then click on the **Create** button. Select **Named Column (RTF)** and click on **Next**:

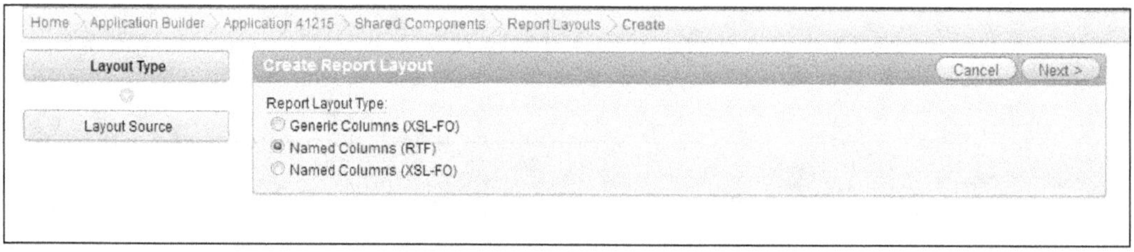

Type the layout name in the **Layout Name** field and select the RTF template. Then click on **Create Layout** to finish:

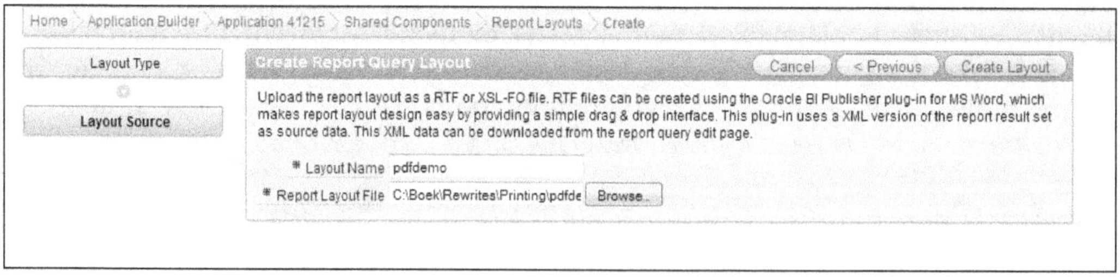

Linking the report to your application

The final step is to link the report to your application. Now, open the report query that was created earlier and select the report layout that has just been created. See the following screenshot:

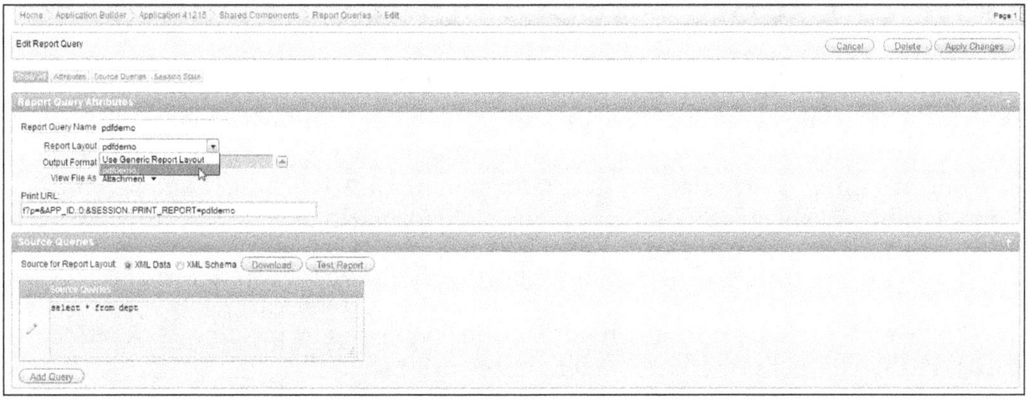

Now the report layout is associated with the report query.

To make these reports available to end users, integrate them with an application. For example, you can associate a report query with a button, list item, branch, or other navigational components that allow you to use URLs as targets.

The next step is to add a button in the APEX application page so that the users can click on that button to open the BI Publisher report.

1. Select **Create Button** from the menu.
2. Fill in the fields on the **Create Button** page to create a button. In this example, I have created the `P1_PRINT` button and set both the label name and the request name to be printed:

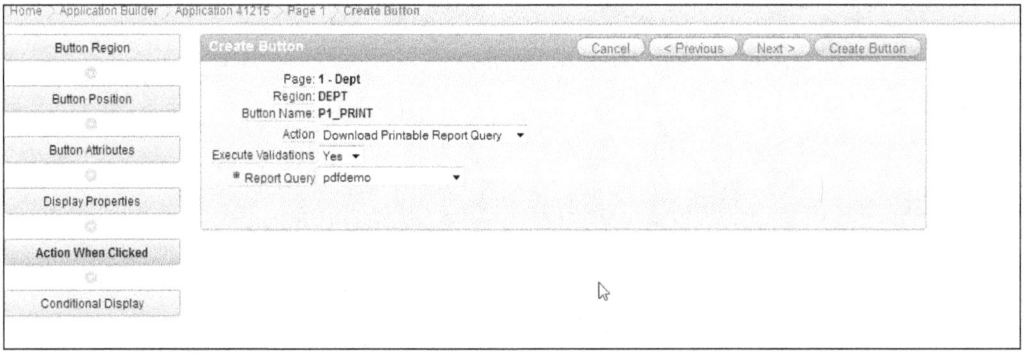

3. And that's it! Now, you are ready to generate a BI Publisher report from your APEX application. When you run the application you should see the **Print** button.

How to create a report that can deliver output in different formats

Apache FOP is only capable of PDF printing. The other printing format options (Word, Excel, and HTML) are available if the BI Publisher configuration is been used or if you are using Oracle Reports in combination with Application Express. Oracle Reports is capable of creating reports in multiple formats.

This example describes how to create a report with different output formats.

The first step is to create a simple report and to enable report printing as described earlier in this chapter under the header Simple print test.

The second step is to create the `select list` item based on a static list of values. Let your users select the kind of report output type to be used. You can do so by creating an item with the `select list` type.

Display value	Return value
PDF	PDF
Word	RTF
Excel	XLS
HTML	HTM
XML	XML

The `select list` item has a list of values attached as follows:

```
Static2:PDF;PDF,Word;RTF,Excel;XLS,HTML;HTM,XML;XML
```

Choose, for example, PDF as the default format.

Under the **Print Attributes** tab in the **Printing** section, the output format needs to have the value-derived output:

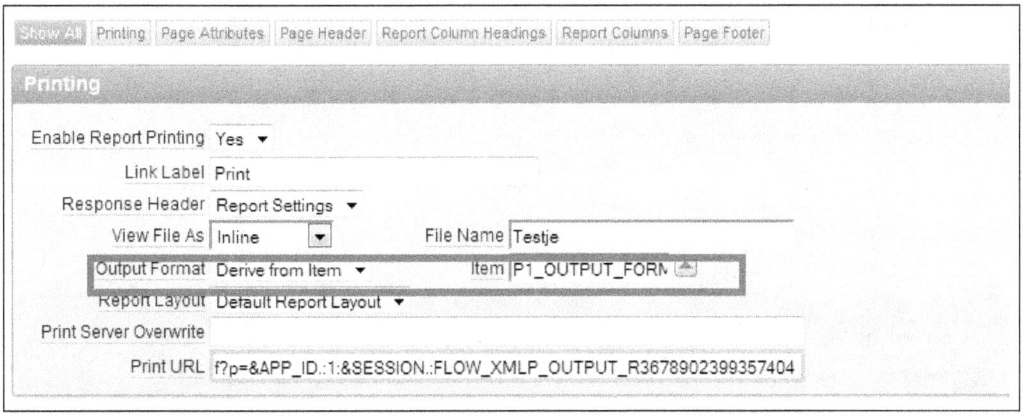

The last step is to add a button with a redirect to the print. In the report printing attributes screen, cut and paste the report printing URL. A report printing URL has the following format:

```
f?p=&APP_ID.:<appid>:&SESSION.:FLOW_XMLP_OUTPUT_R<random number>
```

This is shown in the following screenshot:

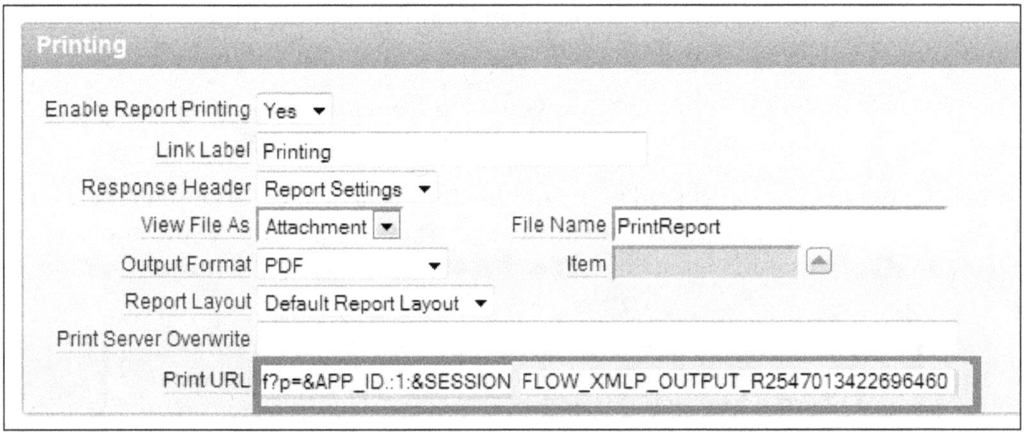

Cut and paste the `FLOW_XMLP_OUTPUT_R###` section from the **Print URL** field. Since you are going to invoke the print from the button, you can remove the **Printing** from the **Link Label** field and a branch needs to be created, as shown in the following screenshot:

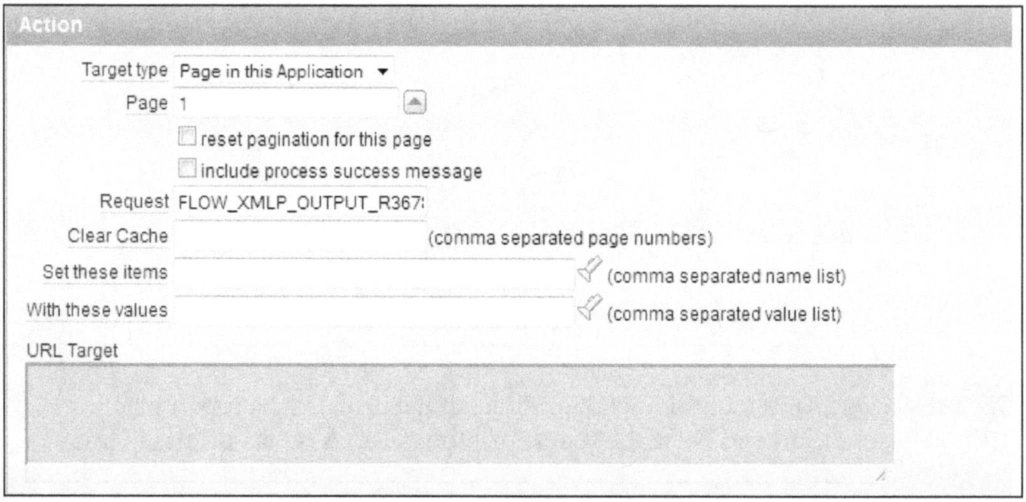

How to add a chart to a report

It's actually quite easy to use the BI Publisher Template Builder plugin for Microsoft Word and BI Publisher as the PDF rendering engine for Application Express.

The Template Builder plugin can be downloaded from `http://www.oracle.com/technetwork/middleware/bi-publisher/downloads/index.html`.

Report layouts can be developed by using the BI Publisher Word Template Builder. Using the Template Builder, you can create a chart and report definition, and save this as an RTF file, which can be uploaded back into Application Express.

> It's important to understand however, that this is not a printer-friendly version of your web page. So if you have, for example, a Flash chart region and a report region on your page, you can't simply print this as a PDF.

The PDF printing feature in Application Express generates XML data of your report's result set, using an XSL-FO report layout (or RTF template). This XML data is then transformed into PDF (or other supported output format). The transformation is sent back to the browser for download.

Creating a chart in a report

In order to create a PDF document that contains a chart and report, you need to create a report query and associate that report query with an RTF-based report layout:

1. The first step is to export the report data in XML format. You can save the generated XML data on your local machine and the BI Publisher Template Builder software will be used to create the RTF layout. See the following screenshot:

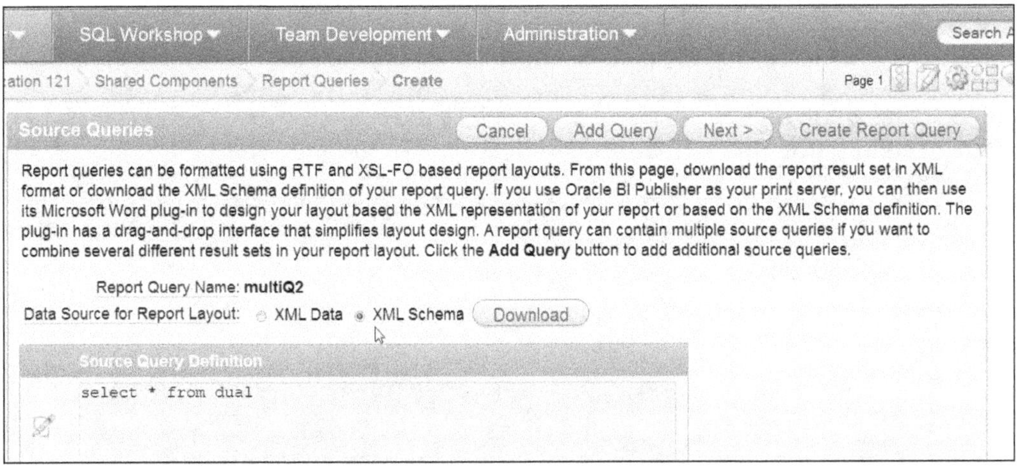

2. The next step is to load the XML file in BI Publisher Template Builder. Navigate to **Oracle BI Publisher | Data | Load Sample XML Data**.

   The following screenshot shows the successful loading of the XML data into the Template Builder:

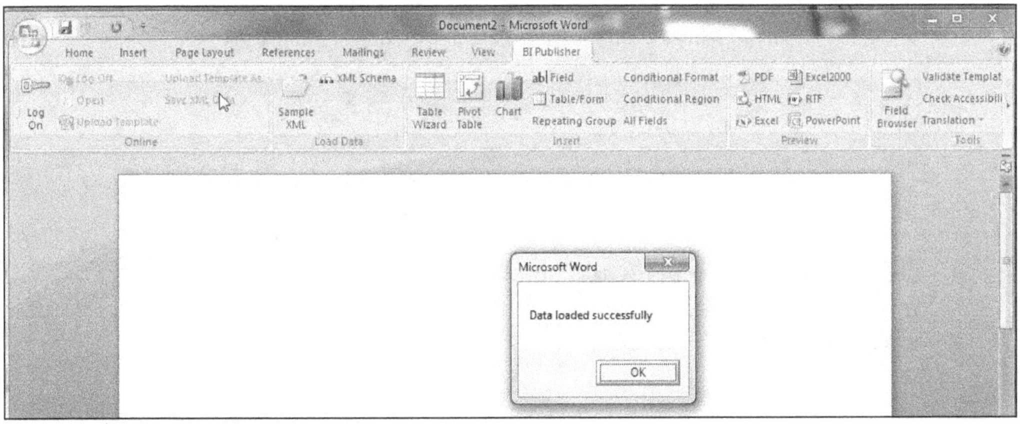

3. Note that nothing appears on the page yet. You need to add the columns to your report. Insert report objects as fields, tables, or charts using the wizard. Navigate to **Oracle BIPublisher | Insert** and select **Field**, **Table**, or **Chart**:

4. Save the layout in the RTF file format.
5. The following screenshot shows the RTF file created by using the Template Builder from BI Publisher:

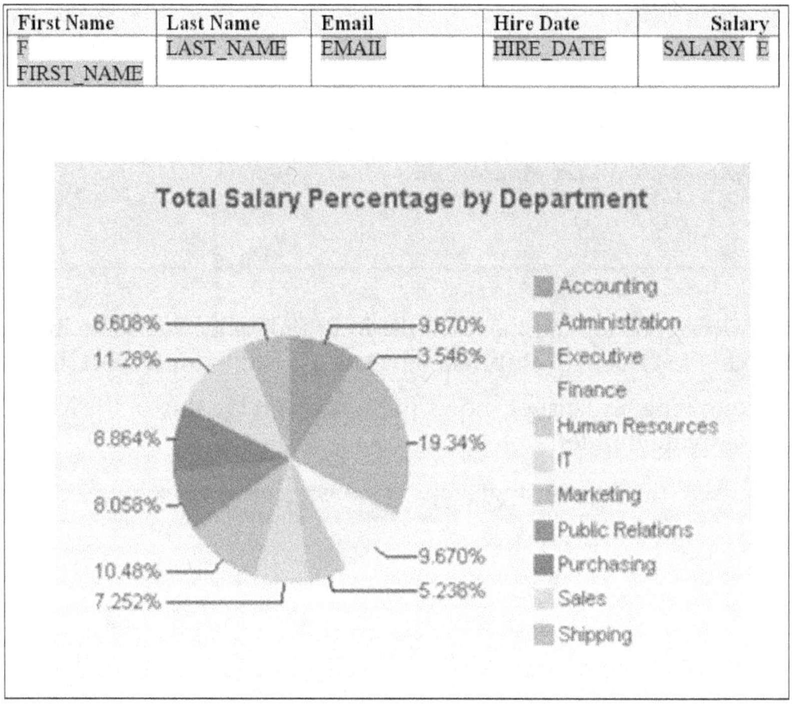

6. Deploy the RTF template to Application Express and associate it with a report query or region. The steps to perform this are described in this chapter in the *Uploading layout* section.

7. The last step of the process is to create a button to print the report. The next screenshot shows you how to do this:

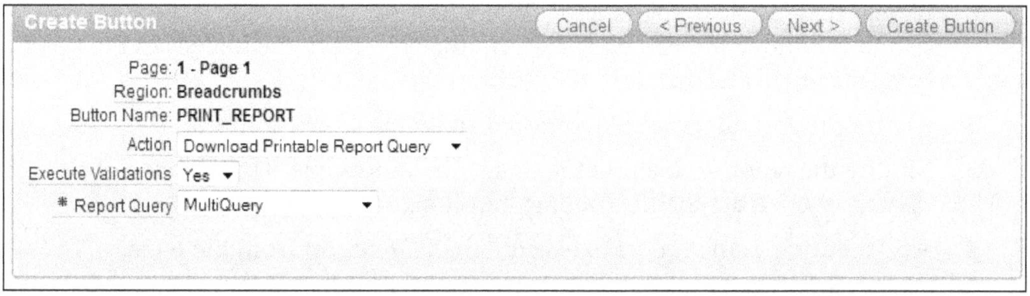

8. Test the report by running the page. In this example, when I press the **PRINT_REPORT** button, I'm getting a PDF document with the chart included in it.

How to add dynamic images to a report

For static images it's pretty straightforward. Just place the static images into your RTF layout, using MS Word and BI Publisher Desktop. For dynamic images, well that's a little more complicated.

When talking about dynamic images, what I mean is the images that are stored in BLOB columns in database tables. To include the image in the PDF, you need to take care of the following:

- The image needs to be included in the generated XML representation of the report data and the RTF report layout needs to include instructions on what to do with the image information stored in the XML data.
- Before BLOB columns can be included in the XML export, they need to be converted to CLOB by using base64 encoding and the report template needs to reference the image data column by using an XSL-FO expression. So the reports template needs to reference the image data column, using XSL-FO expression.

[Keep in mind the 32K limit on report columns.]

The next few steps show how to accomplish this:

1. Create a function to convert your BLOB data to a CLOB base64-encoded format that can be displayed in a PDF report. If you already have a CLOB column, you need to make sure that you store the images in the base64-encoded format.
2. Create a report query and layout that show the CLOB column.
3. Modify the report to include the image in your report. This step is not necessary to create the PDF report, but it may be useful.
4. Add a button to the report to execute the PDF report from the page.

The following steps are necessary to include images in a report.

Create a function to convert BLOB data to CLOB base64-encoded format.

An example of a function to convert BLOB to CLOB is as follows:

```
CREATE OR REPLACE FUNCTION blob2clobase64 (p_blob IN BLOB)
RETURN CLOB
IS
   pos PLS_INTEGER := 1;
   buffer VARCHAR2 (32767);
   res CLOB;
   lob_len INTEGER := DBMS_LOB.getlength (p_blob);
BEGIN
   -- Create a temporary CLOB
   DBMS_LOB.createtemporary (res, TRUE);
   -- Open it for Read/Write.
   DBMS_LOB.OPEN (res, DBMS_LOB.lob_readwrite);
   LOOP
      -- Get the next 32000 bytes from the input BLOB
      -- encode them into base64
      -- and cast it to a VARCHAR2
      buffer := UTL_RAW.cast_to_varchar2
         (UTL_ENCODE.base64_encode (DBMS_LOB.SUBSTR (p_blob,
          32000, pos)));
      -- If there is still data left add it to the result
      IF LENGTH (buffer) > 0
      THEN
         DBMS_LOB.writeappend (res, LENGTH (buffer), buffer);
      END IF;
      -- Move the pointer
      pos := pos + 32000;
      -- Exit when done
      EXIT WHEN pos > lob_len;
   END LOOP;
   RETURN res;
END blob2clobase64;
```

The UTL_RAW.CAST_TO_VARCHAR2 function converts a raw value into a value of datatype VARCHAR2 with the same number of data bytes. The result is treated as if it was composed of single "8-bit" bytes, not characters. Multibyte character boundaries are ignored. The data is not modified in any way—it is only changed to datatype VARCHAR2.

The UTL_ENCODE.BASE64_ENCODE function encodes the binary representation of the RAW value into base 64 elements and returns it in the form of a RAW string.

The DBMS_LOB.SUBSTR function selects the requested number of characters of a BLOB column from a given starting position.

Create a report query and layout to show the CLOB column:

```
select employee_id,
       first_name,
       last_name,
       blob2clobase64(photo)
from employees
where photo is not null
```

In the report query, invoke the blob2clobase64 function for the photo image.

In addition, because you have many rows in the table that may or may not have photos, you need to add the WHERE clause to select only those records that have a photo.

> The Image element is the name of image_item.

For example, the image item is photo. In the template, you now need to reference the image data. We can use an XSL-FO expression to reference the image:

```
<fo:instream-foreign-object content-type="image/gif">
  <xsl:value-of select="PHOTO"/>
</fo:instream-foreign-object>
```

Notice that the template needs to know the mime type of the image—in this case it is `image/gif`. `IMAGE_ELEMENT` (`PHOTO`) contains the base64-encoded image data. The following screenshot shows that the image (picture) has been converted:

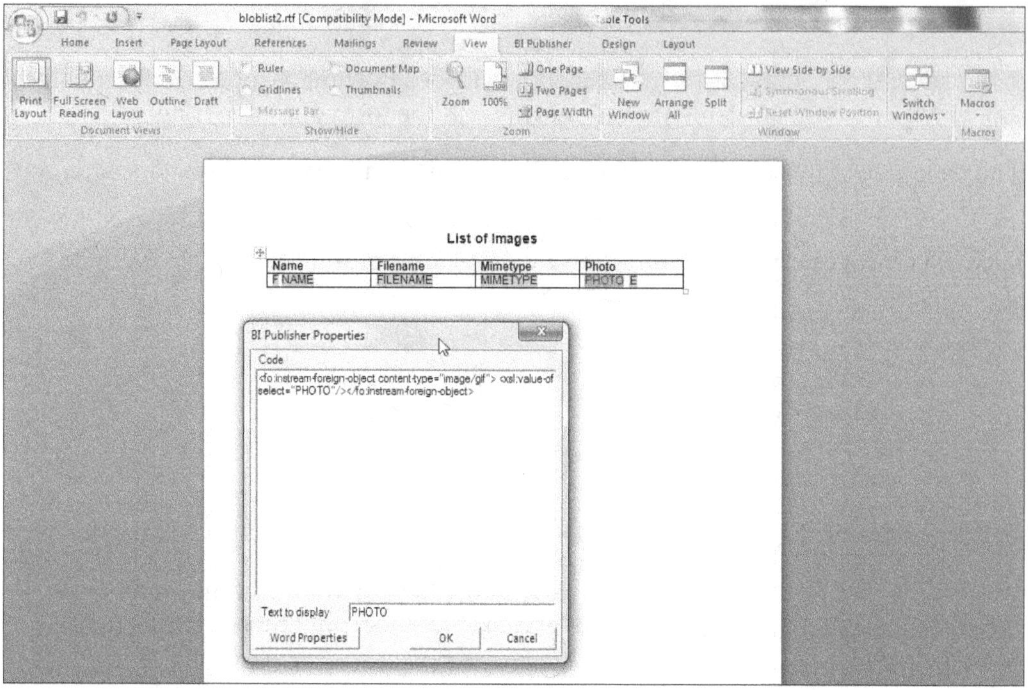

You may also want to include the photo on the report on a page in your application. You can add the `PHOTO` column to the `Report` region, which then needs to be configured in **Report Attributes**.

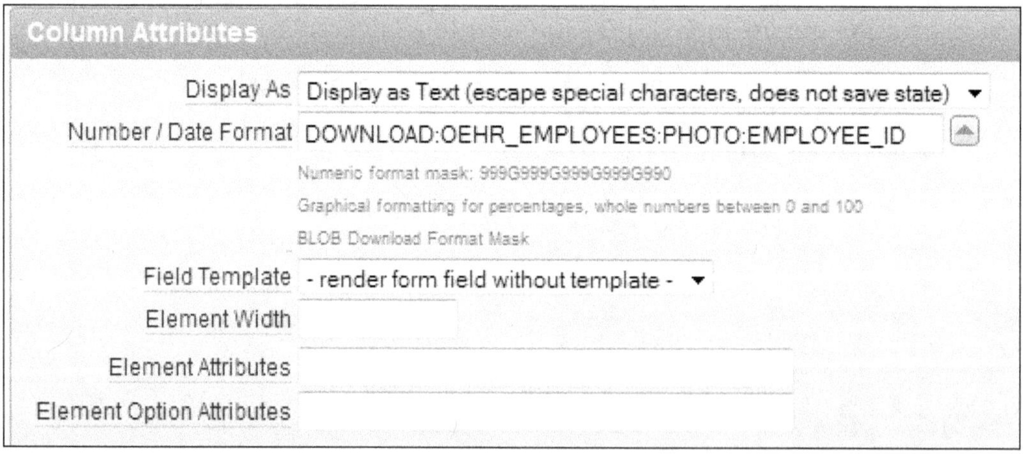

The key to manipulate the download link of a BLOB column is the column's format mask. You specify a format mask for a date or number, in the same way you can format a download link. However, the `DOWNLOAD` format mask requires you to specify at least three parameters, as shown in the following line:

```
DOWNLOAD:EMPLOYEES:PHOTO:EMPLOYEE_ID
```

This is the default format that gets created by the wizard. Additional format options can be added to make the download capability more user friendly (also see the document at `http://docs.oracle.com/cd/E23903_01/doc/doc.41/e21674/advnc_blob.htm#BCGBCHBD`).

Modify the format of the `BLOB_CONTENT` column as follows:

```
DOWNLOAD:TABLE_NAME:BLOB_CONTENT:ID::MIME_TYPE:FILENAME:
LAST_UPDATED:CHARACTER_SET
```

Clicking on the link **BLOB Download Format Mask**, displays a pop up to assist you in entering all the parameters that are necessary for the `DOWNLOAD` format, as you can see in the following screenshot:

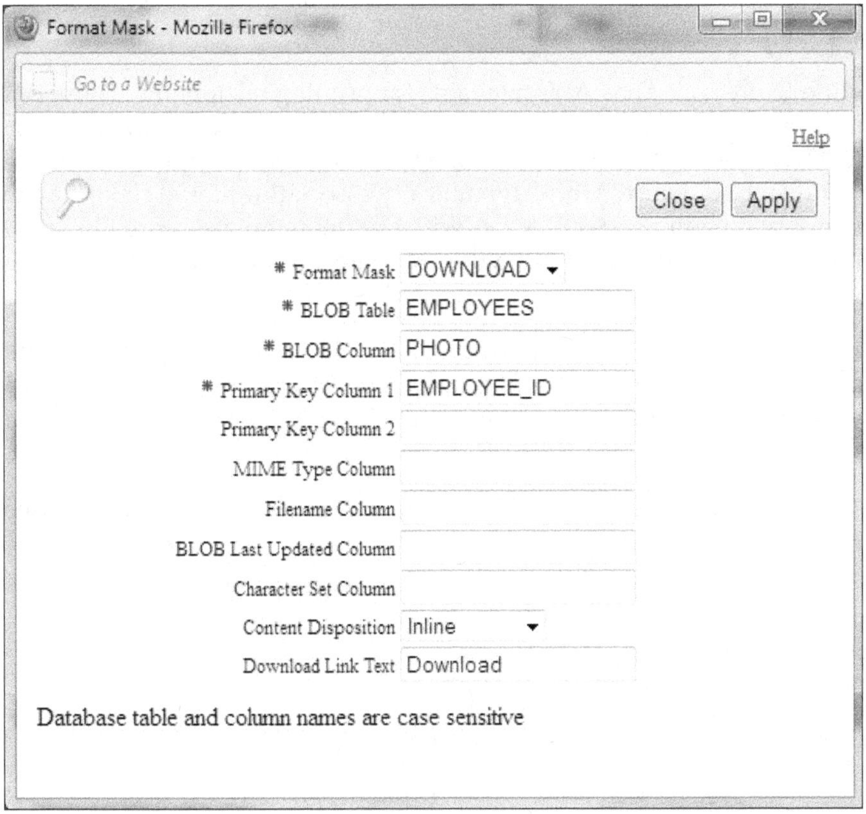

You can invoke the PDF report from within your page by using a button. When you create the button, select **Download Printable Report Query** from the **Action** drop-down list. See the following screenshot:

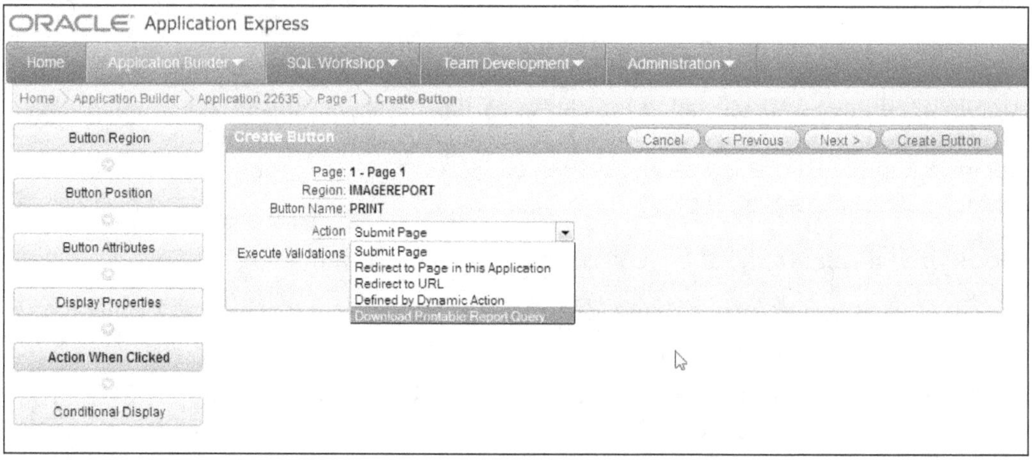

Print API

Application Express also has APIs available for printing documents. These APIs are `apex_util.download_print_document` and `apex_util.get_print_document`. Both Print APIs have four different signatures, which they allow for programmatically downloading report queries while dynamically associating stored report layouts at runtime, downloading report queries with custom templates stored in your own tables, and generating PDF based on your own custom XML by using your own custom templates.

`APEX_UTIL_DOWNLOAD_PRINT_DOCUMENT` initiates download of a print document in four ways. Each has slightly different parameters (you can read more about these parameters at `http://download.oracle.com/docs/cd/E23903_01/doc/doc.41/e21676/apex_util.htm`).

The first option is to use XML-based report data and an RTF- or XSL-FO-based report layout:

```
APEX_UTIL.DOWNLOAD_PRINT_DOCUMENT (
p_file_name IN VARCHAR,
p_content_disposition IN VARCHAR,
p_report_data IN BLOB,
p_report_layout IN CLOB,
p_report_layout_type IN VARCHAR2 default 'xsl-fo',
p_document_format IN VARCHAR2 default 'pdf',
p_print_server IN VARCHAR2 default null );
```

The second option is to use a predefined report query and an RTF- or XSL-FO-based report layout:

```
APEX_UTIL.DOWNLOAD_PRINT_DOCUMENT (
p_file_name IN VARCHAR,
p_content_disposition IN VARCHAR,
p_application_id IN NUMBER,
p_report_query_name IN VARCHAR2,
p_report_layout IN CLOB,
p_report_layout_type IN VARCHAR2 default 'xsl-fo',
p_document_format IN VARCHAR2 default 'pdf',
p_print_server IN VARCHAR2 default null );
```

The third option is to use a predefined report query and a predefined report layout:

```
APEX_UTIL.DOWNLOAD_PRINT_DOCUMENT (
p_file_name IN VARCHAR,
p_content_disposition IN VARCHAR,
p_application_id IN NUMBER,
p_report_query_name IN VARCHAR2,
p_report_layout_name IN VARCHAR2,
p_report_layout_type IN VARCHAR2 default 'xsl-fo',
p_document_format IN VARCHAR2 default 'pdf',
p_print_server IN VARCHAR2 default null );
```

The fourth and last option is to use an XML-based report data (as a CLOB) and an RTF- or XSL-FO-based report layout:

```
APEX_UTIL.DOWNLOAD_PRINT_DOCUMENT (
p_file_name IN VARCHAR,
p_content_disposition IN VARCHAR,
p_report_data IN CLOB,
p_report_layout IN CLOB,
p_report_query_name IN VARCHAR2,
p_report_layout_type IN VARCHAR2 default 'xsl-fo',
p_document_format IN VARCHAR2 default 'pdf',
p_print_server IN VARCHAR2 default null );
```

Reports can be captured and stored in database tables, using the Application Express Print API. `apex_util.get_print_document` retrieves the report in BLOB format. So the `apex_util.get_print_document` function always returns a document as BLOB.

The first option is to use XML-based report data and a RTF- or XSL-FO-based report layout:

```
APEX_UTIL.GET_PRINT_DOCUMENT (
p_report_data IN BLOB,
p_report_layout IN CLOB,
p_report_layout_type IN VARCHAR2 default 'xsl-fo',
p_document_format IN VARCHAR2 default 'pdf',
p_print_server IN VARCHAR2 default NULL
) RETURN BLOB;
```

The second option is to use a predefined report query and a predefined report layout:

```
APEX_UTIL.GET_PRINT_DOCUMENT (
p_application_id IN NUMBER,
p_report_layout_name IN VARCHAR2,
p_report_query_name IN VARCHAR2,
p_report_layout_name IN VARCHAR2 default null,
p_report_layout_type IN VARCHAR2 default 'xsl-fo',
p_document_format IN VARCHAR2 default 'pdf',
p_print_server IN VARCHAR2 default null
) RETURN BLOB;
```

The third option is to use a predefined report query and an RTF- or XSL-FO-based report layout:

```
APEX_UTIL.GET_PRINT_DOCUMENT (
p_application_id IN NUMBER,
p_report_query_name IN VARCHAR2,
p_report_layout IN CLOB,
p_report_layout_type IN VARCHAR2 default 'xsl-fo',
p_document_format IN VARCHAR2 default 'pdf',
p_print_server IN VARCHAR2 default null
) RETURN BLOB;
```

The fourth and last option is to use an XML-based report data and an RTF- or XSL-FO-based report layout:

```
APEX_UTIL.GET_PRINT_DOCUMENT (
p_report_data IN CLOB,
p_report_layout IN CLOB,
p_report_layout_type IN VARCHAR2 default 'xsl-fo',
p_document_format IN VARCHAR2 default 'pdf',
p_print_server IN VARCHAR2 default NULL
) RETURN BLOB;
```

How to bypass the 32K limit

One issue, which will be addressed in the next version of Application Express, is the 32K limit on report columns. This means that only fairly small images are currently supported when using the technique with report queries or report regions. If the XML data is generated some other way, and the PDF rendering is done using the Print API, the use of larger images would be possible as well.

The 32K limit on report columns can be bypassed by using the Print APIs—`apex_util.download_print_document` and `apex_util.get_print_document`. With these APIs, you can generate PDF and other documents through a simple PL/SQL API call. These APIs take care of all the communication with BI Publisher or Apache FOP.

The `apex_util.get_print_document` API can be called to generate and retrieve the print document as a BLOB in the database for further processing, such as storing the document in tables, and so on.

The `apex_util.download_print_document` API can be called in an Oracle Application Express page process to generate and download the print document straight to your client.

An example of this mechanism can be downloaded from `http://marcsewtz.blogspot.com/2012/02/dynamic-images-in-pdf-what-32k-limit.html`.

Alternatives to use for PDF printing

Beside the use of Apache FOP or BI Publisher, PDF documents can be created in Oracle Application Express by making use of alternative methods such as calling Oracle Reports, using plugins, and so on.

Integration with Oracle Reports

Oracle Reports, a component of Oracle Fusion Middleware, is a high-fidelity enterprise reporting tool. It enables businesses to provide instant access to information to all levels within and outside of the organization in a scalable and secure environment.

More information about Oracle Reports can be found on the Oracle Technology Network website (`http://www.oracle.com/technetwork/middleware/reports/overview/index.html`).

Oracle Reports Developer includes Oracle Reports Builder and Oracle Reports Services. Oracle Reports Builder is used to develop the report and Oracle Reports Services executes, distributes, and publishes your reports for enterprise-wide reporting.

This paragraph has been added just to show you the possibility of integrating Oracle Reports with Oracle Application Express.

The Oracle report is called as follows:

```
http://hostname:port/reports/rwservlet?module=example.rdf&userid=hr/
hr@tnsalias&destype=cache&desformat=pdf&p_empid=10
```

In Application Express, the only thing needed is to define a substitution variable to integrate Oracle Reports with Application Express.

Substitution strings use the `&variable` notation. They can be used anywhere in your APEX application such as in an HTML region or even in a template.

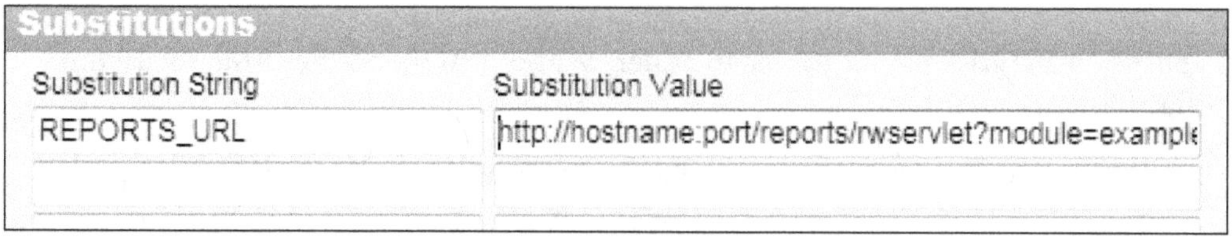

The navigation path for creating a substitution string is `Application Builder Tab/Edit Application properties/Substitution section`.

Enter `REPORTS_URL` under the **Substitution String** field.

Enter `http://hostname:port/reports/rwservlet?userid=hr/hr@tnsalias&P_EMPID` under the **Substitution Value** field.

The Oracle report can be called by pressing a button. A button is created with the URL target as follows:

```
&REPORTS_URL.&module=example.rdf&destype=cache&desformat=
&P1_DESFORMAT.&p_empid=&P1_EMPID
```

Integration with Cocoon

You may prefer another XSL-FO processing engines, which are Apache Cocoon and Apache Tomcat. Cocoon is a web framework other than APEX, of course. For full explanation and a step-by-step approach, follow this link:

`http://carlback.blogspot.com/2007/03/apex-cocoon-pdf-and-more.html`

Integration with JasperReports

JasperReports is a powerful alternative to Oracle Reports. The important design patterns can be translated, using JasperReports.

Architecture

The architecture for JasperReports is as follows:

1. User clicks on link in APEX application.
2. PL/SQL API calls a Jasper report and passes parameter (by using `utl_http`).
3. Jasper Reports creates a JDBC connection to Oracle, executes the report, and returns the report output (for example, PDF) directly.

More on step-by-step integration into the sample application can be found at the following links:

- `http://www.opal-consulting.de/downloads/free_tools/JasperReportsIntegration/Opal-Consulting-JasperReportsIntegration.pdf`
- `http://www.opal-consulting.de/downloads/presentations/2012-06-28-ODTUG-KScope12/2012-06-28-ODTUG-KScope12-jasper-reports.pdf`

Plugins

Plugins allow the Application Express framework to be extended with custom item types, region types, processes, and dynamic actions. Once defined, plugin-based components are created and maintained very much like standard Application Express components. Plugins enable developers to create highly customized components to enhance the functionality, appearance, and user friendliness of their application. Third-party plugins can be found at `http://www.apex-plugin.com/`.

There are two alternatives available for printing PDF files.

Reports 2 PDF

This plugin is a process type plugin. It uses the source queries of all report regions on a page—either a classic or interactive—and puts the results of these queries in a PDF file, ready for download. No print engine, such as Apache FOP or BI Publisher, is needed.

Embedded PDF

This is a plugin that can be used to get the output of a query as a PDF, which is embedded in your application. Also no print-server, such as Apache FOP, BI Publisher, or Cocoon is required.

> These plugins are third-party plugins, which means that they are officially not supported by the Oracle Company.

Summary

This chapter gave you an overview of the possibilities for printing in Application Express.

There are different choices for implementing reports printing/PDF printing:

- Apache FOP by using OC4J
- BI Publisher
- Or alternatives such as Oracle Reports, Jasper Reports, and Plugins

We started with the two most commonly used architectures in Application Express printing—Apache FOP and BI Publisher. Then we saw how to install and configure both Apache FOP and BI Publisher. After the installation, we discussed how to investigate printing problems.

We also dealt with layout of your report and discussed how to include charts and images.

Finally, we discussed some alternatives that can be used for PDF printing, and also plugins.

4
Security

The main question is: How secure is "Secure Enough"?

The answer to this question depends on what you're protecting, who you are protecting it from, and the likelihood of someone wanting to steal what you are protecting. You also need to understand the repercussions you would face if someone was able to successfully steal the things you are protecting. To summarize, you need to think about the questions: Who/what/how can data be accessed?

The definition of security is subjective. My idea of security may be different from yours as a reader of this book. In my view, the secured data can only be seen and edited by people who are qualified and authorized, and that data is protected from people who are not.

Security must be designed into applications from the outset, starting with database design, continuing through application design, development, and testing, and finally with implementation and training. So, plan security and the architecture, and make sure people know the security basics. Have people in your organization who are responsible for security, patching, and so on.

This chapter describes how to provide security for Oracle Application Express. Oracle Application Express is secure, but developers can make it insecure. There is a difference between administrators and developers. Administrators are responsible for the installation from Application Express, and developers are responsible for developing a secure application. Both views and responsibilities are discussed.

The first part of the chapter will discuss the responsibilities of an administrator:

- Installation from Application Express
- Installation from patches
- Security in the database
- Security in the web server
- Session time out
- Password rule(s)

The second part of the chapter will discuss the security aspects for the Oracle Application Express developer. For application developers, security can be a very difficult subject. The application must be tested from the perspective of a hacker or someone who deliberately wants to do harm. Security aspects for developers are as follows:

- Cross-site scripting
- SQL injection
- Authentication
- Authorization
- Session state protection
- Browser security

Securing Oracle Application Express for administrators

Oracle Application Express is secure, but developers can make it insecure.

Protecting the database environment

Oracle Application Express runs in the database, so the database environment needs to be protected.

Follow the principle of least privilege, so a user only has access to the resources required. Lock or remove unused users. Use sensible passwords, and do not use the same password for `SYS` and `SYSTEM`.

> This document provides a checklist for security in the Oracle database
>
> Document # 131752.1: Security Checklist at the My Oracle Support website.

The best way to secure data in your APEX application, or any application, is to secure your data in the database. You can do this by using Oracle's Virtual Private Database.

Virtual Private Database

A very powerful feature of the Oracle database is **Virtual Private Database** (**VPD**). This feature is only available with the Enterprise edition. Virtual Private Database, also known as **Row Level Security** or **Fine Grained Access Control**, is a very popular choice of security when the standard object privileges and database roles are not sufficient. With VPD, you can specify which part (rows and/or columns) are accessible to the user. The policies that you specify can be as simple or complex as required.

VPD policies are defined against the database tables and are enforced whenever the table is accessed, regardless of the user interface that is being used. When the data is accessed through APEX or SQL*Plus, the same VPD policies are enforced and only the data is accessible, which is allowed by the policy.

When you define a VPD policy on a database table, a predicate is added whenever the table is accessed. With the VPD policy, you can define when the predicate is applied to the database table; for example, with `SELECT` or `UPDATE`. The user will not see the predicate being added to the issued statement.

VPD policy

The VPD policy is the key to using VPD. In the VPD policy function, you enforce the security rules that need to be implemented. Depending on your requirements, the VPD policy can be very simple or immensely complex.

Using VPD is a two-step process. The first step is to define a VPD policy and the second step is to apply the policy to the relevant table.

The VPD policy function is a regular database function, which can be in a package. It is highly recommended to place the VPD policy function in a package, as you would place all functions in packages.

The main purpose of the VPD policy is to return a predicate. The VPD policy function needs to adhere to a certain signature. The signature is as follows:

```
function get_predicate (p_schema_name  in   varchar2
                       ,p_table_name   in   varchar2
                       )
   return varchar2
```

The name of the VPD policy function as well as the names of the parameters can be whatever you want. There must be two input arguments of data type `VARCHAR2`. The first argument will contain the schema name, and the second argument will contain the object name. The purpose of the arguments is not quite clear. The documentation on VPD states the following:

> *Define input parameters to hold this information, but do not specify the schema and object name themselves within the function.*
>
> *The function will return the predicate as a VARCHAR2. This predicate will be used when you apply the policy to the database table.*

Be that as it may, the VPD policy function still needs the two arguments defined. In order to show a complete example of what VPD is capable of, two database users are created and some sample data is set up.

```
SQL> create user admin identified by admin
  2  /

User created.

SQL> grant connect, resource to admin
  2  /

Grant succeeded.

SQL> grant select on scott.emp to admin
  2  /

Grant succeeded.

SQL>
SQL> create user noadmin identified by noadmin
  2  /

User created.

SQL> grant connect, resource to noadmin
  2  /

Grant succeeded.
```

The `ADMIN` user will own a table named `EMP`, similar to the `EMP` table in the `SCOTT` schema.

The `NOADMIN` user will be given the `SELECT` privileges on the newly-created table:

```
SQL> conn admin/admin@odd
Connected.
SQL>
SQL> create table emp
  2  as
  3  select *
  4    from scott.emp
  5  /

Table created.

SQL>
SQL> grant select on emp to noadmin
  2  /

Grant succeeded.
```

To implement VPD, the `ADMIN` user will need to have execute privileges on the `DBMS_RLS` package:

```
SQL> grant execute on dbms_rls to admin
  2  /

Grant succeeded.
```

Now, we are ready to create the VPD policy function, which will return the predicate:

```
SQL> create or replace
  2  function get_predicate (p_schema_name   in    varchar2
  3                         ,p_table_name    in    varchar2
  4                         )
  5     return varchar2
  6  is
  7     l_retval varchar2(150);
  8  begin
  9     if user = 'ADMIN'
 10     then
 11        -- The Admin is allowed to
 12        -- have unlimited access
 13        l_retval := '1=1';
 14     else
 15        -- No access if you are
 16        -- not an Admin
 17        l_retval := '1=2';
 18     end if;
 19     -- return the predicate
 20     return l_retval;
 21  end get_predicate;
 22  /

Function created.
```

In the preceding example, a predicate is returned depending on `USER`. When the user is `ADMIN`, `predicate 1=1` is returned (line 13 and line 20), which doesn't restrict anything. When the user is not `ADMIN`, `predicate 1=2` is returned (line 17 and line 20). Because one is never equal to two, this predicate applied to any table will return nothing.

Note that only the predicate is returned; do not include a `WHERE` clause with the returned predicate. This would lead to invalidations at runtime.

> One of the other names of Virtual Private Database is Row Level Security, hence the name of the built-in package `DBMS_RLS`.
>
> The term Row Level Security does not cover the complete functionality of Virtual Private Database. Since Oracle Database 10g, you can also provide a Column Level Security.

The second step in using VPD is to "connect" the VPD policy function to the table. You handle this by using the `DBMS_RLS` built-in package . The appropriate privileges are already granted, so the VPD policy can be added.

```
SQL> begin
  2      dbms_rls.add_policy
  3         (object_schema    => 'ADMIN'
  4         ,object_name      => 'EMP'
  5         ,policy_name      => 'Simple Policy'
  6         ,function_schema  => 'ADMIN'
  7         ,policy_function  => 'get_predicate'
  8         ,statement_types  => 'SELECT'
  9         ,enable           => true);
 10  end;
 11  /

PL/SQL procedure successfully completed.
```

On lines 3 and 4, you should specify the object to which the VPD policy needs to be applied to; in this case, on the `EMP` object of `ADMIN`. Line 5 specifies the name of the policy; make sure it is a useful name, so you can identify the policy for future reference. On lines 6 and 7, you should specify the location of the VPD policy function, the schema in which it is being called, and what function is called.

With `statement_types` on line 8, you should specify the statement for which the policy needs to be applied. In the preceding example, the policy is applied only for the `SELECT` statements. You can specify `INSERT`, `UPDATE`, `DELETE`, and `INDEX` besides the `SELECT` statement, or a combination of all. By default, all statements except the `INDEX` statement are applied.

The last argument in the VPD policy function is `enable` (line 9). This means that the VPD policy is enabled and effective immediately.

Executing a `Select` statement in the table involved will show different results, depending on the user that is logged in. In the following screenshot, the `ADMIN` user is logged in. As you can see, all the data in the sample table is shown:

```
SQL> select *
  2     from admin.emp
  3  /

     EMPNO ENAME      JOB              MGR HIREDATE         SAL       COMM     DEPTNO
---------- ---------- --------- ---------- --------- ---------- ---------- ----------
      7369 SMITH      CLERK           7902 17-DEC-80        800                    20
      7499 ALLEN      SALESMAN        7698 20-FEB-81       1600        300         30
      7521 WARD       SALESMAN        7698 22-FEB-81       1250        500         30
      7566 JONES      MANAGER         7839 02-APR-81       2975                    20
      7654 MARTIN     SALESMAN        7698 28-SEP-81       1250       1400         30
      7698 BLAKE      MANAGER         7839 01-MAY-81       2850                    30
      7782 CLARK      MANAGER         7839 09-JUN-81       2450                    10
      7788 SCOTT      ANALYST         7566 19-APR-87       3000                    20
      7839 KING       PRESIDENT            17-NOV-81       5000                    10
      7844 TURNER     SALESMAN        7698 08-SEP-81       1500          0         30
      7876 ADAMS      CLERK           7788 23-MAY-87       1100                    20
      7900 JAMES      CLERK           7698 03-DEC-81        950                    30
      7902 FORD       ANALYST         7566 03-DEC-81       3000                    20
      7934 MILLER     CLERK           7782 23-JAN-82       1300                    10

14 rows selected.
```

When the other user, `noadmin`, is logged in, none of the data is shown:

```
SQL> conn noadmin/noadmin@odd
Connected.
SQL>
SQL> select *
  2     from admin.emp
  3  /

no rows selected
```

In both situations, the `SELECT` statement is identical. The VPD policy function generated the predicate, and is applied transparently to the executed statement.

VPD and Application Context

VPD can be used in combination with Application Context, a very common combination of techniques. In this section, Application Context is explained and an example is shown that explains how Application Context can play a role in VPD.

An Application Context is a namespace, which you can define yourself and where you can store name-value pairs. It may sound complicated, but it is not. It will all be explained in the following example.

To work with an Application Context, the first thing that is needed is the Application Context itself. The Application Context is created by issuing the following command:

```
SQL> create context docman_ctx using dm_context_pkg
  2  /

Context created.

SQL>
```

> In order to be able to create a context, the `CREATE ANY CONTEXT` privilege must be granted to the user.

In the preceding code, an Application Context is created with the namespace called `docman_ctx`. Since it is not allowed to manipulate the name-value pairs directly, a package or procedure is needed to do so. Note that the package mentioned in the code (`dm_context_pkg`) has not been created yet. Of course, you can first create the package with all of the required procedures, but this is not strictly necessary.

Now that the Application Context is created, the package needs to be created in order to place the name-value pairs in the Application Context. Name-value pairs are placed inside the Application Context using the `DBMS_SESSION` built-in package. In this built-in package, there is a procedure appropriately called `SET_CONTEXT`, which takes three mandatory parameters, `NAMESPACE`, `ATTRIBUTE`, and `VALUE`. There are two more arguments that the procedure can take, but these are beyond the scope of this chapter to cover.

Manipulating the Application Context directly using the `DBMS_SESSION` built-in package is not allowed. This needs to be done by the package (or procedure) that is mentioned when the Application Context is created. This package will act as a wrapper around the `DBMS_SESSION` package.

```
SQL> create or replace
  2  package dm_context_pkg
  3  is
  4
  5     procedure set_department (p_deptno in number);
  6
  7     procedure clear_department;
  8
  9  end dm_context_pkg;
 10  /

Package created.

SQL>
SQL> create or replace
  2  package body dm_context_pkg
  3  is
  4     procedure set_department (p_deptno in number)
  5     is
  6     begin
  7       dbms_session.set_context
  8         (namespace => 'DOCMAN_CTX'
  9         ,attribute => 'DEPARTMENT'
 10         ,value     => to_char (p_deptno)
 11         );
 12     end set_department;
 13
 14     procedure clear_department
 15     is
 16     begin
 17        dbms_session.clear_context
 18         (namespace => 'DOCMAN_CTX'
 19         ,attribute => 'DEPARTMENT'
 20         );
 21     end clear_department;
 22
 23  end dm_context_pkg;
 24  /

Package body created.
```

In the preceding package, there are two procedures, one called `SET_DEPARTMENT` and the other called `CLEAR_DEPARTMENT`. In the package body, the procedures are implemented to act as a wrapper around the `DBMS_SESSION` package.

`SET_DEPARTMENT` places its argument value in the context that was created earlier. It does this by passing three parameters to the `DBMS_SESSION` package.

The first argument (`namespace`), on line 8 of the package body, is the name of the Application Context. The second argument (`attribute`), on line 9, is the name of the attribute, which you will use to retrieve the value. This brings us to the third argument (`value`), on line 10, the actual value. Since you can only store `VARCHAR2` in the Application Context, the `TO_CHAR` function is used on line 10.

The second procedure in the package effectively erases the value for the department. This will be useful when VPD is implemented in the APEX application.

Setting the value in the Application Context is as easy as calling the packaged procedure:

```
SQL> begin
  2      dm_context_pkg.set_department
  3          (p_deptno => 10);
  4  end;
  5  /

PL/SQL procedure successfully completed.
```

In the preceding code, the department number is passed into the packaged procedure, which is subsequently stored in the Application Context.

To access the stored values in the Application Context, use the `SYS_CONTEXT` function:

```
SQL> select sys_context ('DOCMAN_CTX'
  2                      ,'DEPARTMENT'
  3                      )
  4    from dual;

SYS_CONTEXT('DOCMAN_CTX','DEPARTMENT')
--------------------------------------

10
```

The first argument that is passed to the `SYS_CONTEXT` function is the name of the Application Context. The second argument is the name of the attribute value that we need to retrieve. The `SYS_CONTEXT` function can also be used in PL/SQL.

Why would you use an Application Context in combination with VPD? You can use the `SYS_CONTEXT` anywhere in the SQL statement, and it will act as a bind variable. The following statement shows the use of the `SYS_CONTEXT` function in the predicate:

```
SQL> select *
  2    from admin.emp
  3   where deptno = sys_context ('DOCMAN_CTX'
  4                              ,'DEPARTMENT'
  5                              )
  6  /

     EMPNO ENAME      JOB              MGR HIREDATE         SAL       COMM     DEPTNO
---------- ---------- --------- ---------- --------- ---------- ---------- ----------
      7782 CLARK      MANAGER         7839 09-JUN-81       2451                    10
      7839 KING       PRESIDENT            17-NOV-81       5001                    10
      7934 MILLER     CLERK           7782 23-JAN-82       1301                    10
```

Instead of altering all the statements used in the application, define a VPD policy function to return the predicate. Alter the VPD policy function that was created earlier, and look at the effect:

```
SQL> create or replace
     function get_predicate (p_schema_name   in    varchar2
                            ,p_table_name    in    varchar2
                            )
        return varchar2
     is
        l_retval varchar2(150);
     begin
        l_retval :=
        q'[deptno = sys_context ('DOCMAN_CTX', 'DEPARTMENT')]';
        -- return the predicate
        return l_retval;
     end get_predicate;
     /

Function created.

SQL>
SQL> select *
       from admin.emp
     /

     EMPNO ENAME      JOB              MGR HIREDATE         SAL       COMM     DEPTNO
---------- ---------- --------- ---------- --------- ---------- ---------- ----------
      7782 CLARK      MANAGER         7839 09-JUN-81       2451                    10
      7839 KING       PRESIDENT            17-NOV-81       5001                    10
      7934 MILLER     CLERK           7782 23-JAN-82       1301                    10
```

The function returns the predicate that uses the `SYS_CONTEXT` function.

Alternative quoting

It can be quite a challenge to use the correct number of single quotes (`'`) to construct the predicate, which needs to be returned in the VPD policy function. When a string needs to be enclosed in single quotes, these need to be double up. In the preceding function, the `get_predicate` alternative quoting is utilized to ease this burden. The predicate is enclosed between alternative quoting characters. The alternative quoting expression is as follows:

```
q'<quote_delimiter> the actual string
<quote_delimiter>'
```

Alternative quoting starts with the letter `q`, followed by a single quote and a character (the sample code used a bracket, but it can be any character that you want). After this sequence of characters, the actual string is included, followed by the following combination: the quote delimiter and a single quote.

Implementing VPD in APEX

Now that all the hard work is done, implementing VPD in the APEX application is easy.

From the **Application** home page, press the **Edit Application Properties** button:

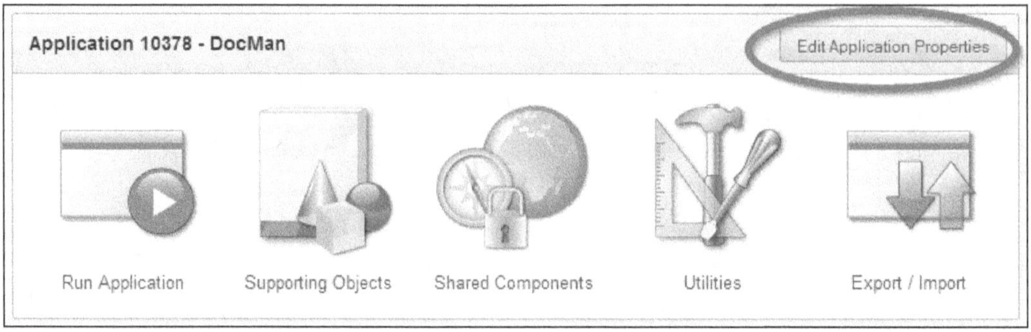

Choose the **Security** tab:

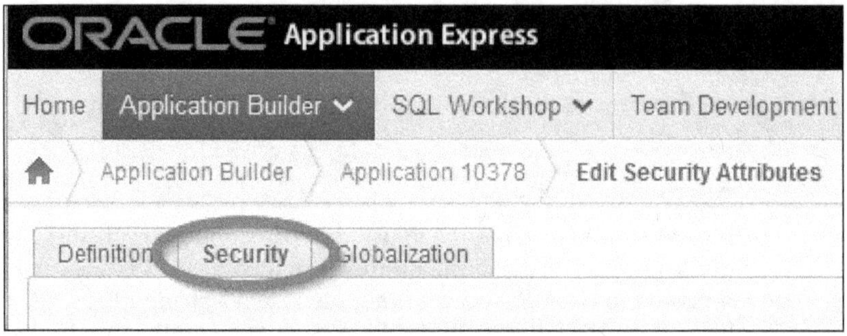

At the bottom of this page, in the section named `Database Session`, there are two sections. In the **Initialization of PL/SQL code** section, the value is set in the context. In the **Cleanup PL/SQL Code** section, the packaged procedure is called to clear the department from the context.

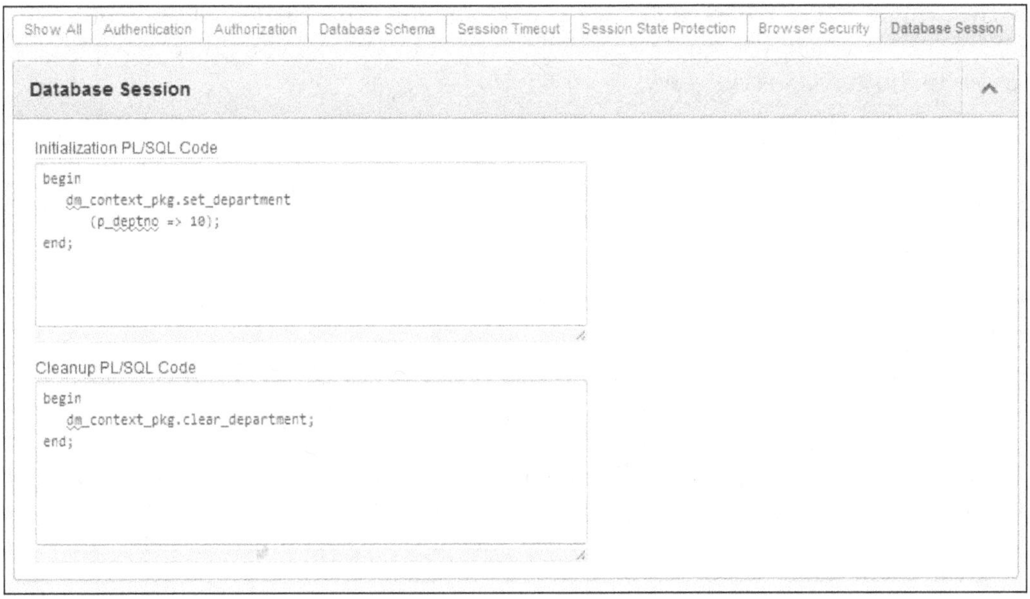

This is all the change that you have to make to the application. Because the predicates are applied at table level, and not at the statement level, all the queries being executed against the base tables will get the VPD predicate applied automatically.

What to do when you get a runtime exception

The predicate is dynamically added to the statement, so an error will show up when you execute the following statement:

```
SQL> select *
  2     from emp
  3  /
  from emp
       *
ERROR at line 2:
ORA-28113: policy predicate has error
```

The error encountered informs you that there is something wrong with the policy predicate. The easiest way to determine where the mistake is made is by looking in the trace file.

To determine where the trace files are generated, you must issue the following statement, for which you might need help from your DBA, if you do not have access to the `V$PARAMETER` view:

```
SQL> select value
  2    from v$parameter
  3   where name = 'user_dump_dest'
  4  /

VALUE
-----------------------------------------------------------
/home/oracle/app/oracle/diag/rdbms/orcl/orcl/trace
```

In the preceding location, you will find all the trace files that are generated from the database; tracking down the correct file can be quite a challenge. When you search the folder for the exception number, `ORA-28113`, the number of files can be greatly reduced.

When you open up the correct trace file, you can see the culprit. The statement that you issued as well as the added predicate done by the VPD Policy function results in two `WHERE` clauses for the SQL statement:

```
Error information for ORA-28113:
Logon user      : ADMIN
Table/View      : ADMIN.EMP
Policy name     : ALL_OR_NOTHING
Policy function: ADMIN.GET_PREDICATE
RLS view  :
SELECT  "EMPNO","ENAME","JOB","MGR","HIREDATE","SAL","COMM","DEPTNO" FROM
"ADMIN"."EMP"   "EMP" WHERE (where 1=1)
ORA-00936: missing expression
-------------------------------------------------------------
```

The trace file indicates the error that was encountered, the user, the table, the name of the VPD policy, and the VPD policy function that was used. Under the section labeled **RLS view**, you can see the issued statement.

Examining this statement will point you directly to the—now obvious—mistake. As you can see, there are two `WHERE` keywords in the statement

Securing the web listener

Oracle Application Express utilizes a web browser on the user's computer, communicating through a web server to the Oracle database.

There are three distinct architectures that can be deployed for Oracle Application Express:

1. Using Oracle HTTP application server with MOD/PLSQL.
2. Using XDB HTTP protocol server with the embedded PL/SQL gateway (EPG).
3. Using the Oracle Application Express Listener against:
    - Oracle WebLogic
    - GlassFish
    - OC4J

There is one golden rule: Give away as little as possible about your environment. Don't publicize names/versions of your running software.

HTTP server

The following screenshot shows the HTTP server request processing:

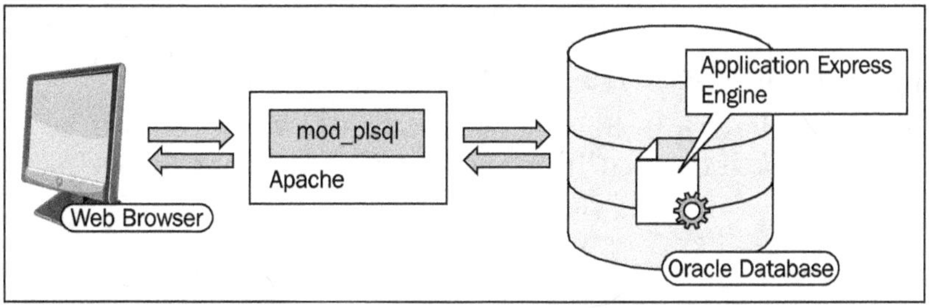

When the HTTP server is installed on a different machine, it will be more secure because the database and HTTP server are separated from each other.

The HTTP server gives full flexibility with rewrite rules, access rules, and so on.

Rewrite

Rewrite relies on the `mod_rewrite` module from APACHE to rewrite an incoming URL and modify the URL dynamically. You enable `mod_rewrite` by adding `RewriteEngine` in the `httpd.conf` configuration file.

For example:

```
#LoadModule rewrite_module modules/mod_rewrite.so
RewriteEngine on
RewriteRule ^/application$ http://hostname:port/pls/apex/f?p=102:
```

This rewrite rule causes the application in the URL to be rewritten to `hostname:port/pls/apex/f?p=102`.

So, application number `102` will show that `http://hostname:port/application` is rewritten to `hostname:port/pls/apex/f?p=102`.

You need to restart the Web Server before the rewrite rule is taken into account. The syntax is as follows:

```
RewriteRule    url-pattern   new_url [flag optional]
```

Additional information about rewrite rules can be found in the Apache documentation at `http://httpd.apache.org/docs/2.0/misc/rewriteguide.html`.

Security considerations in the HTTP server

You would like to give as little information as possible about yourself. So, you also need to think about the security aspects when configuring the web server, HTTP server.

Some important security considerations related to the HTTP server are as follows:

```
ServerSignatureOff (Removes server info from error pages)
ServerTokensProd (Removes server version from HTTP header)
```

Obfuscate the password in the `dads.conf` configuration file. The parameter `PlsqlDatabasePassword` specifies the password for logging in to the database. You can use the `dadTool.pl` utility to obfuscate passwords in the `dads.conf` file. You can find the `dadTool.pl` utility in the following directory:

`ORACLE_HTTPSERVER_HOME/ohs/modplsql/conf`

For example:

```
PATH=$ORACLE_HOME/Apache/modplsql/conf:$PATH
export PATH
PATH=$ORACLE_HOME/perl/bin:$PATH
export PATH
LD_LIBRARY_PATH=$ORACLE_HOME/lib:$ORACLE_HOME/lib32: -$LD_LIBRARY_PATH
export LD_LIBRARY_PATH
PERL5LIB = $ORACLE_HOME/perl/lib/5.6.1
cd $ORACLE_HOME/Apache/modplsql/conf
perl dadTool.pl -o
```

Embedded PL/SQL gateway

The following screenshot shows the **Embedded PL/SQL Gateway** request processing:

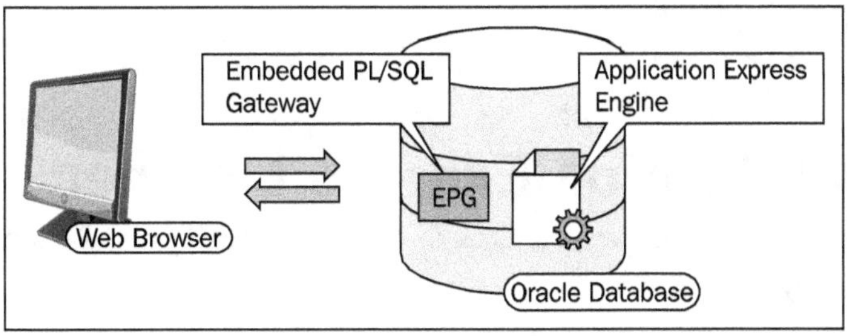

The embedded PL/SQL gateway is a method that exists in RDBMS version 10.2 and higher, but is officially supported in APEX against version 11 of RDBMS. Embedded means that the web server is running inside the Oracle database. From a security point of view, this is not a recommended configuration when running Internet applications. In the HTTP server setup, there are several log files automatically created, such as the `error_log` and `access_log` files. In the case of an Embedded PL/SQL gateway, you need to activate the log option with the following:

```
SQL> execute dbms_epg.set_global_attribute('log-level', 3)
```

So, you need to make use of an API to turn on logging, and it's therefore much harder to get the necessary log information. `wwv_flow_epg_include_local.sql`, included with Oracle Application Express, contains a request-validation function named `wwv_flow_epg_include_modules.authorize`. This function specifies access restrictions appropriate for the standard DAD configured for Oracle Application Express. During installation, scripts also name this function in the request-validation function directive in the XDB configuration file.

At the installation time, the installer also creates a PL/SQL function in the Oracle Application Express product schema (`FLOWS_XXXXXX or / APEX_XXXXXX`). You can change and recompile this function in order to restrict URL access procedures within the DAD. The source code for this function is not wrapped and can be found in the database administrator's product core directory in the file named `wwv_flow_epg_include_local.sql`.

Additional information can be found at the following URLs:

- `http://docs.oracle.com/cd/B25329_01/doc/appdev.102/b25309/adm_wrkspc.htm#BEJDIJAH`
- `http://docs.oracle.com/cd/E14373_01/appdev.32/e11838/sec.htm`

Oracle Application Express Listener

The following screenshot shows the Oracle Application Express Listener request processing:

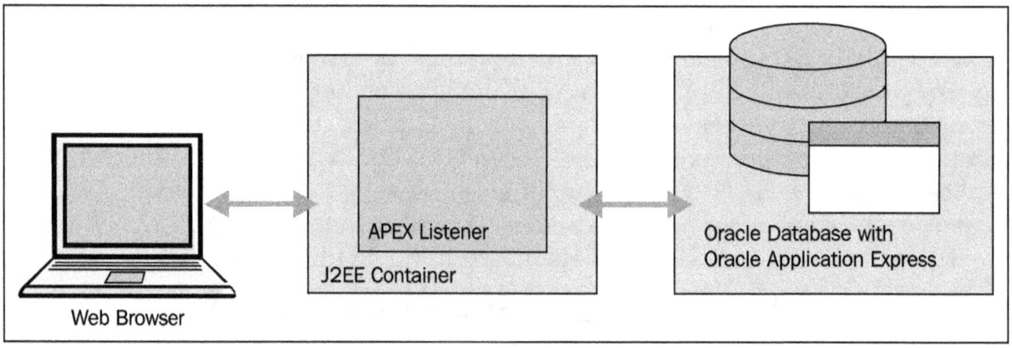

The Oracle Application Express Listener is configurable from a web page, and includes a rich set of configuration options including security options, database connectivity options, and caching options. The Oracle Application Express listener is the recommended architecture from Oracle because of integrated security in front of the database. Apart from this, the Oracle Application Express listener has a graphical user interface, which makes configuration easy.

The listener provides greatest security for Oracle Application Express implementations:

- Allowed procedures: Checks if the procedure name is in the inclusion list
- Blocked procedures: Checks if the procedure is NOT in the exclusion list
- Database validation function: Checks if the procedure name is valid
- Caching: Specifies procedure names to allow the caching of files

The following screenshot shows the security implementation in the Oracle Application Express listener:

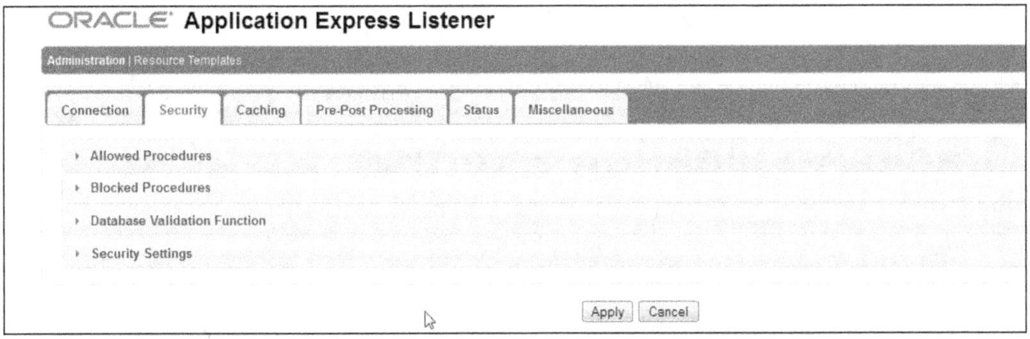

Enabling SSL for the web server

The **Secure Socket Layer** (**SSL**) encrypts all the traffic between the web browser and the web server. It prevents data from being sent over an unprotected communication channel. The HTTP server responds by sending a certificate back to the browser. The browser checks if this certificate has been signed by a trusted authority listed in the browser.

To configure Oracle Application Express for SSL, the web server used must be configured in the SSL mode. This will be one of the following:

- The HTTP Server
- The Embedded PLSQL Gateway (EPG), if using an 11g DB
- The frontend web server (OC4J, Web Logic or Glassfish) for the 11 Oracle database (Oracle Application Express version 3.2.1 and above)

Enabling SSL for the web server enables only the SSL to the web server and not to the RDBMS; this needs to be configured separately. Enabling SSL for the RDBMS can be performed within the advanced security option of the database. Advanced security is an option available in the Enterprise edition of the database.

The following screenshot shows SSL at instance level (navigation path: `APEX_ADMIN/Manage Instance/Security`):

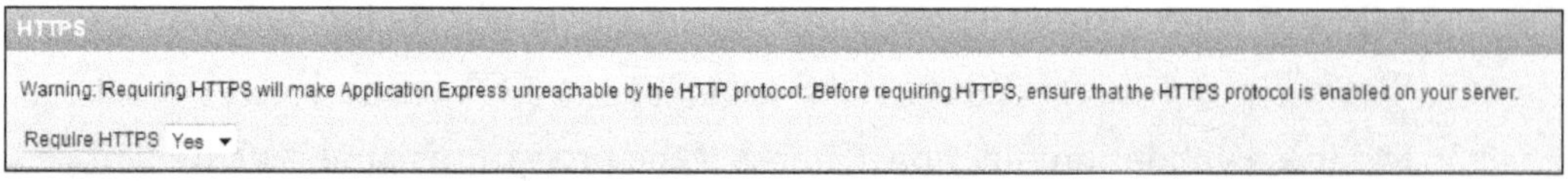
HTTPS
Warning: Requiring HTTPS will make Application Express unreachable by the HTTP protocol. Before requiring HTTPS, ensure that the HTTPS protocol is enabled on your server.
Require HTTPS Yes

When you enable SSL at the administration website of APEX, you need to ensure that the HTTPS protocol is enabled on your web server. Additional information about security considerations in web servers can be found at `http://docs.oracle.com/cd/E14571_01/security.htm`.

Security considerations when installing Oracle Application Express

Even before installing Application Express, you need to think about security measures to be taken during each step of the installation process.

Runtime installation

An Oracle Application Express runtime environment enables you to run production applications, but it does not provide a Web interface for administration or direct development of these applications. So, this makes it more an indurate environment. The runtime environment is a more secure environment, because only the necessary objects and privileges are installed and configured.

You administer the Oracle Application Express runtime environment using SQL*Plus or SQL Developer and the `APEX_INSTANCE_ADMIN` API. The `ADMIN` account is not used in a runtime environment, but is created anyway. It will be used if the runtime environment is converted to a full development environment.

To determine if only the runtime environment is installed, connect as `SYS` and run the following query (Oracle Application Express version 4.x):

```
Select count(*) from APPLICATION_EXPRESS_040200.WWV_FLOWS where id =
4000;
```

The query checks if the runtime is installed. The ID is always equal to `4000`, so do not enter your application ID. If the count is `0`, it is a runtime; if the count is `1`, it is a full development environment.

There are scripts provided to completely remove/re-install the application builder. The scripts to install or remove the application builder are `apxdevrm.sql` and `apxdvins.sql`. The scripts are installed in the APEX main directory.

Access Control Lists (ACLs)

Network services needs to be enabled when attempting actions related to the following:

- Sending outbound mail in Oracle Application Express.
- Using Web services in Oracle Application Express.
- PDF/report printing.
- Searching for content in online **Help** (that is, using the find link). The following screenshot shows the find link:

In Oracle RDBMS 11gR1, a new feature called fine grained access control to external networks was introduced. This feature gives the administrator a control over which database users are permitted to access external network services, and on which ports access is permitted. If an application relied upon the PL/SQL packages `UTL_TCP`, `UTL_SMTP`, `UTL_MAIL`, `UTL_HTTP`, or `UTL_INADDR`, they would now need to be given permission to access the external network service via a Network ACL.

If you are running Oracle Application Express against Oracle RDBMS 11g and later releases, you need to use the new `DBMS_NETWORK_ACL_ADMIN` package to grant connect privileges to any host for the `FLOWS_XXXXXX/APEX_XXXXXX` (version) database user and any other user who may need to interact with network services, such as `UTL_HTTP`, `UTL_SMTP`, `UTL_TCP`.

The instructions for accomplishing this are included in the Oracle Application Express Installation Guide, which is available at the Oracle Technology network under the documentation library (*Oracle Database Oracle Application Express Installation Guide*). Information about ACL can be found in the section entitled *Enable Network Services in Oracle Database 11g*. This document can be found at `http://www.oracle.com/technetwork/developer-tools/apex/documentation/index.html`

If you are running a different version of Oracle Application Express, then you will need to change the reference to the appropriate Oracle Application Express schema. This script should normally be run as `SYSTEM`.

> If you are encountering the error, `ORA-29273: HTTP request failed ORA-06512: at "SYS.UTL_HTTP", line 1577 ORA-24247: network access denied by access control list (ACL)`, when running a custom application, then the script must be run for the `Database` account associated with the workspace containing the application. In other words, it needs to be run for the application's parsing schema.

There have been two changes in this feature in Database 11gR2, which may have an impact on Oracle Application Express users:

- In **Database 11gR2 11.2.0.1**, the precedence order in the evaluation of the network ACL entries has been changed to most specific to least specific. More information on this topic is discussed in the sections to follow.
- In **Database 11gR2 11.2.0.2**, the network ACL now applies to any use of `DBMS_LDAP`.

For additional information, refer to the following URL:

```
http://joelkallman.blogspot.co.uk/2010/10/application-express-
network-acls-and.html
```

Enabling builders in Oracle Application Express

Instance administrators can control which components are available within an Oracle Application Express instance. Configurable components include Web sheets, SQL workshop, application builder, and team development.

> Navigation path: `Home/Administration/Manage Service/Workspace preferences`

The following screenshot shows the configurable components:

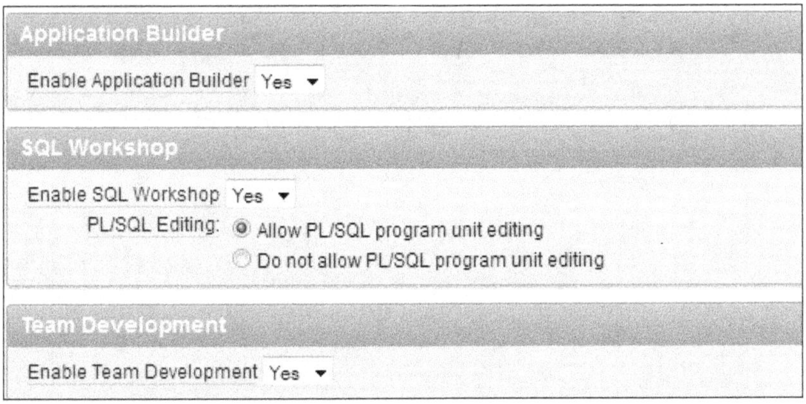

Session timeout

An essential way to indurate your application is to configure a session timeout.

Session timeout is the number of minutes after which a running session times out. It allows developers/administrators to kill a user's session, if the user has been idle for a certain amount of time, and avoids unauthorized people from accessing the application. It can be defined at instance level and application level by setting the maximum session length and idle time for APEX developer logins.

Maximum session length specifies the number of seconds a session exists and is used by the application. **Maximum session idle time** specifies the maximum time between one page request and the next one. An example of session timeout can be found at the following URL:

`http://www.oracle.com/webfolder/technetwork/tutorials/obe/db/11g/r2/prod/appdev/apex/apexsec/apexsec09.htm#t5`

Instance level

In Oracle Application Express Builder, you can find the session timeout settings under the **Security** tab page at instance level:

1. Connect with the `INTERNAL` workspace or browse to `http://<host name>:8080/apex/apex_admin`.
2. Navigate to **Home | Manage Instance | Instance Settings | Security section | Session Timeout for Oracle Application Express**.
3. Change the **Maximum Session Length in Seconds** and **Maximum Session Idle Time in Seconds** properties according to your needs.

The following screenshot shows the security settings at instance level:

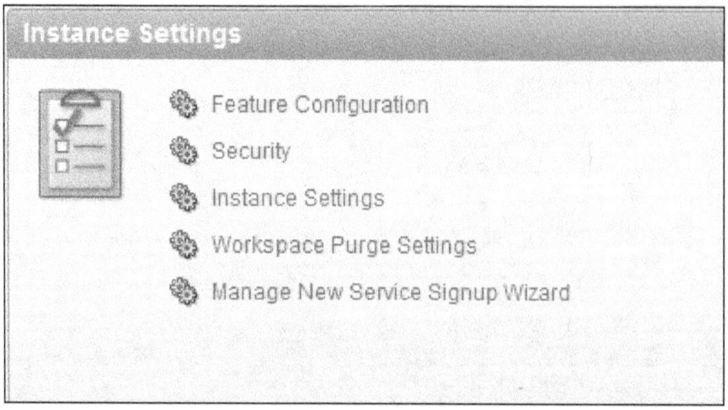

The following screenshot shows the session timeout at instance level:

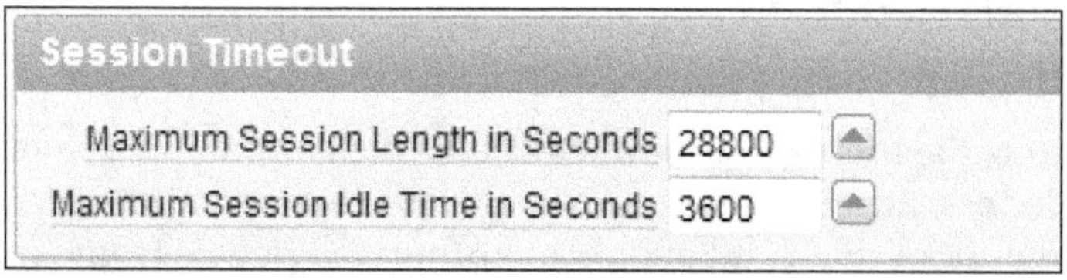

Application level

Session timeout settings are not just available for the Oracle Application Express Development environment; you can also use them in your applications to make your application even more secure!

1. Navigate to **Shared Components** | **Security** | **Security attributes section** | **Session Timeout**.
2. The new section has several properties to define the session timeout behavior of your application

The following screenshot shows the breadcrumb to reach the security attributes section in Oracle Application Express:

The following screenshot shows the **Security Attributes** section:

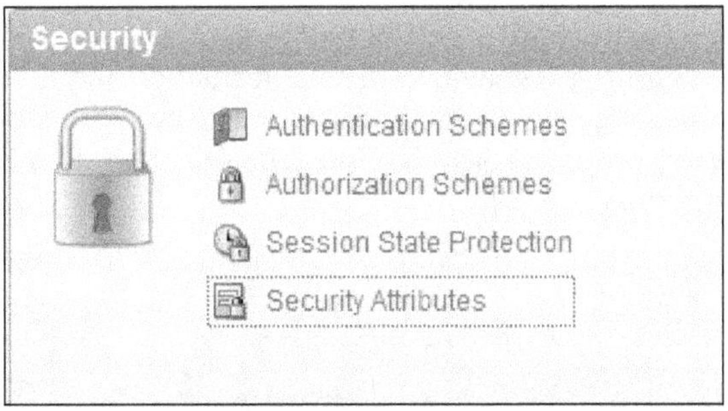

Time out\settings can also be set programmatically during runtime. This can be performed with the `APEX_Util.set_session_lifetime_seconds` and `APEX_Util.set_session_max_idle_seconds` API procedures.

Password complexity rules

The Oracle Application Express administrator can create password complexity rules or a policy, for the passwords from the available accounts in an instance. These rules apply to all the accounts in the installation, across all the workspaces. You can set multiple complexity rules and re-use rules across an instance.

The following are examples of password complexity policies of passwords:

- It should contain at least one uppercase character
- It should contain at least one numeric digit
- It must be at least six characters long

You can set all the available parameter values within the `APEX_INSTANCE_ADMIN` package. You should be able to set the password preferences, such as `PASSWORD_NOT_LIKE_USERNAME`, `PASSWORD_NEW_DIFFERS_BY`, and `PASSWORD_ONE_ALPHA`, using the `APEX_INSTANCE_ADMIN` API.

Additional documentation about the `APEX_INSTANCE_ADMIN` package can be found at: `http://docs.oracle.com/cd/E23903_01/doc/doc.41/e21676/Oracle Application Express_instance.htm#CHDFGJEI`.

Do not allow debug for a production site

For a production application, it is a good idea to disable debugging. Give away as little information about yourself as possible. The navigation path for turning off debugging the application is **Application | Application definition | properties.**

The following screenshot shows how to turn debugging on and off:

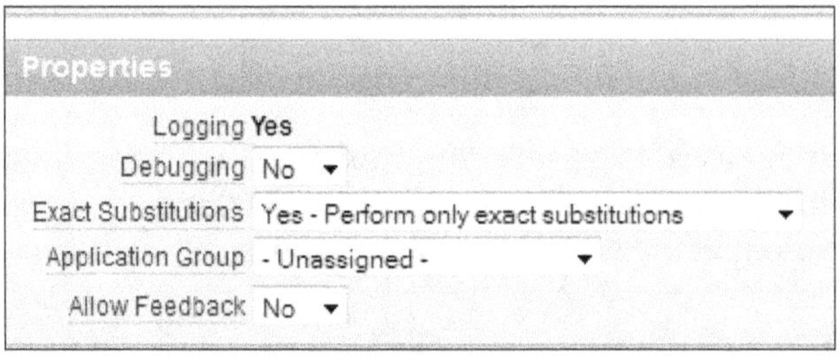

Patching strategy

Patching your software is very important from a security point of view. Patching does not only mean software patching, but it also means that operating system patches are important.

Oracle Corporation delivers a security patch (CPU patch) every quarter for all its software components. It is important to install the quarterly delivered patches. Via My Oracle Support or the Oracle technology network, you can subscribe for the CPU patches. In this way, you indurate different components in your system.

It is also important to install the normal patch sets when they are released. You can download patches and patch sets at the My Oracle Support website.

Security considerations for the developer

From the first day of a project, you should be thinking about security. Each piece of code has consequences for security. So, each piece of code should be reviewed carefully for security vulnerabilities. In practice, we very often consider security an "after thought". Only after making security mistakes do we start to think about it.

Browser attacks

The different browser attack methods are discussed in this section.

Cross-site scripting (XSS)

Cross-site scripting (also referred to as **XSS**) is a security breach that takes advantage of dynamically generated Web pages.

Cross-site scripting is "injection" of Java script. This may be in the database, URL, or an upload from files. XSS is often not that dangerous on its own, but when combined with bugs in a browser, a virus, or a worm, it can be serious. In most cases, the application express developer of the application is unaware of the issue, and it goes undetected for a long time.

An **attacker** injects JavaScript in an application in order to attack other users. When an XSS attack occurs, it means that an unwanted script is performed by the browser. Examples of attacks are data being stolen, hijacking of session tokens, and performance of unauthorized actions. The script can be rendered in different parts of the application, such as HTML regions, during the page rendering process of Application Express. To prevent the introduction of malicious code into the session state, the Oracle Application Express engine escapes characters in certain cases. When components in an Oracle Application Express page use the sys.htp package to emit the values of page items or application items to the browser, special precautions are necessary to protect against cross-site scripting attacks.

For example: http://hostname:port/pls/Apex/f?p=25186:1:1461001897587701::::P1_HIDDEN:<script>alert(document.cookie);</script>.

There is a computation (before header) at the item named P1_HIDDEN. The computation has the following content: P1_HIDDEN:<script>alert(document.cookie);</script>.

The output from this URL is cookie information sent to the browser. The following screenshot shows the cookie information:

ORA_WWV_F4000_P4150_TREE=RenderingTree%3ARenderingTree_after_show_items_regions%3A5377496350076244104; ORA_WWV_ATTRIBUTE_PAGE=4651
%2C%23ALL; ORA_WWV_R1=%23ALL; ORA_WWV_R2=%23ALL; ORA_WWV_R3=%23ALL; s_nr=1337767135928;
__utma=7204706.1279156844.1337780533.1338627205.1338713386.5; utmz=7204706.1337780533.1.1.utmcsr=(direct)|utmccn=(direct)|utmcmd=(none); __atuvc=1|21;
ORA_UCM_INFO=3~00027147766664288412908416870092 BIGipServerapex-ext_oracle_com_http=1680380557.24862.0000;
__utmb=7204706.4.10.1338713386; __utmc=7204706

An alert displaying the cookie information may not be a security problem. This technique illustrates that a malicious user can get the application to send information to the browser, contrary to the developer's intention. As a result, the user can potentially mount harmful security attacks using similar methods.

To prevent XSS vulnerability, change the code used in your Oracle Application Express region to escape the text sent to the browser.

An example of this code is: `sys.htp.p(sys.htf.escape_sc(:P1_SOMETHING));`.

The following screenshot shows the PL/SQL code to prevent XSS. The code is prefixed with **sys**.

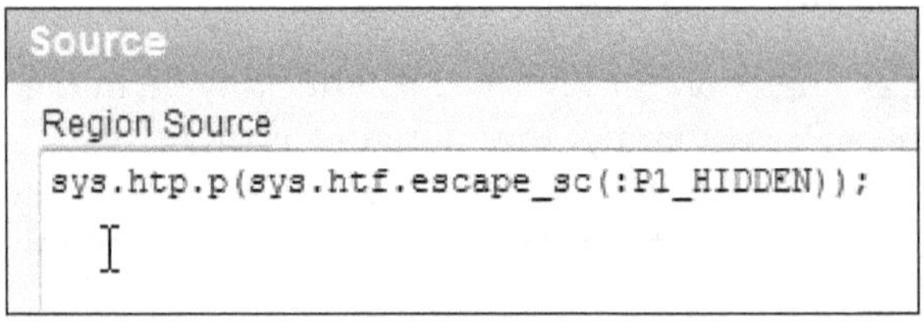

Why prefix the code with `sys`? If the PL/SQL code is not prefixed with `sys`, hackers get the opportunity to make a local package to define the same name. When making use of the `htp` or `htf` package, you need to prefix with `sys`. When the text is escaped, the information in the URL is displayed in the browser window. However, there can be a case that the value in the session state is not escaped. As a result, malicious information can still be manipulated in the session state (`WWV_FLOW_DATA`).

When the session state is referenced, the value posted to the page will not have special characters (`<`, `>`, `&`, and `"`) escaped. If the referenced item is one of the following safe item display types, the value will be escaped.

The following item display types can be used safely:

- **Display as Text (does not save state)**
- **Display as Text (escape special characters, does not save state)**
- **Display as Text (based on LOV, does not save state)**
- **Display as Text (based on PL/SQL, does not save state)**
- **Text Field (Disabled, does not save state)**: This field is a read-only item; the end user cannot type into the field and the value is not saved into a session state.

An example of a "safe" item type is an item type with the following property: **Display as text**. In this way, the text is escaped in the browser and in the session state.

The following screenshot shows a safe item type. The text is escaped in the browser and in the session state.

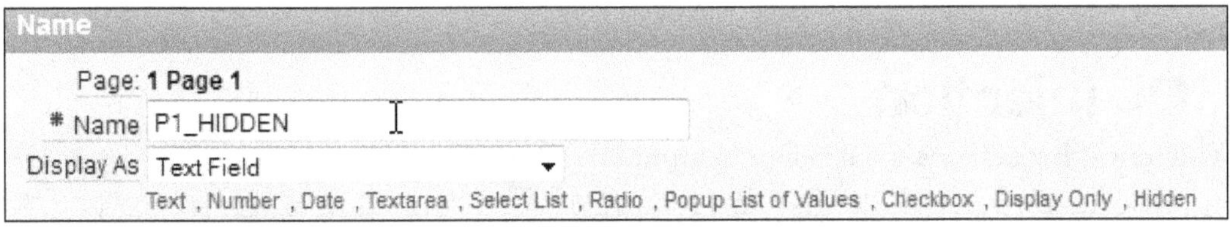

Protecting HTML regions and other static areas

Session states can be referenced by the `&ITEM` notation.

Protecting dynamic output

Items fetched and rendered should explicitly escape special characters.

Protecting reports regions

In Application Express 4.1 and higher, report attributes have the default value of **Display as Text (escape special characters, does not save state)**. Any extra embedded HTML code will be ignored during page rendering.

The following screenshot shows an item of the type **Display as Text (escape special characters)**:

Protecting form items

When form items, including hidden items, obtain their values during the generation of the form page to be sent to the browser, the resulting text is escaped before rendering.

The rules for cross-site scripting that must be taken into account are as follows:

- Escape Special Characters (<> &) and / or escape output.
- Use of `sys.htf.escape_sc`.

- Use this "fully qualified". Fully qualified means that you need to prefix this package with `sys`. This avoids the opportunity for hackers to make a local package with the same name.

SQL injection

The following screenshot is taken from `http://xkcd.com/327`:

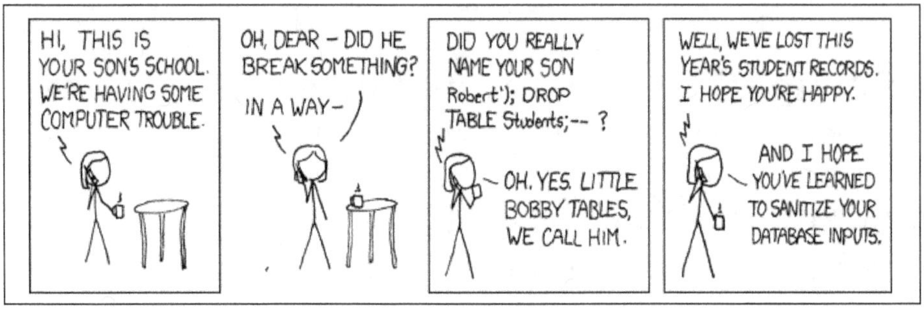

SQL injection is a technique for maliciously exploiting applications that use client-supplied data in SQL statements. SQL injection can be used to "inject" SQL code. This SQL code can be used to create and delete objects or to access data at unauthorized locations. Attackers trick the SQL engine into executing unintended commands. When using dynamic SQL (`DBMS_SQL`), you need to be aware of SQL injection. Web applications are at a higher risk, because an attack can occur without database connection or application authentication.

Some standard rules must be observed to prevent SQL Injection:

- **Use of the bind variable syntax** . The use of bind variables is important in the use of static and dynamic SQL. Its usage decreases the change for SQL injection and improves performance.
- **Make use of the** `SYS.DBMS_ASSERT` **Oracle package**: This package includes functions to check and validate user input.
- **Check of parentheses and commentary** (`- / **`): When literals are used, enclose them in double quotes. (A document providing an example can be found at the My Oracle Support website: *Doc ID # 101458.1*: *How to change user password*.)
- **Dismiss database privileges that are not necessary**: Give away as little as possible from yourself. This does not eliminate SQL injection, but helps to restrict the impact of a possible attack.

The following screenshot shows the flow chart that shows how to start assessing vulnerability:

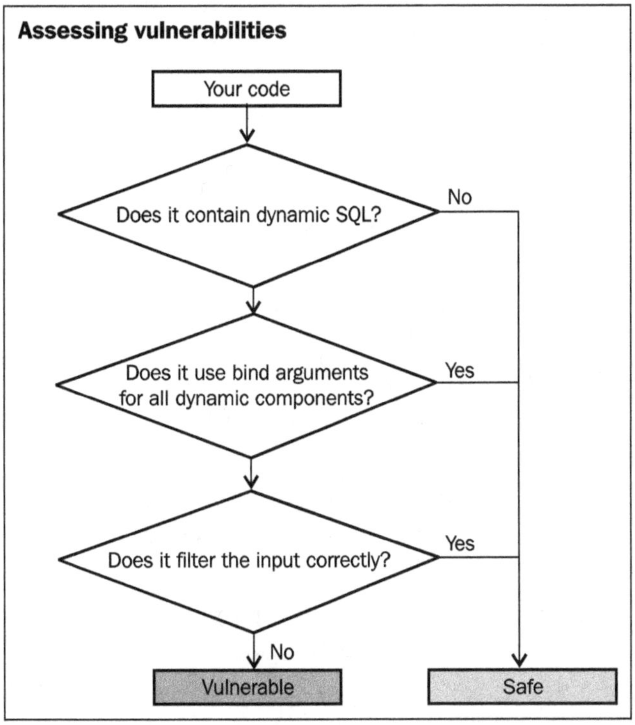

Insecure use of variables

To start, I would like to mention that this example can be found at the following location:

`http://www.oracle.com/technetwork/issue-archive/2009/09-jul/o49browser-091379.html`

In **Application Builder**, click on **Create Page**, select **Blank Page** as the page type, and click twice on **Next**.

1. Enter `SQL Injection` for **Name** , click twice on **Next**, and click on **Finish**.
2. Click on **Edit Page**.
3. In the **Regions** area, click on the **Create** icon, select **HTML**, click on **Next**, select **HTML** again, and click on **Next**.

4. For **Title** enter Locate Employee Number, click on the **Next** button, and create a new **Region**.
5. Create a new item, select **Text** as the value for **Item Type**, enter Employee Number for **Item Name**, select **Locate Employee Number** for **Region**, and create the item.
6. Create a new button, select **Locate Employee Number**, and click on the **Next** button. Select **Create a button in a region position**, and click on the **Next** button. Enter Locate for **Button Name**, and create the button.
7. Create a region and select **PL/SQL Dynamic Content**, click on **Next**, enter **Employee Data** for **Title**, and click on **Next**.
8. Enter the following for PL/SQL source :

```
FOR c1 IN (SELECT ename FROM emp
WHERE empno = &P<1>_EMPNO.) LOOP
   htp.p('<br>Employee Name:'||c1.ename);
END LOOP;
```

9. Click on **Next**, select **Value of Item in Expression 1 Is NOT NULL** for **Condition Type**, enter P<1>_EMPNO for **Expression 1**, and click on **Create Region**.
10. Run the application. Enter 7521 for **Employee number**, and click on **Locate**. The employee name, **Ward**, is displayed.
11. Now, enter 0 or 1=1 for **Employee number**, and click on **Locate**. Because of the SQL injection, all the employee names are listed.

The following screenshot shows all the employee records after the bind variable syntax is omitted:

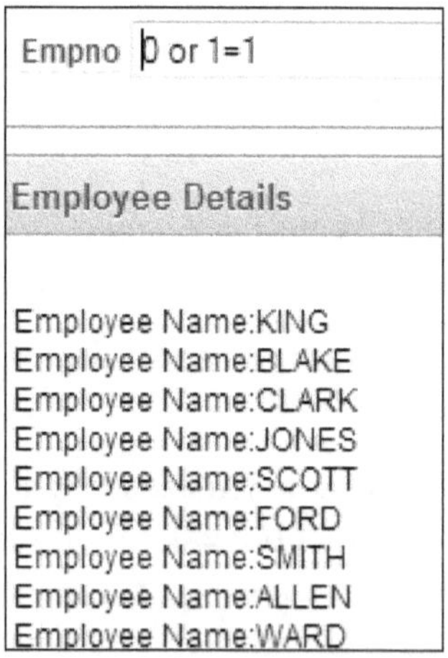

Correct use of Bind variables

This example shows the appropriate way of using bind variable syntax and to avoid possible SQL Injection:

1. Navigate to **Application Builder** for **page <1>**, and in the **Regions** area, click on **Employee Details**.
2. For **Region Source**, change **WHERE empno = &<1>_EMPNO** to **WHERE empno = :P<1>_EMPNO**.
3. Make sure the **Do not validate PL/SQL code (parse PL/SQL code at runtime only)** box is checked. Click on **Apply Changes**.
4. Run the **SQL Injection** page.
5. Enter `7521` for **Empno**, and click on **Search**. The employee name, **Ward**, is displayed.
6. Enter `0 or 1=1` for **Empno**, and click on **Search**. This time you should see an error message, because the PL/SQL uses a bind variable.

SYS.DBMS_ASSERT

Sometimes, you cannot prevent SQL injection by using bind variables (`select * from P1_TABLE` is not valid in SQL). You have to rely on filtering and/or validation. The `SYS.DBMS_ASSERT` package contains a number of functions that can be used to filter and sanitize input strings, particularly the ones that are meant to be used as Oracle identifiers. In Oracle Application Express, a validation is created from the type: function returning a Boolean value.

This example of the `SYS.DBMS_ASSERT` function checks the name of the table, an item level validation from the function returning a Boolean type:

```
begin
if dbms_assert.simple_sql_name(:P<N>_TABLE) = :P<N>_TABLE then
    Return true;
end if;
exception when others then
   Return false;
end;
```

`SYS.DBMS_ASSERT` contains many functions against SQL injection. Additional information about `SYS.DBMS_ASSERT` can be found at the following URL:

`http://www.oracle-base.com/articles/10g/dbms_assert_10gR2.php`

Additional information about SQL injection can be found at the Oracle Technology Network (OTN):

http://www.oracle.com/technetwork/database/features/plsql/overview/how-to-write-injection-proof-plsql-1-129572.pdf

Additional examples of SQL Injection can be found at the following URL:

http://st-curriculum.oracle.com/tutorial/SQLInjection/index.htm

Security attributes

The **Edit Security Attributes** page is divided into the following sections:

- **Authentication**
- **Authorization**
- **Database Schema**
- **Session State Protection**
- **Browser Security**
- **Database Session**

The following screenshot shows the security attributes:

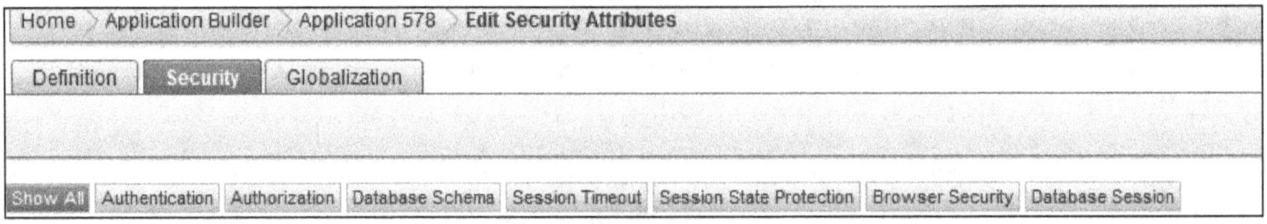

Authentication

After creating an application, you want to ensure that only authorized users can access the application. Authentication is confirming user credentials before allowing access to the application. This is done through a login page. Only if the login succeeds can the user view any component of the application. When your application uses an authentication scheme, Oracle Application Express prompts each user for a username and password when they try to log in. The credentials are evaluated, and the user is accordingly allowed or denied access to the application. After user is identified, the Oracle Application Express engine keeps track of the user by setting the value of `APP_USER. The APP_USER` is a built-in variable representing the current user running the application. The Oracle Application Express engine uses `APP_USER` to track each user's session state. An authentication schema is executed only once per session.

If you choose not to authenticate your application, Oracle Application Express does not check user credentials. All the pages of your application are accessible to all users.

The following screenshot shows the flow of the authentication mechanism:

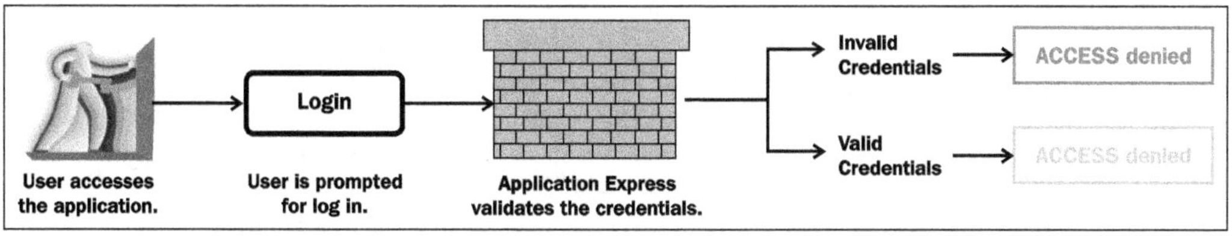

Oracle Application Express provides out-of-the-box, pre-configured schemes and customized authentication. The "best" choice for a production system is an **Lightweight Directory Access Protocol** (**LDAP**) solution. Examples are Microsoft Active Directory, Single Sign On (Oracle Internet Directory), Open LDAP, and Oracle Access Manager. The authentication delegation is outside of Oracle Application Express. In addition, there is also a choice that can be made for custom authentication. This method is the most flexible solution. This methodology allows users to be authenticated against tables, web services, and so on.

To create security mechanisms for an application, navigate to the shared components page and select the appropriate link in the **Security** list.

The following screenshot shows the **Shared Components** section with the **Security** list components:

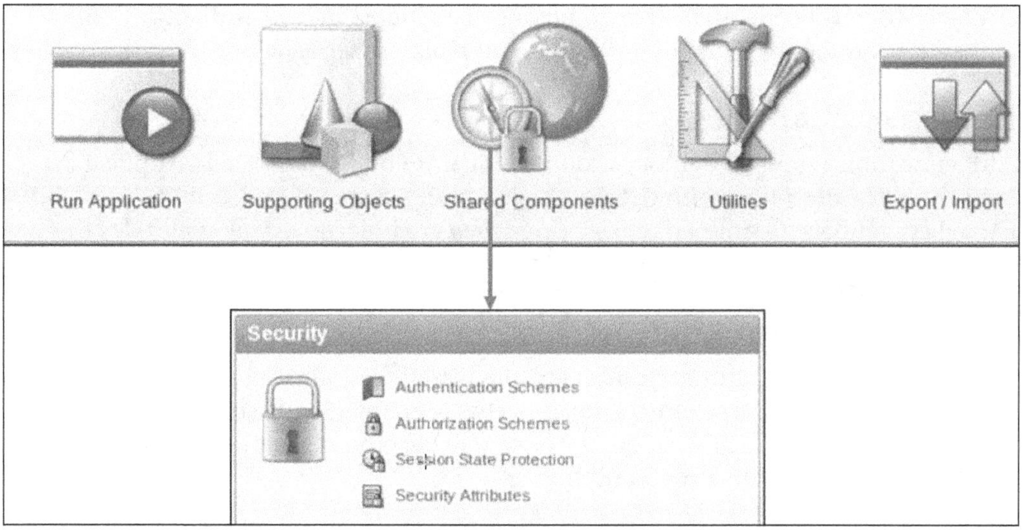

Available 'out of the box' authentication schemes

The following screenshot shows the available pre-configured schemas in Oracle Application Express:

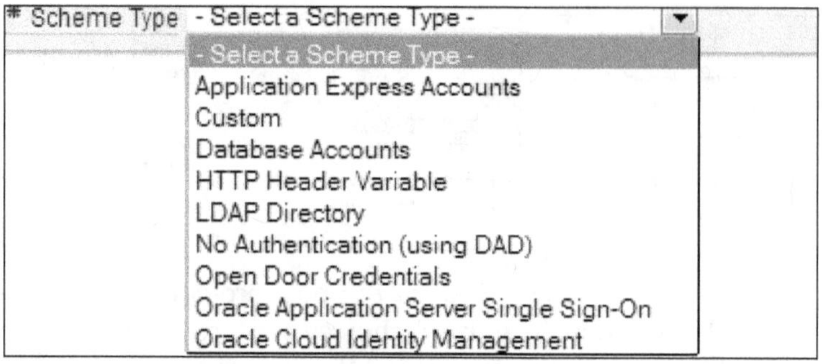

Oracle Application Express accounts

This type of authentication validates against Oracle Application Express user credentials stored in an internal repository. These user accounts are created and managed by an Oracle Application Express Workspace administrator.

Custom

It is sometimes necessary to write custom authentication schemes to meet specific requirements. Credentials verification is performed through custom PL/SQL code. By creating your own custom authentication schema, you are in full control over how and where your user repository is stored. An example of when custom authentication is needed, is when you make use of table driven authentication. So authentication occurs against your own set of tables or repository..

Database accounts

Authentication against database accounts will authenticate an Oracle Application Express application user with database username/password (for example `scott/tiger`) credentials. Granted database privileges are ignored; it only validates the correct combination of username and password of the database user.

HTTP header variable

HTTP header variable authentication is authentication against the Oracle Access Manager authentication schema. Oracle Access Manager 11g is supported with APEX 4.1 and above. HTTP header variable will become available in Oracle Application Express version 4.2 and higher.

Additional details about Oracle Application Express and Oracle Access Manager can be found at the following URL:

`http://www.oracle.com/technetwork/developer-tools/apex/learnmore/apex-oam-integration-1375333.pdf`

LDAP directory

The username and password are entered in a login page by using an LDAP. LDAP is an Internet protocol used to look up directory information. To use this scheme, you must have access to an LDAP directory. Additional information can be found here:

`http://www.oracle.com/technetwork/developer-tools/apex/how-to-ldap-authenticate-099256.html`

> **Note**
>
> The `apex_ldap.authenticate` function in 4.1.1 and older versions calls the following piece of code:
>
> ```
> dbms_ldap.simple_bind_s (g_session, 'cn='
> ||p_username||case when p_search_base is not
> null then ','||p_search_base end,p_password )
> ```

Tests with `ldapsearch` on the command line against the LDAP server shows that searches should be against the `uid` attribute:

```
DECLARE
  vSession DBMS_LDAP.session;
  vResult PLS_INTEGER;
BEGIN
  DBMS_LDAP.use_exception := TRUE;
  vSession := DBMS_LDAP.init
     ( hostname => 'ldap_server', portnum => 389 );
  vResult := DBMS_LDAP.simple_bind_s
     ( ld => vSession
     , dn => 'uid=xx,cn=Users,dc=xx,dc=org'
     , passwd => 'password1');
  DBMS_Output.put_line('User authenticated!');
  vResult := DBMS_LDAP.unbind_s(vSession);
END;
```

LDAP `auth` in 4.2 has a new attribute, **Username Escaping**, that escapes special characters in the username, to prevent LDAP injection.

No authentication

There can be a requirement that NO authentication is necessary for the Oracle Application Express application. This is named a public application; no login page is shown, and all the pages of an application are accessible to all users.

Open door credentials

A built-in login page is displayed and you are prompted for a username. You can enter any string, which then serves as the user identifier for the session.

Single sign on

In the **Single Sign On** (**SSO**) scheme, you must register the Oracle Application Express site as a partner application with the Oracle Application Server - SSO server. This method will be replaced in future releases with Oracle Access manager, because SSO will be phased out in near future.

Oracle Cloud identity management

In Oracle Cloud identity management authentication you need to authenticate against the Oracle Cloud identity management. This option will become available in Oracle Application Express version 4.2 and higher.

Authorization

An authorization scheme specifies which data can be seen or not seen by users or groups of users. Authorization may take place several times during the use of the application. It determines the power of seeing or not seeing a particular data set, and restricts access to specific pages, components (for example forms, reports, or items), or to a particular column in a report. Authorization is a process of determining whether an authenticated or identified person is permitted to access a resource or do an operation. Authorizations are implemented by using authorization schemes. If the component-level authorization succeeds, the user can view the component. If the application-level or page-level authorization fails, Oracle Application Express displays a predefined message. There are various types, such as Exists, SQL Query, and PL/SQL functions.

An authorization scheme can be applied to any of the following:

- Application
- Page
- Component on a page (form or chart)
- Item, such as a button or a text field
- Column in a report

There are three ways to create and implement an authorization scheme:

- In the shared components from the application:
    1. Create an authorization scheme from scratch.
    2. Copy an authorization scheme from an existing scheme.
- To create an access control administration page. This automates the step of creating the authorization schemes:
    1. Create an access control page.
    2. Set the application mode.
    3. Add users to the access control list.
- Apply the authorization scheme to application components.

Creating an authentication schema from scratch

The following screenshot shows the shared components from the application—the creation of an authorization schema:

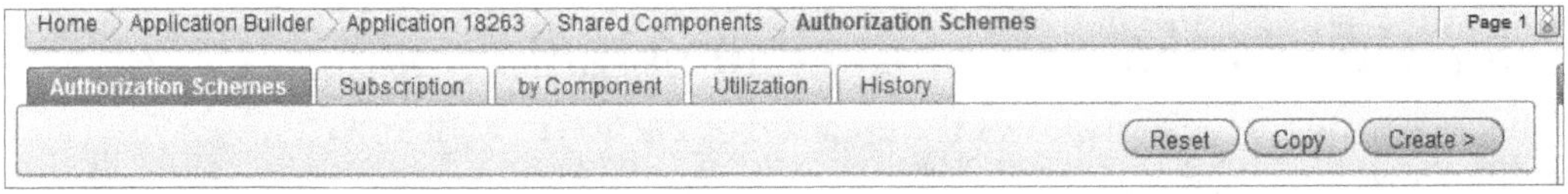

The following screenshot shows the creation of the authorization schema from scratch:

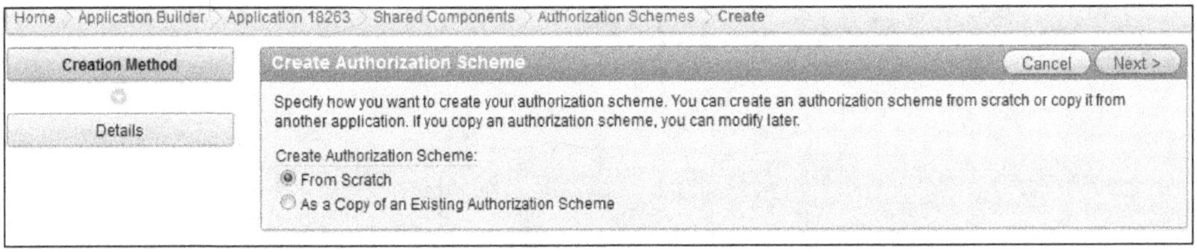

The following screenshot shows the last step of the creation of the authorization schema:

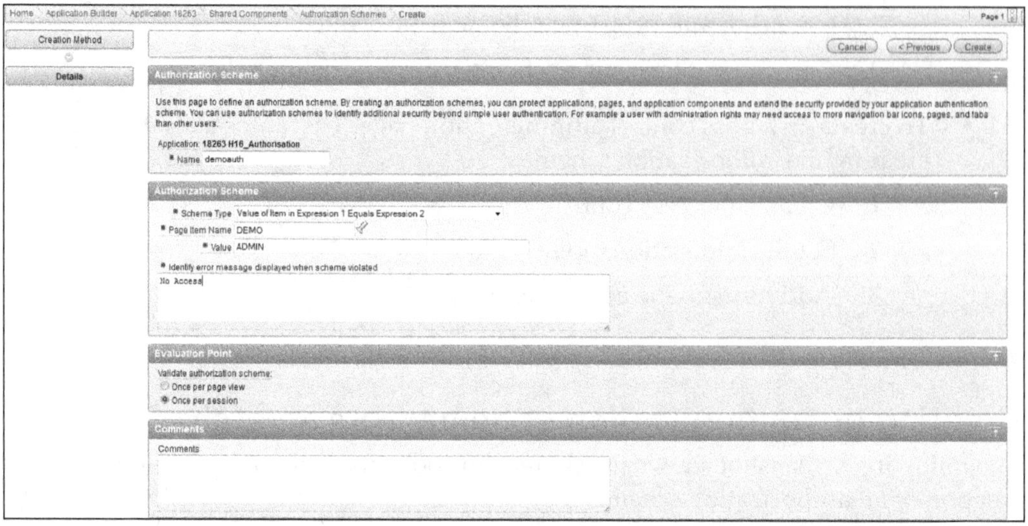

Creating an access control administration page

The following screenshot shows the creation of the access control administration page:

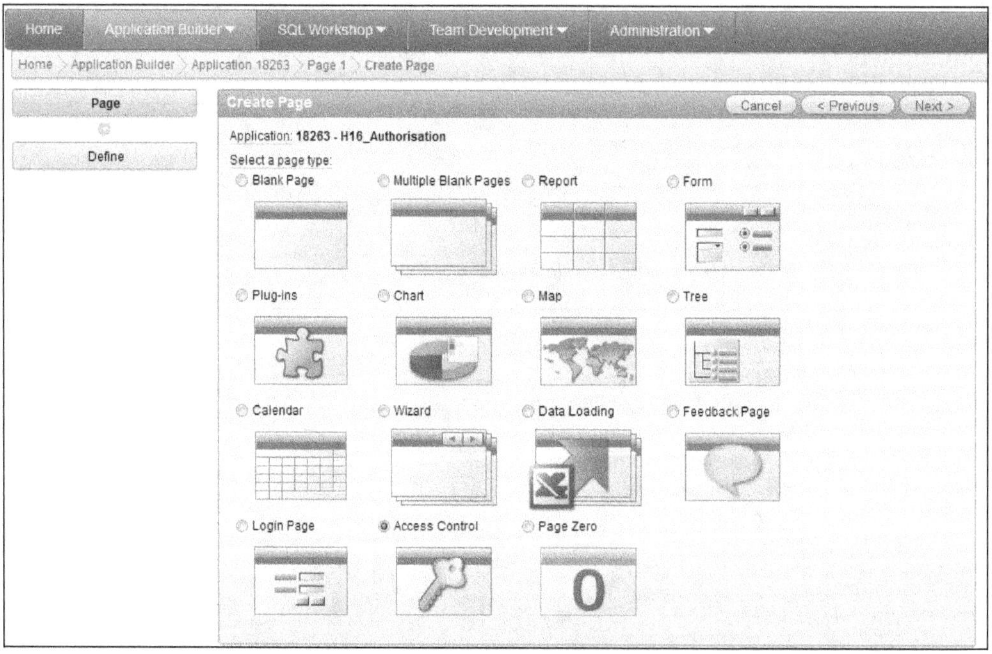

The following screenshot shows the wizard for the access control administration page:

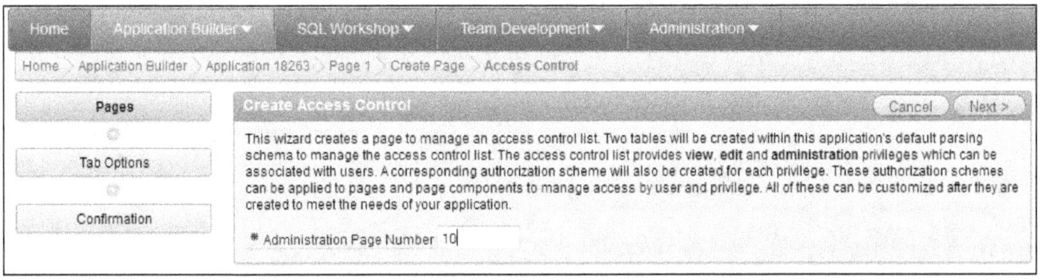

The following screenshot shows the second page in the wizard—the creation of tab pages:

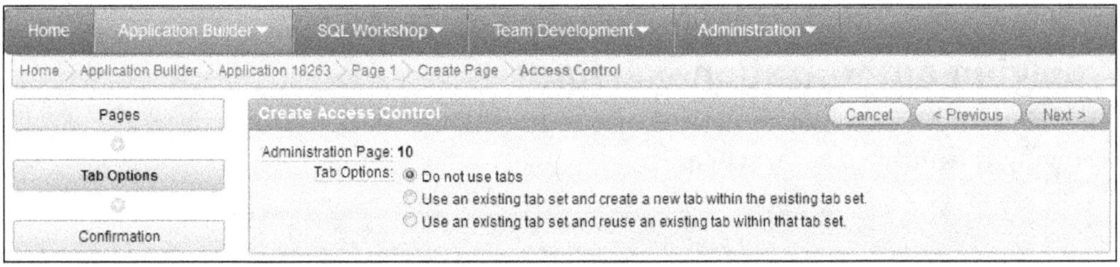

The following screenshot show the last step of the wizard—a summary is given:

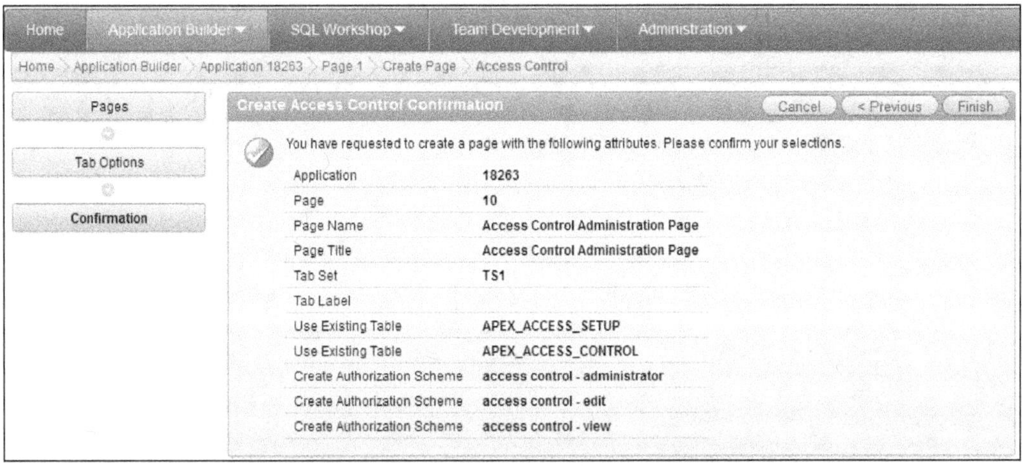

The following screenshot shows the configuration of the access control administration page:

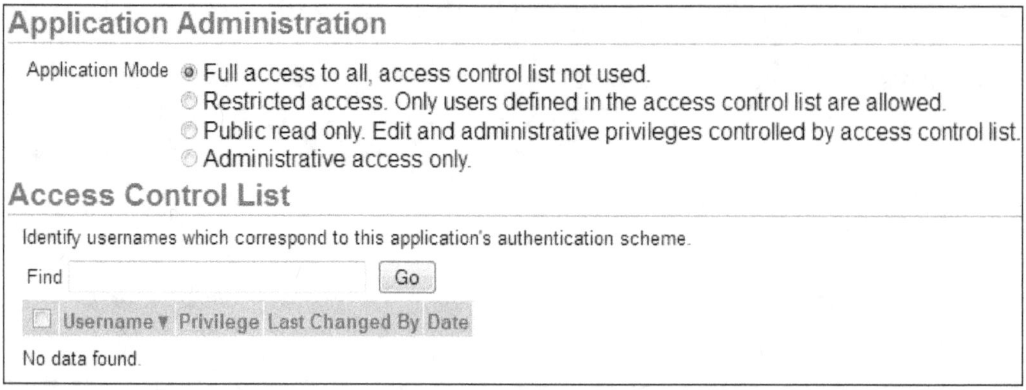

Applying authorization schemas

The following screenshot shows the option to edit application properties for applying the authorization schema:

The following screenshot shows the edit application property/security part:

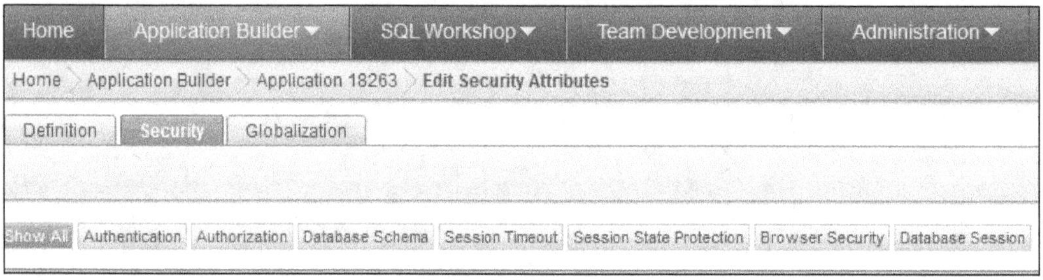

The following screenshot shows the last step of applying the authorization schema to the application:

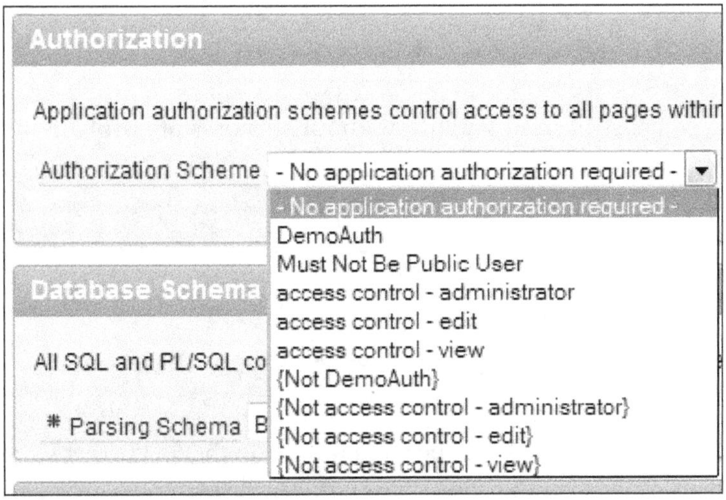

Database schema

All SQL and PL/SQL commands issued by this application will be performed with the rights and privileges of the database schema defined. The domain of the available schemas is defined per workspace.

URL tampering

For URL tampering, no extra programming code is necessary, there are no special circumstances, and anyone can learn how to do it. URL tampering can adversely affect the program logic, session state contents, and information privacy. A lot of developers are unaware of URL tampering, and the results can be disastrous.

Session state protection against URL tampering

You need to always be protected from people who deliberately want to harm. A classic example in an Oracle Application Express application is a form that is linked to a report. A record is selected from the report, and is presented in a corresponding form. So, you need to protect passing values from one page to another through a URL. If session state protection is not on, one is able to automate the ID in the URL change (URL tampering), and data from another record will be displayed. This will give the information from another record, without passing through the application.

> Therefore, session state protection should always be on. Session protection enabled is performed in two steps. In the later sections of this chapter, you will learn how to turn on session state protection.

The following screenshot shows a URL without session state protection turned on:

A URL consists of the following components:

```
F?P= APP PAGE: SESSION: REQUEST: DEBUG: CLEAR CACHE: AMES ITEM:
ITEM VALUES
```

The `EmpID` attribute at the URL can be changed, and when a correct value for `EmpID` is entered, the information about the other employee is shown.

The following screenshot shows a URL with session state protection turned on:

The `EmpID` value at the URL cannot be changed. Any attempt to do so will end in an error message.

Session State Protection is accomplished in two steps. In the first step, the feature is turned on, as follows:

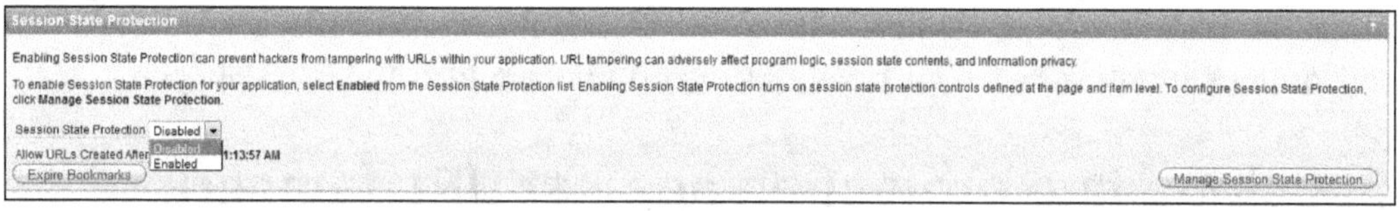

The navigation path is: **Edit application properties | Security | Session State Protection**.

In the second follow-up step, the page and item security attributes are defined:

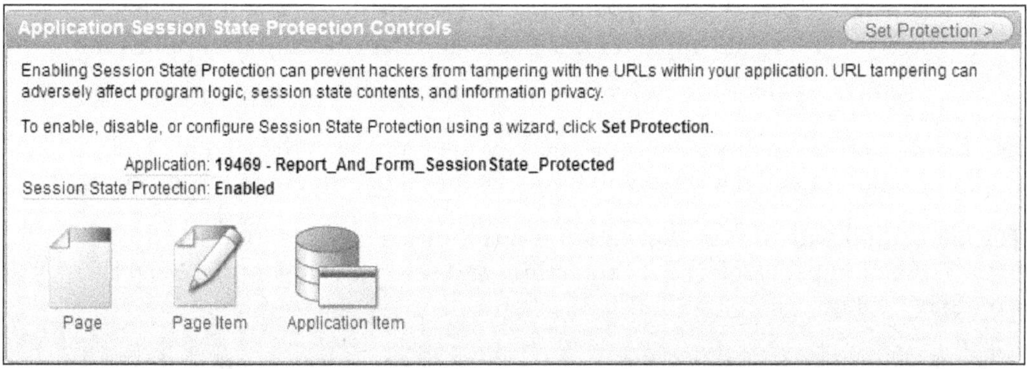

Then starts the configuration of session state protection by making use of the wizard:

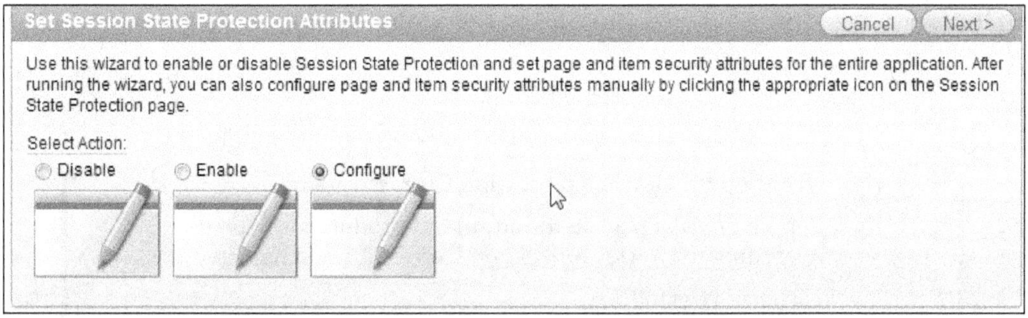

The following screenshot shows the summary page of the configuration of the session state protection:

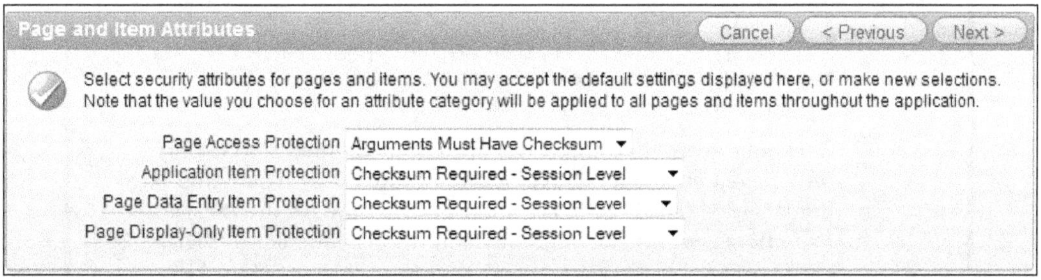

To summarize, you can configure security attributes in the following two ways:

- Use a wizard and select a value for specific attribute categories. Those selections are then applied to all pages and items within the application.
- Configure values for individual pages, items, and/or application items.

You can configure session state protection by making use of the wizard. The selections applied in the wizard will be active for all pages within the application.

The navigation path to start the wizard is as follows: Navigate to **Session State Protection** page, select **Set Protection**, and select a value for the **Select Configure** option.

When session state is enabled, the page uses the page protection attributes and a checksum added in the URL. Session state protection protects against unauthorized access and URL tampering. In Application Express the MD5 checksum is used.

In the following screenshot, you can see the checksum at the end of the URL:

> **Heads up for Oracle Application Express version 4.x**
>
> Certain types of page items on submit produce an error after upgrading to Oracle Application Express 4.1 and higher.
>
> The error is as follows:
>
> **`Session state protection violation: This may be caused by manual alteration of protected page item PX_XX. If you are unsure what caused this error, please contact the application administrator for assistance.`**
>
> The change of behavior for **Display Only** page items, where **Save Session State = Yes**, is an intentional change in Oracle Application Express 4.1.1.
>
> This more restrictive check has been implemented for **Display only** page items where **Save Session State = Yes**, **Text Field** page items where **Disabled = Yes** and **Save Session State = Yes**, and **Page Items**, where the read only condition evaluated to **TRUE**.
>
> It is no longer possible to change the session state for **Display Only** page items through JavaScript/dynamic actions if the **Save Session State** flag is set to **Yes**.

Even though session state protection helps to prevent URL tampering, there really should be other security measures on the pages, or even better in the database to prevent unauthorized access. On the page, you can prevent access to the whole page or objects on the page using authorization schemes. The best approach is making use of database triggers, instead of triggers, check constraints or Virtual Private Database. (VPD)This to prevent unwanted access.

Browser security attributes

Oracle Application Express 4.1 added two new Browser Security attributes: **Cache** and **Embed in Frames**. These attributes can be found by navigating to **Shared Components | Security Attributes | Browser Security (region)**.

The following screenshot shows the **Browser Security** attributes region in the shared components:

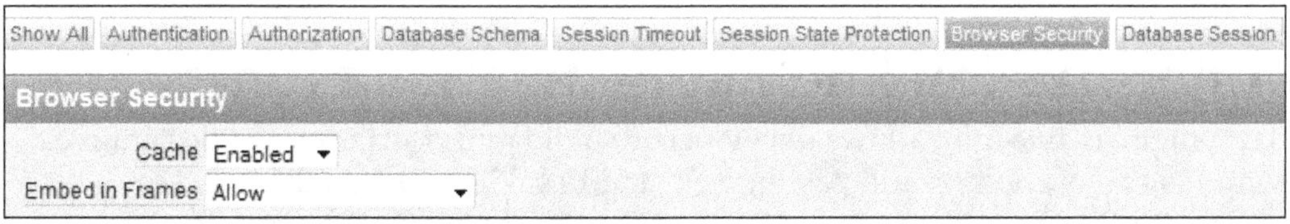

Cache

Oracle Application Express 4.1 and higher contain two browser security attributes. The attributes are named **Cache** and **Embed in Frames**.

> This feature requires browsers that support the HTTP header response variable `cache-control`.

Embed in Frames

Embed in Frames means that the browser is allowed to display application pages within a frame.

Valid values are as follows:

- **Deny**: The page cannot be displayed in a frame
- **Allow from same origin**: The page can only be displayed in a frame as the same origin or the page itself
- **Allow**: The page can be displayed in any frame

> This feature requires browsers that support the HTTP header response variable `X-Frame-Options`.

Additional information can be found here: `http://docs.oracle.com/cd/E23903_01/doc/doc.41/e21674/bldr_attr.htm#CHDDDHHF`.

Database session

Use the database session attribute to enter a PL/SQL block that sets a context for the database session associated with the current "show page" or "accept page" request. The block you enter here is executed at a very early point during the page request, immediately after the `APP_USER` value is established. Use this attribute to enter a PL/SQL block that runs at the end of page processing. It can be used to free or clean up resources that were used, such as VPD contexts or database links.

Authorization and authentication plugin

The plugin architecture allows developers to build authorizations in a declarative way, instead of copying and pasting SQL and PL/SQL code. Authentication and authorization plugins are included in Oracle Application Express version 4.1 and higher.

Plugins provided by Oracle can be found here:

`http://www.oracle.com/technetwork/developer-tools/apex/application-express/apex-plug-ins-182042.html`

Plugins found on this website are fully supported by Oracle and checked on security vulnerability issues. The danger of third-party plugins is that you are never guaranteed against security, such as SQL injection and XSS attacks. So, be careful using third-party plugins. The use of third-party plugins is at the owner's "risk".

An authorization scheme is created mostly using an existing SQL query. Many times, the query is copied to different authorization schemes within the application. Copying the code over and over is very hard to maintain. A plugin can help to encapsulate the authorization code in one place and prevent mistakes.

This is an example of coding an authorization plugin.

The code checks if the user is authorized to see a certain part of the application. An example of the PL/SQL code that can be used in an authentication plugin is as follows:

```
function is_authorized (
    p_authorization in apex_plugin.t_authorization,
    p_plugin        in apex_plugin.t_plugin )
    return apex_plugin.t_authorization_exec_result

is
   v_group  varchar2(4000) := p_authorization.attribute_01;
   v_count  number;
   v_result apex_plugin.t_authorization_exec_result;
begin
    select count(*)
    into v_count
    from apex_workspace_group_users
    where user_name  = p_authorization.username
    and group_name = v_group;
    v_result.is_authorized := l_count > 0;
    return v_result;
end is_authorized;
```

Applying the authentication schema can be performed with the following steps:

1. Go to **Shared Components | Authorization Schemes**.
2. Click on **Create**.
3. Click on **Next**.
4. Enter `Is SalesManager` for **Name**.
5. Enter `APEX Group Authorization [Plug-in]` for **Scheme Type**.
6. Enter `SalesManager` for **Group Name**.
7. Enter `This part of the application is ONLY for sales managers` for **Error Message**.
8. Click on **Create**.

Secure items in an application

The various security aspects in items will now be discussed.

Item encryption

In version 3.2.1 from Oracle Application Express and higher, it is possible to store data encrypted in session state. Item security is a property of an item.

The following screenshot shows the item security property named **Store value encrypted in session state**:

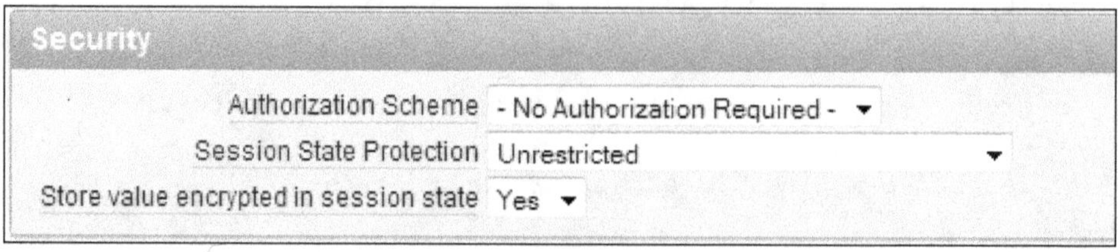

Hidden items protection

Oracle Application Express has two types of hidden items:

- **Hidden**: A form element that is not visible within the HTML page
- **Hidden and protected**: A form element, but the value is checked by the server to ensure the value has not been modified

The following screenshot shows a hidden and protected item:

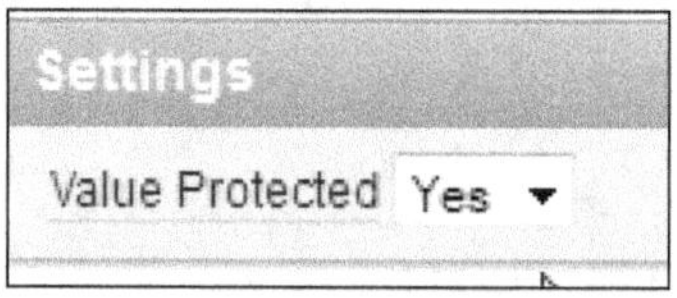

It is safer to use a value that is **Hidden and Protected,** by default, for maximum security. The reason is that a hidden item will very probably not change and this will protect against unwanted change of the value by a client-side script.

> **The Oracle Application Express User's Guide states:**
>
> "For maximum security, use **Hidden and Protected** instead of **Hidden** unless your page has client-side behavior; for example, JavaScript that alters the item value after the page is rendered by Oracle Application Express."

Let's look at an example.

An application may contain a page to display user information, and allow the user to update their details. If this page has a hidden username field that is used by the application to know which user to update, then a user could update another user's details by modifying the hidden field.

If the item was hidden and protected, the application would raise an error when the modified value was submitted.

> **Recommendation**
>
> Change all **Hidden** items to be **Hidden and Protected**, unless they are modified by client-side code.

For Oracle Application Express version 4.0 onward, set the **Value Protected** item in **Settings** on the item. Additional documentation covering hidden and protected items can be found at the following URL:

`http://download.oracle.com/docs/cd/E10513_01/doc/appdev.310/e10499/bldapp.htm#BCEGHEAJ`

Items of type password

Password items enable users to enter passwords without saving them to the session state. This prevents the password from being saved in the database in the session state tables.

There are reports provided to identify at-risk password items:

1. Navigate to the **Workspace** home page.
2. Click on the **Application Builder** icon.
3. The **Application Builder** home page appears.
4. On the **Tasks** list, click on **Cross Application Reports**.
5. Under **Security**, click on **Password Items**.

The following screenshot shows a report of **Password Items**:

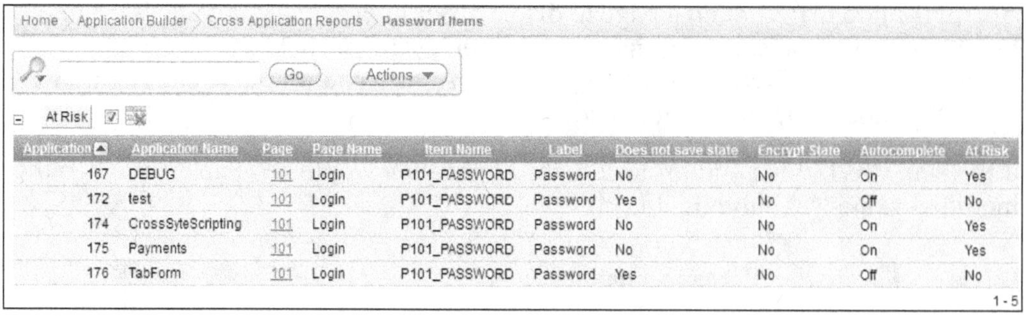

Application	Application Name	Page	Page Name	Item Name	Label	Does not save state	Encrypt State	Autocomplete	At Risk
167	DEBUG	101	Login	P101_PASSWORD	Password	No	No	On	Yes
172	test	101	Login	P101_PASSWORD	Password	Yes	No	Off	No
174	CrossSyteScripting	101	Login	P101_PASSWORD	Password	No	No	On	Yes
175	Payments	101	Login	P101_PASSWORD	Password	No	No	On	Yes
176	TabForm	101	Login	P101_PASSWORD	Password	Yes	No	Off	No

1 - 5

File upload items

The APEX_APPLICATION_FILES database view will only show those files associated with "your" database account (or workspace). You need to prevent the files from being accessed by unauthorized people. Use the **Allow Public File Upload** attribute to control whether unauthenticated users can upload files in the application or not.

Managing instance security

An Application Express instance can be secured in different ways.

> Navigation path: APEX_admin/manage instance/security.

The following screenshot shows the security section from the instance at the administration site:

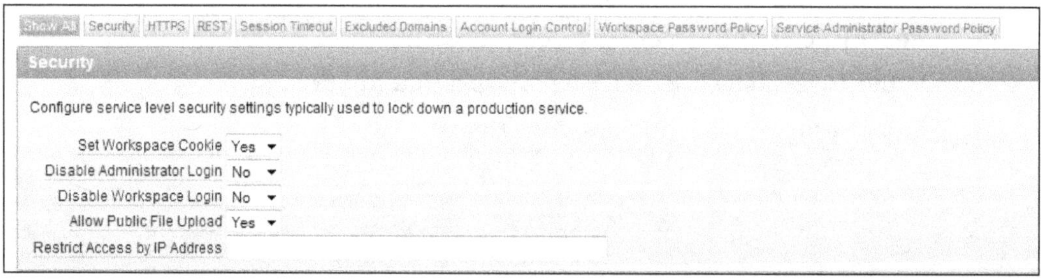

Application data

In Oracle Application Express, it is possible to download a report to different formats. In a classic report, it is possible to define a column restriction such as: "Not allowed to include in Export". Unfortunately, column restriction is not available in Interactive reports and therefore you need to write your own customized code to create this kind of column restriction. An alternative can be to write your own customized PL/SQL code to download reports to XML. This technique is very well explained at the following blog:

`http://spendolini.blogspot.co.uk/2006/04/custom-export-to-csv.html`

An own export routine prevents downloading all data by any authenticated user. In this way, you can restrict downloading of data to certain groups of users.

The following screenshot shows the column restriction attribute in a classic report:

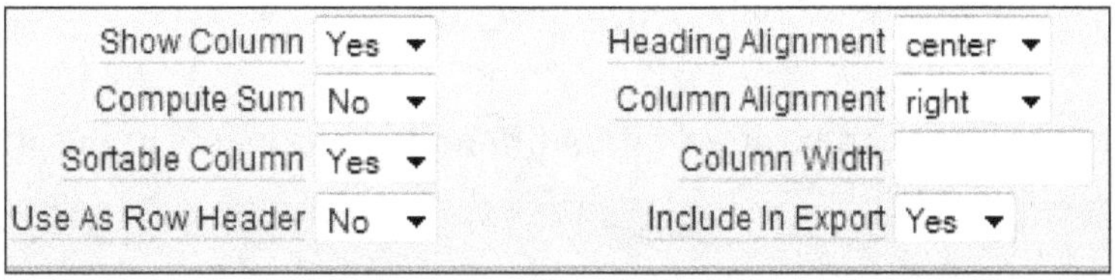

Fake input

When you use HTML controls, such as select lists, checkboxes, or radio buttons, you might think that you don't need to validate the input from these since the values are constrained. However, you cannot count on this. A select list can easily be converted to a normal text input field. In Firebug or a web developer, there is an option available in the menu to convert all select lists on the current page to text fields. So take care and validate all input. Use a database trigger, a foreign key constraint, or a check constraint to restrict the values entered by the user.

A classic example from fake input via the Firebug add-on is changing a value that is selected in a list of values to another value. Fake input via Firebug can be avoided by creating extra validations within the database.

The following is an example of fake input via the Firebug add-on:

```
        <input type="hidden" value="2270853644859806859" name="p_arg_names">
      ⊟ <select id="P1_EMPNO" class="selectlist" size="1" name="p_t01">
            <option value=""> </option>
            <option selected="selected" value="7839">KING</option>
            <option value="7876">ADAMS</option>
            <option value="7900">JAMES</option>
            <option value="7934">MILLER</option>
        </select>
      ⊞ <a class="eLink" tabindex="999" href="javascript:popupURL('f?p=4000:371:22517628845
      </td>
    </tr>
</tbody>
```

Additional information and a nice solution against fake input with the firebug add-on can be found at the following URL:

`http://www.talkapex.com/2009/05/enhancing-apex-security-explanation.html`

Authorization schemas can be attached to different components in the application (button, region, and so on).

A malicious user can perform the process (through JavaScript) without requiring the actual button to be accessible. This means that securing the button is not sufficient by having only an authorization schema.

> **General advices**
>
> Using Zero as Session ID: This is critical for `PUBLIC` applications to ensure no cross-user contamination will occur. Zero session ID means not being included in application URL.
>
> For example, where you might normally code the link to page 1 as `f?p=&APP_ID.:1:&APP_SESSION`, you would code `f?p=&APP_ID.:2:0`.
>
> When users access Oracle Application Express application pages, numerous links containing session IDs become visible in the Web browser's location window.

Saving state before branching

The "Save state before branch" feature for branches was deprecated, because the existing implementation had some serious restrictions that confused numerous developers in many different situations.

- If `clear page` was specified, it was performed when the page was rendered. So the value which was set during "accept" processing was cleared out when the page was actually rendered.
- If a page item was set, which was based on a database column and it wasn't the primary key column, the value didn't show up when the page was rendered. When someone used **Save state before branch** = **No**, it would work as expected.

Workaround:

- Use a computation or a process to set the session state before branches are fired
- In the branch, simply specify the page and do not include page items

The preceding workaround is doing the same as **Save state before branch** = **Yes**, and will work fine for primary key page items or page items that are not based on a database column.

Utilities

There are different utilities in Application Express that can be handy to ensure security.

Application dashboard

To access the **Utilities** page, click on the **Utilities** icon on the application home page. From the **Utilities** page, you can access application utilities as well as page-specific utilities.

Security lists the current authentication scheme, the number of public and non-public pages, and the number of authorization schemes.

The following screenshot shows the security part of the application dashboard:

[Navigation path: `Application home page/Utilities`.]

How to check the security of your application

Oracle Application Express has different in-built tools available to ensure security within an application.

Oracle Application Express Advisor

The built-in Oracle Application Express Advisor is a tool that can be used to check for performance issues, as well as performing checks for errors, security issues, usability, and quality assurance. This utility is available in 4.0 and above. The Advisor functions like a compiler or LINT flagging suspicious behavior or errors. **LINT** is a utility that examines and analyses programs for style, usage, and portability issues. By running the Advisor, you can check the integrity of your application based on the underlying metadata.

> **Note**
>
> When running the Advisor with all the checks checked, the following error is thrown:
>
> **`ORA-01460: Unimplemented or unreasonable conversion requested.`**
>
> **`Work-around is easy, hit the apply button.`**

The following screenshot shows the Advisor utility in Oracle Application Express:

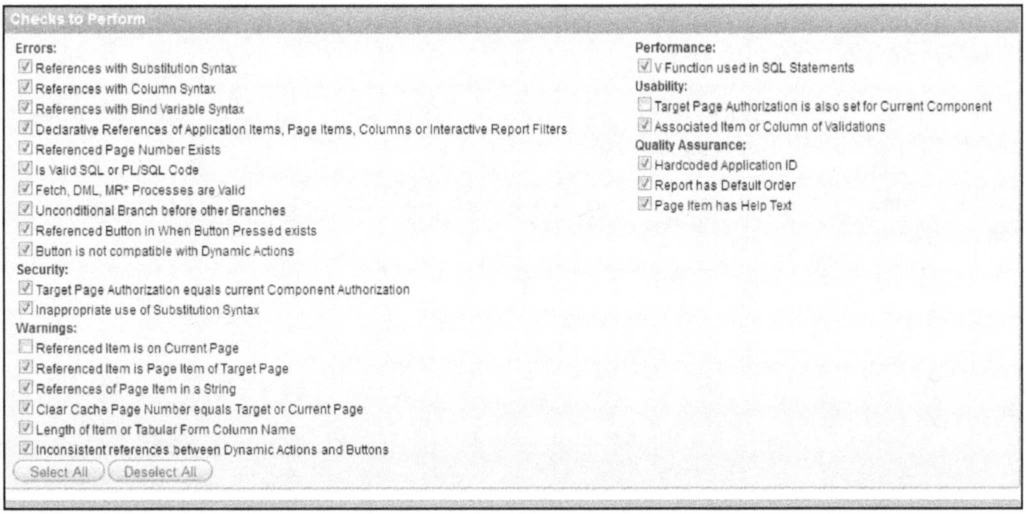

Third-party tools to check on security

There are third-party tools available to check the security from your application. The ApexSec Security Console is designed to import and analyze your Oracle Application Express application for issues with security implications. Demonstration of the tool can be found at the following website:

`https://secure.recx.co.uk/apexsec/help.jsp`

Sumneva also provides a security scan tool for Oracle Application Express applications, at the following URL:

`http://www.sumneva.com/apex/f?p=15000:1070:0`

Summary

Security is not an easy subject, and should be considered all the time and with each piece of code that you write. All layers involved with Oracle Application Express should involve insecurity; this means the web server, database, and the application itself. There is a fine balance between security and productivity. Too much security means a hard time doing your job, and too little means exposing the system to a security breach. Basic security hardening is just a matter of knowing where the weaknesses are. Organizations need to have their patches and CPU patches strategy in place. Patching is very important when hardening security. Think about security before it is too late, as it could have negative consequences for you and your organization!

A general advice is making use of Application Express built-in security capabilities and the Application Express Advisor.

Besides this, perform an Application Express analysis by making use of third-party analysis tools.

5

Debugging and Troubleshooting

Debugging Oracle Application Express can be a conundrum. Oracle APEX is a blend of technologies - PL/SQL and SQL that generates HTML pages using CSS, templates, and JavaScript. Tracking and resolving problems in this multi-layer environment necessitates a blend of tactics to examine what is happening in each component of the application.

This chapter will cover the following topics:

- Debugging in APEX
- Remote debugging using Oracle SQL Developer
- Web development tools
- Reports available in Application Express for troubleshooting
- Advisor

Debugging an APEX page

Before you can start by debugging a page, there are some prerequisites. First of all, the debugging property needs to be set to `Yes`, and second the developer toolbar needs to be visible. Although this last requirement is not strictly necessary, it is very convenient when the development toolbar is visible.

By default, the debugging property is set to `No`. To switch the debugging property to `Yes`, follow the steps listed here:

1. Navigate to the application home page.
2. Click on **Edit Application Properties**.
3. In the **Properties** section, set the value for **Debugging** to **Yes**.

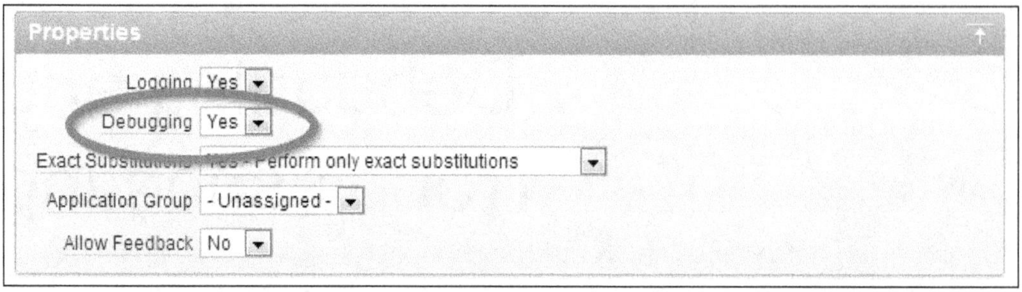

In the preceding screenshot, the Debugging property is set to **Yes**. This property enables debugging for the entire application.

By default, the developer toolbar is visible when the application is run starting from the development environment in the same browser. The developer toolbar offers a quick way to edit the current page, create a new page, region, or page control, view the session state, or toggle in and out of the debug mode. The development toolbar is shown at the bottom of each page.

It is possible to control whether the developer toolbar is shown by changing the **Status** attribute on the **Edit Application Definition** page. When you start the application from the development environment and the developer toolbar does not show, then take the following steps:

1. Navigate to the application home page.
2. Click on **Edit Application Properties**.

3. In the **Availability** section, set the value for **Status** to **Available with Edit Links**:

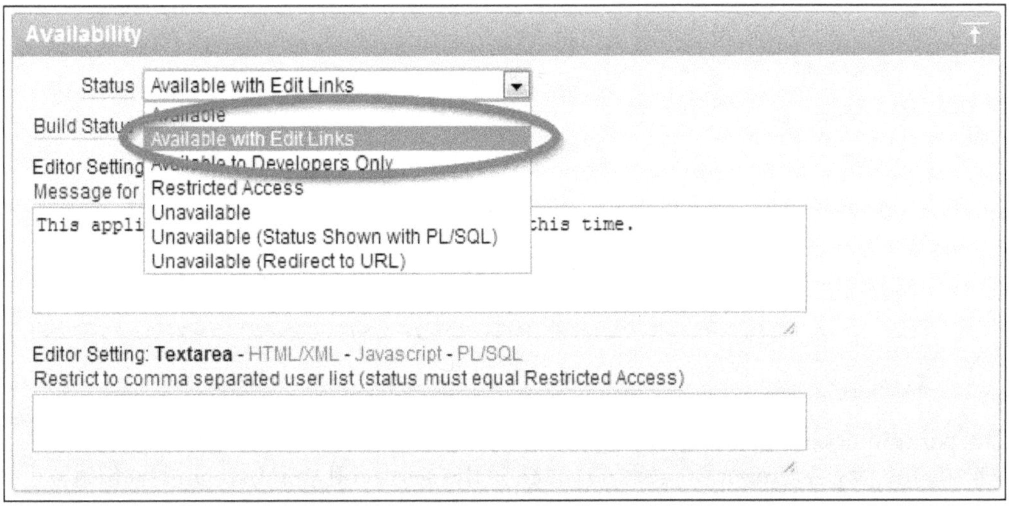

In the preceding screenshot, **Status** is set to **Available with Edit Links**, which is the default value for this property. Only developers running the application will see the development toolbar with the setting at default.

After meeting these prerequisites, the actual debugging can begin. In the application development bar, shown in the following screenshot, click on the **Debug** option:

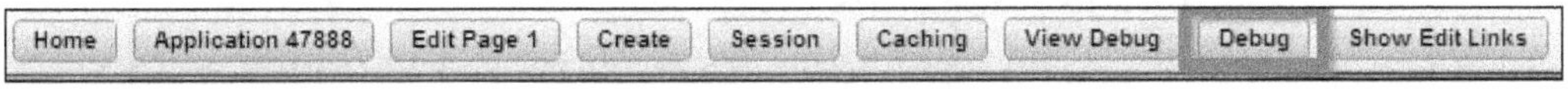

The page gets refreshed and the debugging information gets captured. The label on this button will be changed to **No Debug**.

Besides using the button in the development toolbar, it is also possible to manipulate the URL to toggle the debugging. A complete URL might look as follows:

```
http://host:port/DAD/f?p=100:1:2345678912345::YES
```

The fifth parameter in the URL is the debug toggle; the parameters are as follows:

- Application ID
- Page number or page alias
- Session ID
- Request
- Debug toggle
- Clear cache
- Item names
- Item values
- Printer friendly
- Tracing toggle

The parameters are listed after `f?p=` in the preceding URL; `100` is the Application ID, `1` is the page number, `2345678912345` is the session ID, and so on. The fifth parameter is set to `YES`, which means that debugging is enabled.

Using the URL to toggle debugging can be convenient when the development bar is not visible.

> **In Application Express 4.2**
>
> Where the `f?p` URL syntax arguments are described, the argument `Debug` should be extended as follows:
>
> - Valid values for the `DEBUG` flag are `YES`, `LEVEL1` to `LEVEL9` or `NO`
> - Setting this flag to `YES` will display details about application processing
> - Setting this flag to `LEVELn` (where `n` is between `1` and `9`) controls the level of debug detail, from least details (`LEVEL1`) to most details (`LEVEL9`)
> - The value `YES` is equal to `LEVEL4`

Now that debugging is enabled, it is possible to see exactly what APEX is doing and how long it takes, including page rendering and page processing.

> Page rendering is the process of generating a page from the database. The HTML page is assembled and displayed. During the page rendering process, the following actions occur: computations, processing, and region- and item rendering.
>
> Page processing computations and processes are performed when the page is submitted to the APEX engine. For page processing, the following actions take place: computations, validations, processes, and branching.

Reviewing this information and comparing the listed actions with the intended actions helps to discover where events are or are not firing, with correct or incorrect values.

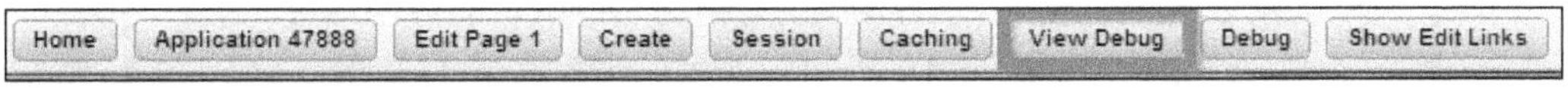

To review the debug messages, use the button in the development toolbar labeled **View Debug** (see the previous screenshot). This will open up a new window similar to the following screenshot:

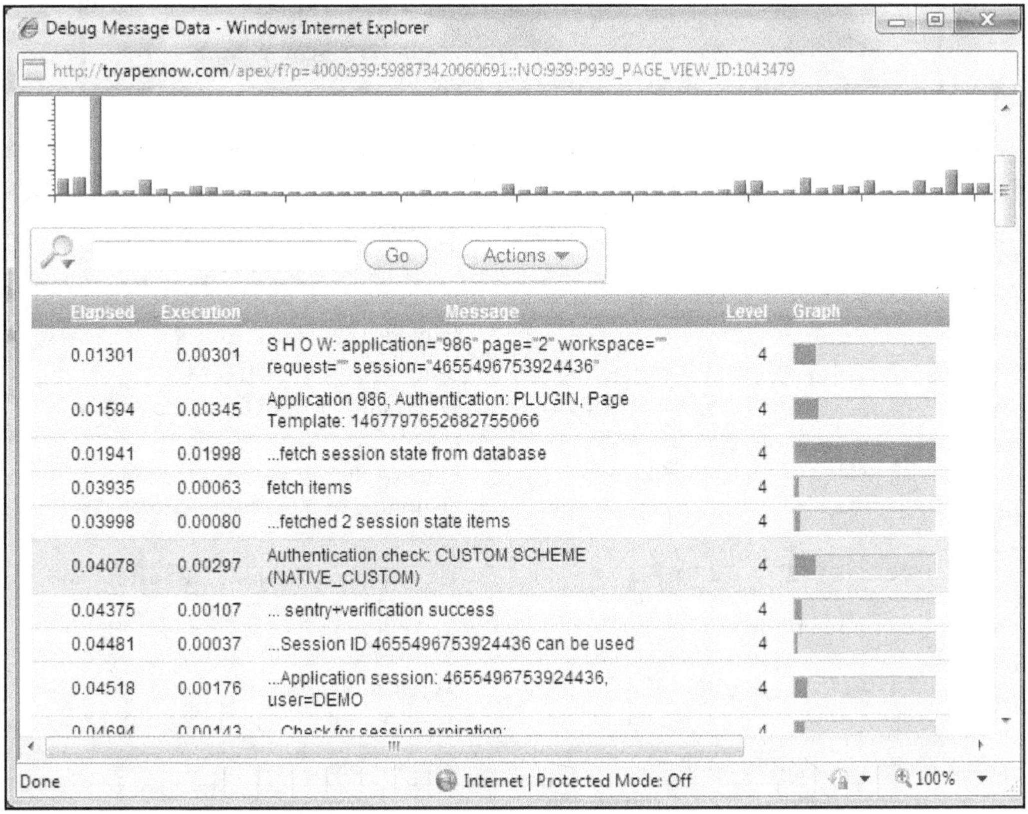

At the top of the **Debug Message Data** window (see the previous screenshot), there is a graphical representation of the execution times. This makes it easy to narrow down where most of the time is spent on the page. Clicking on the graph on the top will navigate to the appropriate line in the report. A similar graph is shown per line in the report; the wider the bar, the more time this line takes.

The previous screenshot shows the information that can be found in the debug information: authentication information, validation checks, assignments and session state information, values assigned in queries, and much more.

> Debug information can also be queried through the `APEX_DEBUG_MESSAGES` view. The actual debug information is stored in two data dictionary tables: `WWV_FLOW_DEBUG_MESSAGES` and `WWV_FLOW_DEBUG_MESSAGES2`.

> **In Application Express 4.2**
>
> The `APEX_DEBUG_MESSAGE` has been renamed to `APEX_DEBUG`. In the top-level description, it should be specified that the module can still be accessed by its previous name, `APEX_DEBUG_MESSAGE`, for compatibility reasons, but the new name is preferred.

The following table lists the columns in the `APEX_DEBUG_MESSAGES` view:

Column name	Data type	Remark
`ID`	`NUMBER`	
`PAGE_VIEW_ID`	`NUMBER`	Page view identifier, which is a unique sequence generated for each page view recorded with debugging
`MESSAGE_TIMESTAMP`	`TIMESTAMP(6) with time zone`	Timestamp: In GMT that message was saved
`ELAPSED_TIME`	`NUMBER`	Elapsed time in seconds from the beginning of page submission or page view
`EXECUTION_TIME`	`NUMBER`	Time elapsed between the current and the next debug message
`MESSAGE`	`VARCHAR2(4000)`	Message
`APPLICATION_ID`	`NUMBER`	Application identifier
`PAGE_ID`	`NUMBER`	Page identifier within the application
`SESSION_ID`	`NUMBER`	APEX session identifier

Column name	Data type	Remark
APEX_USER	VARCHAR2(255)	Username of the user authenticated to the application
MESSAGE_LEVEL	NUMBER	Can be level 1:7 (importance)
WORKSPACE_ID	NUMBER	Application Express workspace identifier

Instrumentation of the APEX code

Code instrumentation makes it much easier to track down bugs and isolate unexpected behavior more quickly. Code instrumentation is used to diagnose errors and to write trace information. Besides instrumenting the database code (see *Chapter 2, Leveraging the Database*), instrumenting APEX code can also be very beneficial.

You can reference the DEBUG flag using the following syntax:

Substitution string	&DEBUG.
PL/SQL	V('DEBUG')
Bind variable	:DEBUG

When a page is run in the `DEBUG` mode, the debug item is automatically set to `YES`; otherwise, it is set to `NO`. This can be useful to show region content depending on the debug mode variable.

The following example shows a region depending on the value of the `DEBUG` variable:

Create a condition of the type PL/SQL expression.

The value expression `1` has the following value:

```
v('DEBUG') = 'YES'
```

That means when the `DEBUG` variable is equal to `'YES'`, the region is shown; when the `DEBUG` variable is `'NO'`, the region is not shown. This way you can limit your debug code to only execute when running in the debug mode. So you only call the code when you need the code. When running the application in production, the debug mode is turned off and the debug code is ignored by the APEX engine.

APEX_APPLICATION.G_DEBUG

The APEX_APPLICATION package enables users to take advantage of global variables. The apex_application.g_debug variable refers to whether debugging is currently switched on or off. Valid values for this variable are TRUE or FALSE.

Turning debug ON shows details about application processing.

For example:

```
IF apex_application.g_debug THEN
  apex_debug_message.log_message('Custom Validation');
END IF;
```

Including the preceding code in the APEX page, anywhere where PL/SQL is allowed, will add information visible in APEX_DEBUG_MESSAGES, and therefore in the **View Debug** page. This information will only be added when apex_application.g_debug evaluates to TRUE.

The debug Advanced Programming Interface (API)

The APEX_DEBUG_MESSAGE package provides utility functions for managing the debug message log. Specifically, this package provides the necessary APIs to instrument and debug PL/SQL code contained within the APEX application as well as the PL/SQL code in database stored procedures and functions. Sometimes, you need to know where the problem resides. A problem can exist in the rendering part or in the processing part of the page. Using the API, debug messages can be included at page rendering and page processing level. **Page rendering**: before header, **page processing**: after submit.

The APEX debug message

There are several procedures in the APEX_DEBUG_MESSAGE package. These procedures are listed in the following table:

Procedure	Usage
DISABLE_DEBUG_MESSAGES	Programmatically disable debugging
ENABLE_DEBUG_MESSAGES	Programmatically enable debugging
LOG_MESSAGE	Log a message of up to 4000 bytes at a given level
LOG_LONG_MESSAGE	Log a LONG message (split into 4000 byte chunks) at a given level

Procedure	Usage
LOG_PAGE_SESSION_STATE	Emit session state information into the DEBUG table
REMOVE_DEBUG_BY_AGE	Remove debug messages for a given application older than N days
REMOVE_DEBUG_BY_APP	Remove debug messages for a given application
REMOVE_DEBUG_BY_VIEW	Remove debug messages for a given application and page view ID
REMOVE_SESSION_MESSAGES	Remove debug messages for a given session

The following is an example of enabling debug messages for a specific user in the page rendering process—Onload/Before header header.

```
IF :APP_USER = 'XX' THEN
  apex_debug_message.enable_debug_messages;
END IF;
```

The REMOVE_DEBUG_BY_AGE procedure takes two arguments:

```
(p_application_id in number default null,
 P_older_than_days in number default null);
```

This example shows how the REMOVE_DEBUG_BY_AGE procedure is used.

Before we can use the procedure to remove the debug information, we first need to create some debug information. Debug information is created when the **View Debug** button in the developer toolbar is pressed.

The following steps will guide you through this process:

1. Edit the page, and in the **Processes** section, click on the **Create** icon, to add a new process to this page. This will launch the **Create Page Process** wizard.
2. Select category PL/SQL, and click on the **Next** button.
3. Type `Clear Debug Info`, ensure that **Point** is set to **On Load -Before Header**, and click on **Next**.
4. Under the **Source** heading, enter the following code:

```
apex_debug_message.remove_debug_by_age
  (p_application_id   => :APP_ID
  ,p_older_than_days => 1
  );
```

The following screenshot shows the `APEX_DEBUG_MESSAGE.REMOVE_DEBUG_BY_AGE` process:

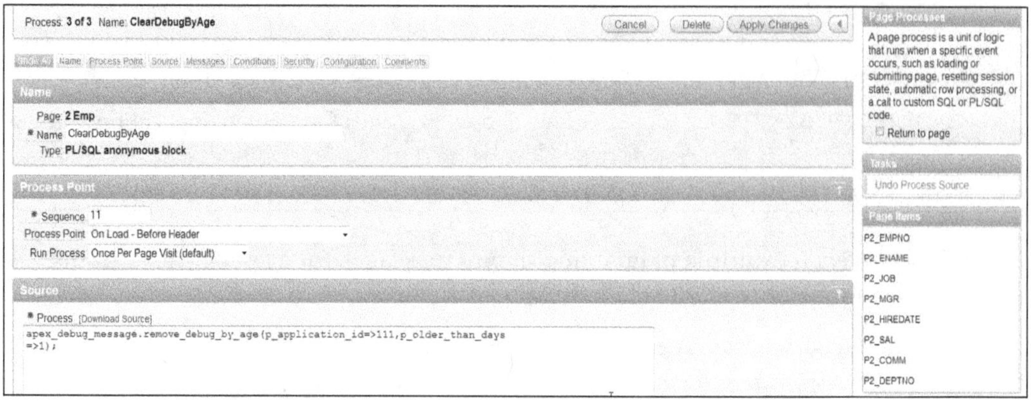

5. In the **Success Message** text areas, type the message `Debug Messages Cleared`, and click on **Next**.
6. Click on **Create Process**.
7. Run the page, and click on **View Debug** in **Developer Toolbar**.

The result is that the debug information for the page older than 1 day will be cleared.

APEX_DEBUG_MESSAGE.LOG_MESSAGE

With the Application Express `APEX_DEBUG_MESSAGE.LOG_MESSAGE` process, you have the possibility to emit messages in the debug output.

For example:

```
apex_debug_message.log_message('Render: Hello');
```

Or:

```
apex_debug_message.log_message('Item Validation');
apex_debug_message.log_message('...Item: '||p_item);
```

In this way, you add debug information to your code and therefore make it easier to troubleshoot your code.

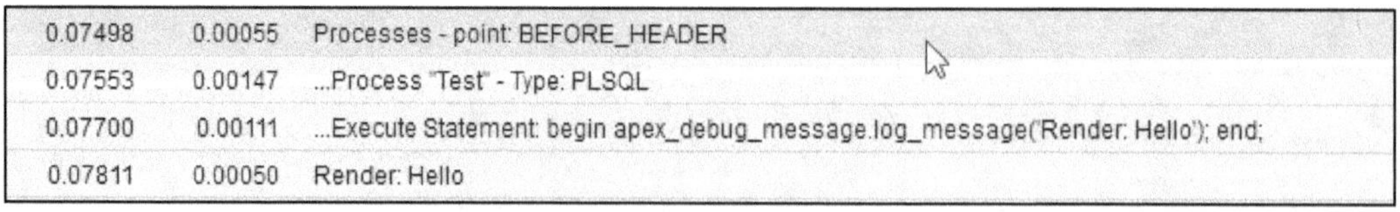
0.07498 0.00055 Processes - point: BEFORE_HEADER
0.07553 0.00147 ...Process "Test" - Type: PLSQL
0.07700 0.00111 ...Execute Statement: begin apex_debug_message.log_message('Render: Hello'); end;
0.07811 0.00050 Render: Hello

This image shows the extra debug information `'Hello'`, which is emitted by the `apex_debug_message.log_message` API.

WWV_FLOW_API.SET_ENABLE_APP_DEBUGGING

This API is not documented in the APEX documentations, and is therefore officially not supported. It allows you to turn debugging `ON` or `OFF` at the application level.

For example:

On:

```
wwv_flow_api.set_enable_app_debugging (:APP_ID, 1);
```

Off:

```
wwv_flow_api.set_enable_app_debugging (:APP_ID, 0);
```

APEX and Oracle SQL Developer

APEX and Oracle SQL Developer can work perfectly together. For troubleshooting PL/SQL code within APEX, remote debugging can be very handy.

Oracle SQL Developer is a graphical user interface that allows you to browse database objects, run SQL statements and scripts, and debug PL/SQL statements. Before concentrating on the integration of Oracle SQL Developer and APEX, we are going to look at how debugging is done in Oracle SQL Developer. Oracle provides two packages for debugging PL/SQL code. The first, `DBMS_DEBUG`, was introduced in Oracle version 8i and not used anymore in Oracle SQL Developer. The second, `DBMS_DEBUG_JDWP`, was introduced in Oracle version 9i and is used by Oracle SQL Developer.

More information and downloads of Oracle SQL Developer can be found at:

`http://www.oracle.com/technetwork/developer-tools/sql-developer/overview/index.html`

To demonstrate debugging with Oracle SQL Developer, create the following procedure:

> The procedure is for demonstrations purposes only; it does not reflect best practices or efficient coding techniques.

```
create or replace
procedure get_emp_list(pmaxrows in number) as
   cursor emp_cursor is
      select l.state_province
            ,l.country_id
            ,d.department_name
            ,e.last_name
            ,j.job_title
            ,e.salary
            ,e.commission_pct
        from locations   l
            ,departments d
            ,employees   e
            ,jobs        j
       where l.location_id = d.location_id
         and d.department_id = e.department_id
         and e.job_id = j.job_id;
   emp_record emp_cursor%rowtype;
   type emp_tab_type is table of emp_cursor%rowtype
      index by binary_integer;
   emp_tab emp_tab_type;
   i       number := 1;
begin
   open emp_cursor;
   fetch emp_cursor
      into emp_record;
   emp_tab(i) := emp_record;
   while (emp_cursor%found)
         and (i <= pmaxrows)
   loop
      i := i + 1;
      fetch emp_cursor
         into emp_record;
      emp_tab(i) := emp_record;
   end loop;
   close emp_cursor;
   for j in reverse 1 .. i
   loop
      dbms_output.put_line(emp_tab(j).last_name);
   end loop;
end get_emp_list;
```

By default, the line numbers are not visible in the worksheet of Oracle SQL Developer. Show the line number by right-clicking in the gutter (the location where the lines are supposed to show up) and choose **Toggle Line Numbers** from the context menu.

To run the procedure, locate the procedure in the connections navigator. Right-click on the procedure and choose run. The results are displayed in the **Running Log** window.

To debug a procedure, it needs to be compiled for debug first. This step adds in the compiler directives required for debugging. Once you have completed the debug, you should compile the procedure again and remove the extra directives.

> When the directives are not removed, performance will be decreased because of the directives available in the code.

Set a breakpoint in the `EMP_LIST` procedure by clicking on the margin at the line where you would like the execution to stop. The line number is replaced with a red dot. This is a breakpoint symbol.

> A breakpoint is a location in the code that you identify as a stopping point. When the code is run in debug mode, execution will stop at the breakpoint.

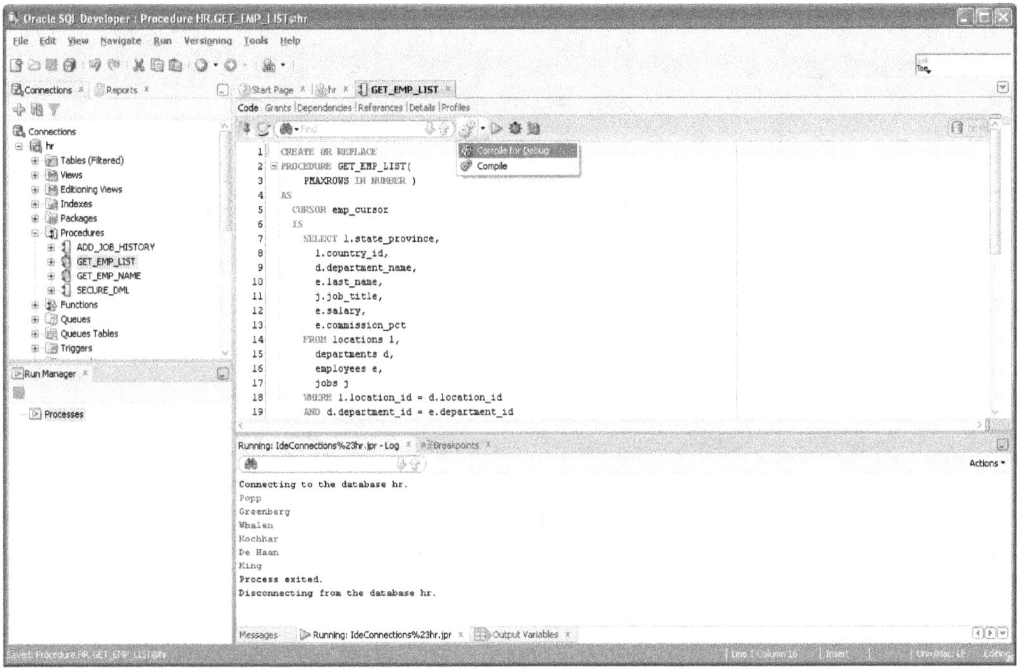

This image shows the compile for debug option in Oracle SQL Developer

After defining the breakpoints, the debug icon ( ) in Oracle SQL Developer can be clicked to start the debug session. Oracle SQL Developer sets the sessions to a debug session and issues the following command:

```
DBMS_DEBUG_JDWP.CONNECT_TCP (Hostname, port )
```

Be aware that you are not restricted by the firewall.

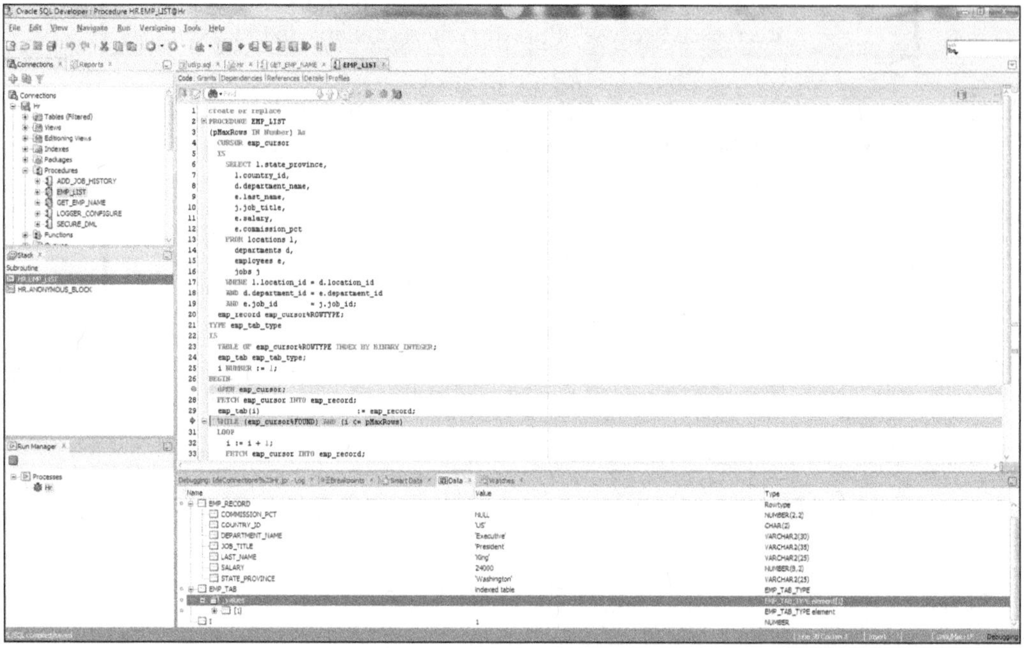

This image shows defining the breakpoint in the `EMP_LIST` procedure:

Item	Remark
The **Data** tab	Collect all values of the variables as you step through the code
The smart data	Keeps track of the same detail as the **Data** tab, but only the values immediately related to the area worked in
Run to cursor	Start debugging and quickly move to another part of the code
Watch	Allows you to watch an expression or code
Inspect	Allows you to watch values

Remote debugging

The easiest way to illustrate remote debugging is to use Oracle SQL Developer with an application in APEX. The subprogram resides in APEX, and Oracle SQL Developer is used to debug it. This capability is especially useful when an application isn't failing but also isn't producing the results you expect. The following grants are necessary before performing remote debugging:

```
grant DEBUG CONNECT SESSION to <schema>;
grant DEBUG on <object> to PUBLIC;
grant DEBUG ANY PROCEDURE to APEX_PUBLIC_USER;
```

Or `ANONYMOUS` when using the embedded gateway.

1. Connect Oracle SQL Developer and import the APEX application.
2. Set a breakpoint in the code that needs to be debugged.
3. Compile the procedure for debug.

   Note that running a package in debug mode severely hampers performance. Once testing is complete, compile the package without debug information.
4. At this point, prepare Oracle SQL Developer for remote debugging. Do this by selecting the connection that will be used for debugging the code, and select **Remote Debug** in the menu.
5. Next, a pop-up window is shown where the port and IP address need to be entered. The port number will be shared by Oracle SQL Developer and the APEX application.

The following image shows the remote debug connection:

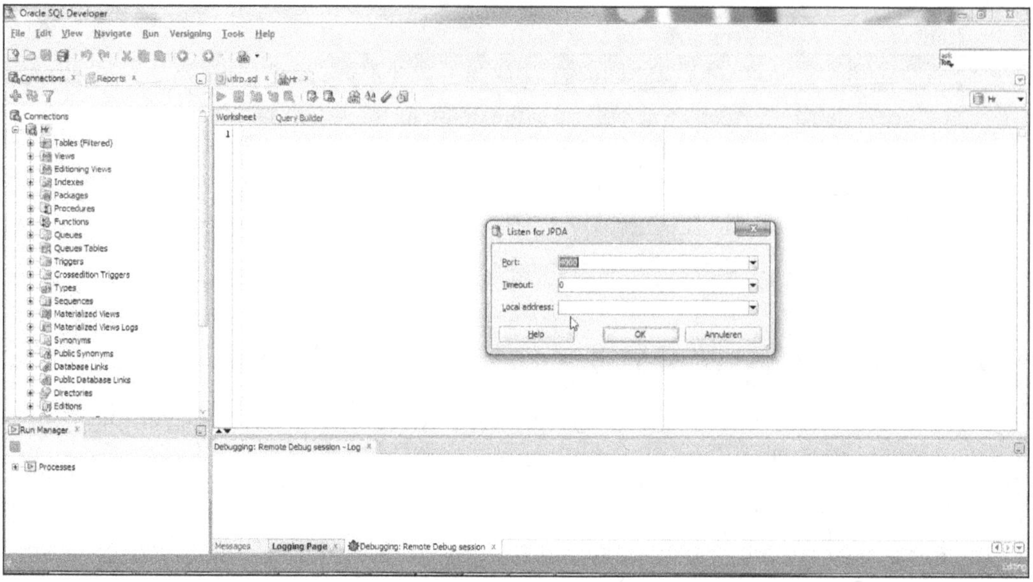

This prepares Oracle SQL Developer for the connection to the debugger and opens the process. Application Express also needs to be prepared for remote debugging. This is done by performing the program in debug mode, and changing `YES` in the URL to `REMOTE` (the fifth position in the URL).

Steps to be performed in APEX

The necessary steps in APEX to perform remote debugging are as follows:

1. Execute the program in Application Express.
2. Click on **Debug** in the developer toolbar when you want to debug.
3. Change the `YES` in the URL to `REMOTE`.

The following is an example of the URL for performing remote debugging out of an APEX application:

```
http://host:port/apex/f?p=103:11:6993768986060180::REMOTE
```

Now, debugging can be performed in Oracle SQL Developer. The APEX application will wait for the debugging process to complete. At this point, it is not possible to continue working with the application. On the other hand, this is not the purpose – keep the application online at this time. When debug is ready, control is given back to the APEX application.

JavaScript console wrapper

Martin Giffy D'Souza has written the **Console Wrapper** utility. For additional information, see `http://www.talkapex.com/2011/01/console-wrapper-previously-js-logger.html`.

Console wrapper allows to view the debug information in a nice console window within browsers. Most of the browsers are console-enabled (exception is the Internet Explorer browser). The utility is designed to easily debug JavaScript within applications. It allows developers to use the JavaScript console without breaking anything.

The most common use of the console is the `console.log` command:

```
console.log('hello world');
```

Removing instrumentation code before going into production can be annoying, especially if you need to debug it later on. To resolve this issue, Martin D'Souza has created a console wrapper. This allows you to leave your debugging calls in production code. Here are some features:

When running APEX in debug mode, the log level is automatically set.

Installation of the console wrapper

Installation steps of the JavaScript Console Wrapper are as follows:

1. To download `$console_wrapper.js`, navigate to `http://code.google.com/p/js-console-wrapper/`.
2. Add the `console_wrapper.js` in the page template.

The different levels can be defined as follows:

- Info
- Exception
- Error
- Log/debug
- Off
- Warn

Using the console wrapper, it is possible to set the debugging level, by issuing the following command:

```
$.console.setLevel('log');
```

Retrieve the information about the current level, by using the following command:

```
$.console.getLevel();
```

Or write a message for a specific level, as follows:

```
$.console.warn('A message at warning level');
```

Another feature available is the function called `logParams`. `logParams` will automatically log all the parameters in your function. This can save a lot of time, since you don't need to manually list all the parameters, and it will detect any extra parameters.

To see the console wrapper in action, navigate to:

```
http://apex.oracle.com/pls/apex/f?p=16406:1200:0:::::&tz=2:00
```

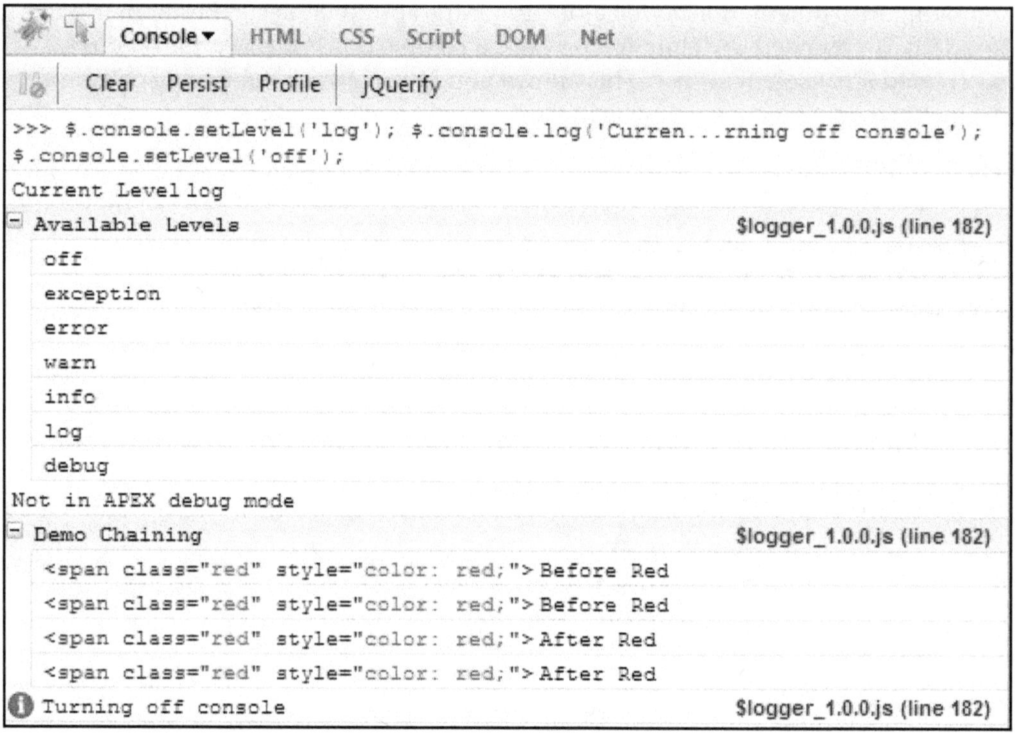

This screenshot shows the console wrapper in action.

> Keep an eye on the Google site, to find out if there is a new release available of the js-console-wrapper.:
>
> `http://code.google.com/p/js-console-wrapper`

Web development tools

When you make use of the Advanced Programming Interface, custom user interface, templates, or specialized JavaScript, a web development tool can be essential. The **Web Developer** plugin authored by *Chris Pederick* is a must have addition to Firefox and Chrome for CSS, JavaScript, and HTML development. The Web Developer add-on can be downloaded from here:

`http://chrispederick.com/work/web-developer/`

Installation is as simple as clicking on the **Install Now** button on the **Download** page from a browser window. The Web Developer extension adds a menu and a toolbar to the browser with various web developer tools. The extension is available for Firefox and Chrome.

This screenshot shows the Web Developer toolbar as it appears in Firefox.

The Web Developer toolbar is a set of tools meant to assist with web development. It provides a large number of useful tools when developing with APEX. Most options in Web Developer interact directly with the page. Changes made in Web Developer are not saved. So, changes are lost when leaving or reloading the page.

Form

ID	NAME	METHOD	ACTION
wwvFlowForm	wwv_flow	post	wwv_flow.accept

Elements

INDEX	ID	NAME	TYPE	VALUE	LABEL	SIZE	MAXIMUM LENGTH	STATE
0	pFlowId	p_flow_id	hidden	129				
1	pFlowStepId	p_flow_step_id	hidden	1				
2	pInstance	p_instance	hidden	1596139063127722				
3	pPageSubmissionId	p_page_submission_id	hidden	3056178308389071				
4	pRequest	p_request	hidden					
5	B18189708231454936		button					
6	B18189912953454936		button					
7	B18189816812454936		button					
8	check-all-rows	x02	checkbox	1	Check All			
9	f01_0001	f01	checkbox	1	Select Row			
10	f02_0001	f02	text	7876	Empno	16	2000	
11	f03_0001	f03	text	ADAMS	Ename	16	2000	
12	f04_0001	f04	text	CLERK	Job	16	2000	
13	f05_0001	f05	text	7788	Mgr	16	2000	
14	f06_0001	f06	text	1100	Sal	16	2000	
15	f07_0001	f07	text		Comm	16	2000	
16	f08_0001	f08	text	20	Deptno	16	2000	
17	f09_0001	f09	text	12-JAN-83	Hiredate	16	2000	
18	fcs_0001	fcs	hidden	C59EE625B0B84590D252F9B61CD08519				
19	frowid_0001	frowid	hidden	AAAW3pAAEAAAASMAAK				
20	fcud_0001	fcud	hidden	U				
21	f01_0002	f01	checkbox	2	Select Row			
22	f02_0002	f02	text	7499	Empno	16	2000	
23	f03_0002	f03	text	ALLEN	Ename	16	2000	

This screenshot shows the Web Developer form, which contains form information.

The Web Developer form can be handy when debugging tabular forms in APEX. Web Developer is especially handy for CSS, JavaScript, and HTML development debugging. APEX developers who add AJAX features will be most interested in the ability to examine the `<div>` element details and JavaScript. Developers who build custom page templates and themes will appreciate the **Form Information** and **Outline** menus, and the myriad of options for displaying HTML element information. In web developer, CSS can be viewed and edited.

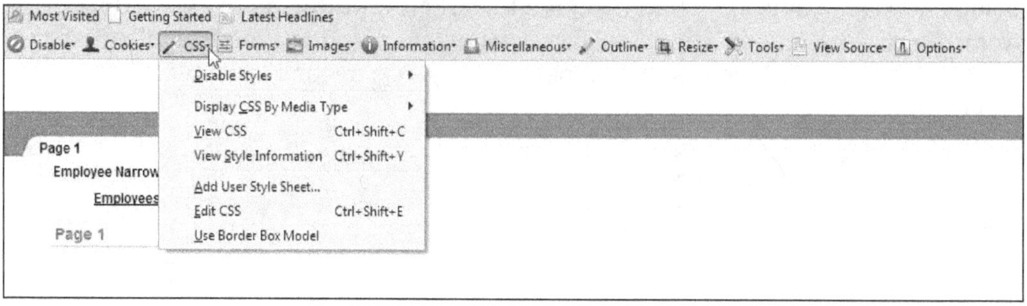

This screenshot shows the CSS sub-menu in the Web Developer tools.

Firebug

Firebug can be downloaded from this location: `https://addons.mozilla.org/nl/firefox/addon/firebug/`. Firebug offers many of the same features as Web Developer, in a slightly different format and package. Firebug is also a Firefox add-in, and is installed by clicking on the **Install Now** button on the Firebug home page. Firebug can be started as a pane in the same window or in a separate window. The main Firebug headings are Console, HTML, CSS, Script (JavaScript), DOM, and NET.

The essential features to view and edit HTML, CSS, and JavaScript are all there. The Firebug JavaScript Console is very helpful for informational messages and testing JavaScript. The **HTML** tab displays all HTML in hierarchical format, expandable by the main HTML tag. The **CSS** tab displays all CSS for the page. The **Script** tab displays all JavaScript and the JavaScript debug interface. The **DOM** tab displays all DOM element descriptions. The **NET** tab displays network header/response information and timing. The JavaScript debugger is a great feature. The use of the Firebug JavaScript debugger is as simple as opening Firebug, selecting the **Script** tab, setting a break, and refreshing the page.

APEX and Firebug

Firebug can be useful for checking images and their location, to check the version of CSS, and JavaScript's currently loaded or used by an APEX application. Firebug allows us to investigate our page, run and debug JavaScript, changing page styles on the fly, and see which files are missing.

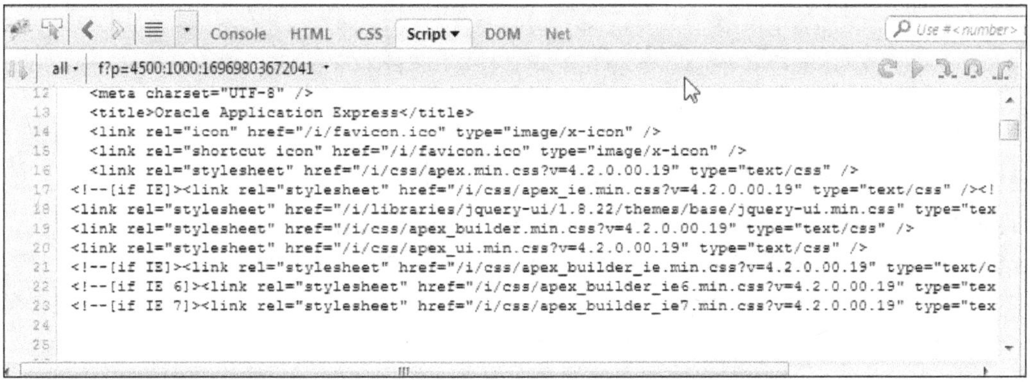

The preceding screenshot shows images and stylesheets used in APEX in the Firebug console.

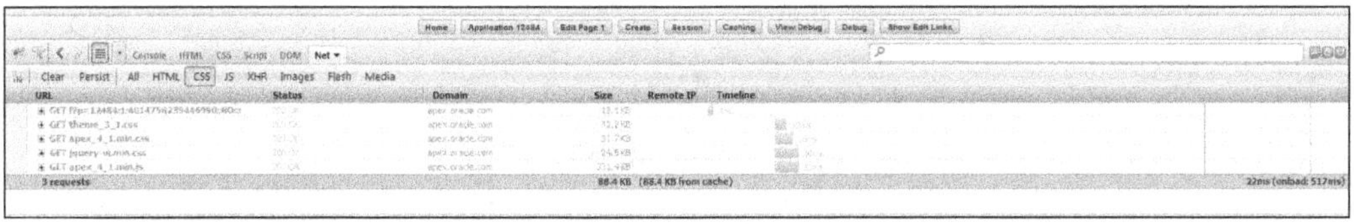

The preceding screenshot shows the CSS sub-menu in the Firebug add-on.

Debugging dynamic actions

Debugging dynamic actions in Application Express is slightly different than other debugging, because much of the processing done with the dynamic action framework is done on the client, not on the server. In order to debug dynamic actions, output the debug information to the browser's JavaScript console.

The Firebug add-on integrates with Firefox. You can edit, debug, and monitor CSS, HTML, and JavaScript live in any web page. Firebug will show the debug information in its Console pane.

The debug information will tell you when a dynamic action fires, the name of the dynamic action, and also specifically which action has fired.

To debug dynamic action, debug needs to be enabled at application level and the page will need to run in the debug mode. Both requirements are described earlier in the chapter. In the Firebug console you will see the JavaScript logging that the dynamic action produces. So, Firebug can be very useful here.

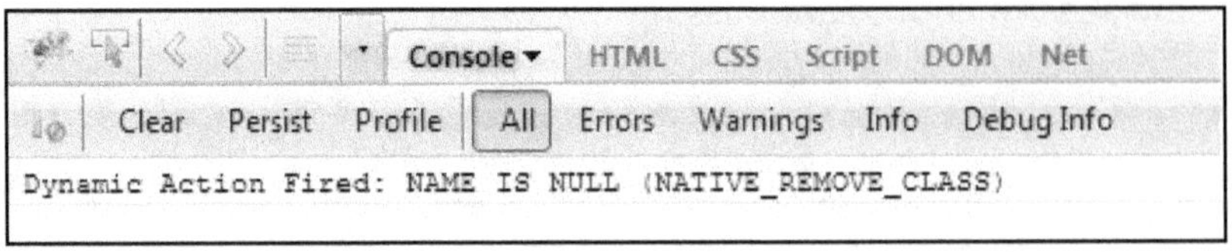

The preceding screenshot shows the output from the Firebug console.

This outputs the name from **Dynamic Action** and the action is fired. The extension **DOM** tab shows all dynamic actions active on current page. Look for `da.gEventList`. The `da` is a short notation for Dynamic Action.

This is the output from the **DOM** tab from Firebug.

If you have defined a dynamic action that fires when a certain item's value changes, change that item's value, and the console will show the debug output if the dynamic action fires.

Yslow

Yslow is a tool to analyze webpages and can be used as a performance indicator. Yslow shows you the size of each resource as well as the time it takes to load each. This information can be very useful when the page takes a long time to load. It helps you pinpoint the problem area. With Yslow, you don't have to guess which resource takes up the most time. Yslow can be downloaded from this location:

`https://addons.mozilla.org/en-US/firefox/addon/yslow/`

Error handling

In Application Express, error handling is dramatically improved. You can define how exceptions are handled in your application instead of being constrained by the APEX engine itself.

This feature can be used if a developer wants to have full control of the error handling when an error occurs in an APEX application. It can not only be used to just log the error, but also for modifying the error message text. You can also define where the message should be displayed.

(Inline with Field and in Notification: Error messages display in notification area; Inline with Field: Error messages displayed within the field label; Inline in Notification: Error message display in the #notifcation_message substitution string or at a specific Error Page.) It is also possible to specify which page item/tabular form column should be highlighted.

1. Install the sample database application.
2. Review the `DEMO_ERROR_HANDLING` function.
3. Rename and tweak to meet your requirements.
4. Modify your application properties to use the **Error Handling** function:

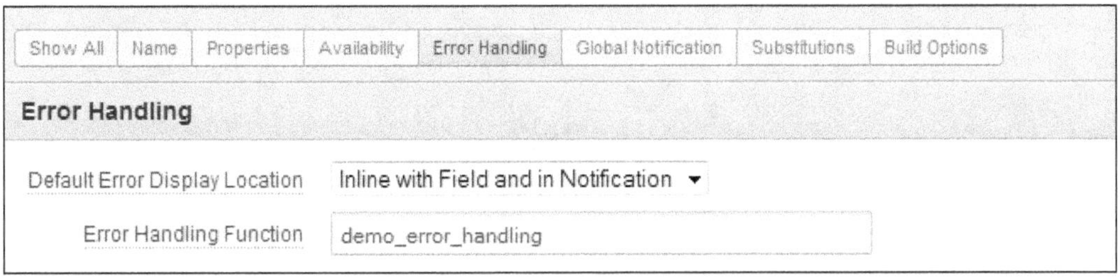

Logging and tracing

It can be quite difficult to debug slow regions or reports. A trace file can help to analyze the slow performance. Append `&p_trace=YES` to the URL, as follows:
`http://hostname:port/apex/f?p=appid:pageid&P_TRACE=YES`

> grant alter session to APEX_PUBLIC_USER
> Otherwise trace file will not be created.

APEX will automatically generate a SQL trace file, and putting it in `USER_DUMP_DEST`. `USER_DUMP_DEST` specifies the pathname for a directory where the server will write debugging trace files on behalf of a user process. The trace files will be located on the database server.

To retrieve the value of the `user_dump_dest` parameter, start a `SQL*plus` session and perform the following statement:

```
show parameter user_dump_dest
```

You can use Oracle SQL Developer and/or **TKPROF** to analyze the trace file. When you have the raw SQL trace (with extension `.trc`) output files, you can display it nicely formatted in Oracle SQL Developer as an alternative to using the `TKPROF` program to format the contents of the trace file. To open a `*.trc` file in Oracle SQL Developer and see an attractive, effective display of the information, navigate to **File | Open**, and specify the file or drag the file's name or icon into the Oracle SQL Developer window:

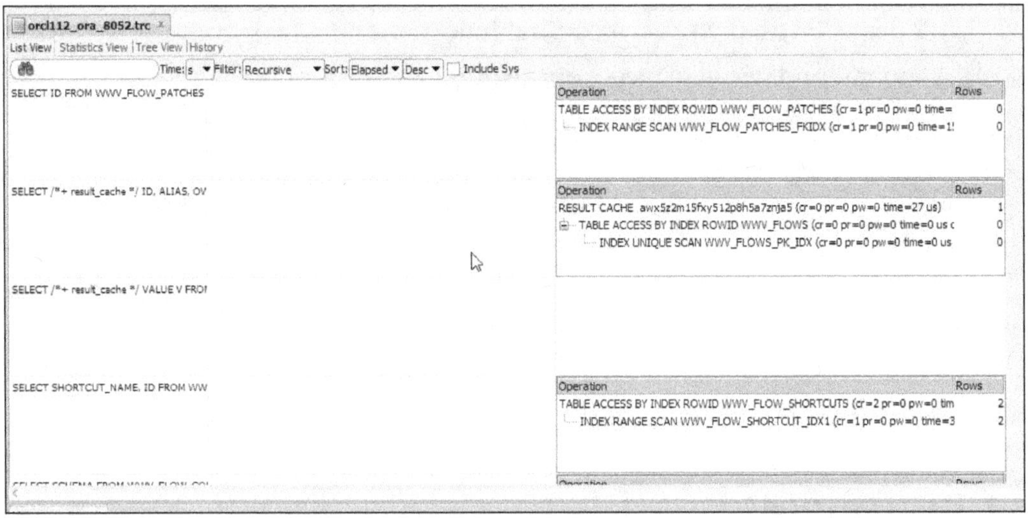

The preceding screenshot shows the nicely formatted trace file in Oracle SQL Developer.

Logging (editing the application definition) determines whether or not the user activity is recorded in the Oracle Application Express activity log. When set to `Yes`, every page view is logged. Records are written to the `APEX_WORKSPACE_ACTIVITY_LOG` Application Express dictionary view.

> Disabling logging may be advisable for high volume applications.

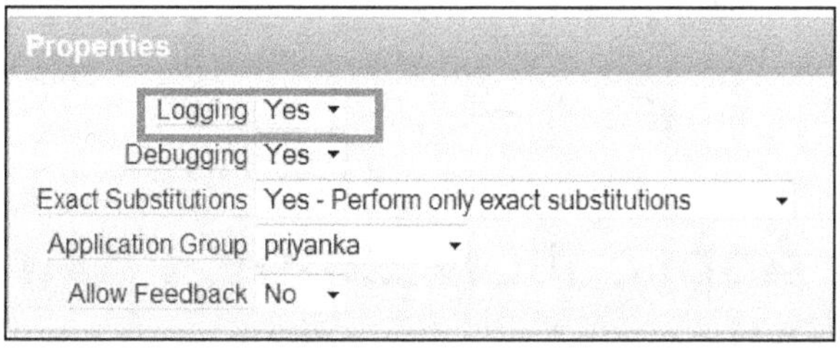

Enabling/disabling logging

There are actually two log tables; each one gets purged roughly every two weeks. Of course, you can make the decision to store the log information in your own log tables.

The `APEX_ACTIVITY_LOG` view records all activities in a workspace, including developer activity and application run-time activity.

Additional Information can be found at: `http://docs.oracle.com/cd/E23903_01/doc/doc.41/e21676/apex_debug.htm`

Also, the `error_message` column can be used to find error messages:

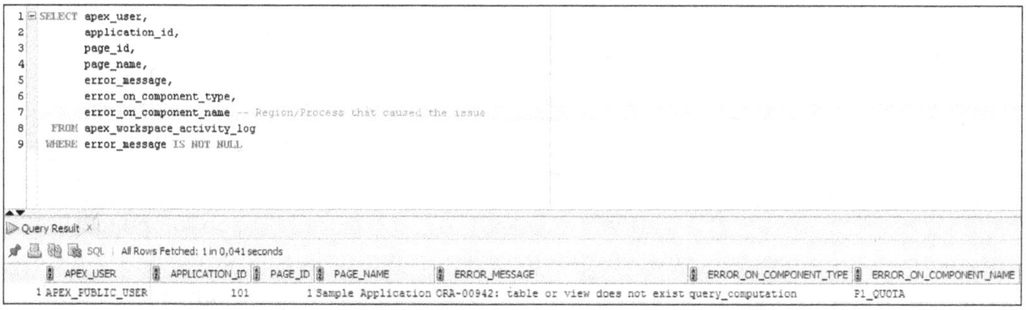

The preceding screenshot shows the output from `apex_workspace_activity_log`. The error message shows the reason for the application not to function correctly.

The activity log identifies both region- and page-level errors. `APEX_WORKSPACE_ACTIVITY_LOG.ERROR_ON_COMPONENT_NAME` identifies the region or process that the error occurred in.

> **Watch out**
>
> When multiple region level errors occur, only the first error is logged in the activity log.

Reports in Application Express that facilitate troubleshooting

APEX comes with a set of utility reports that can aid you in troubleshooting. These utilities are accessible by navigating to **Application Utilities**. The different items on this page will be discussed in this section, some in more detail than others.

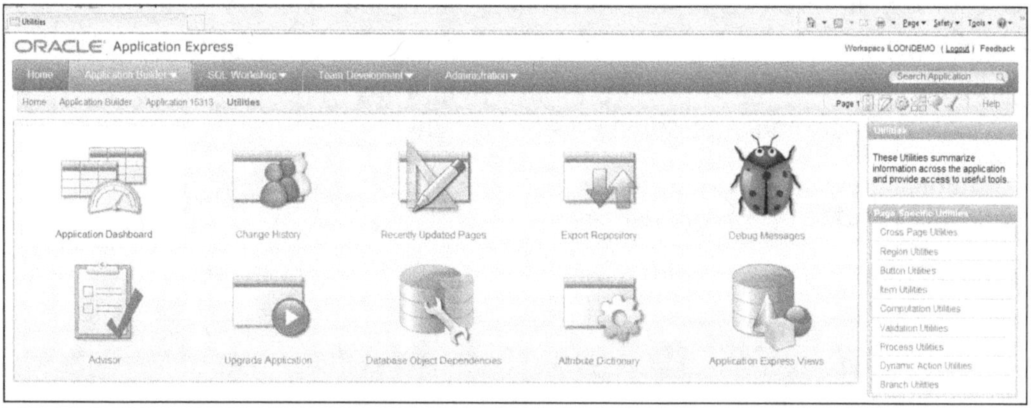

Utilities Page	Remarks
Application Dashboard	Breaks down the metrics of a specific application by overview, security, templates, page by type, application components, and page components.
Change History	Displays who changed what in the application builder. Does NOT provide a before and after image of changes, but only that something is changed. Be careful in using this as it may not correctly identify.
Recently Updated Pages	A list from the most recently updated pages.
Debug Messages	All debug trace information collected from the application can be accessed here for a specific application. Can drill down to specific debug information and debug information can be purged.

Application Express Advisor

The Oracle **APEX Advisor** (or simply **Advisor**) enables you to check the integrity and quality of your APEX application. Advisor functions like a compiler or lint, and flags suspicious behavior or errors. Running Advisor checks the integrity of your application based on the underlying metadata. The Advisor performs several checks on your application, including programming errors, security issues, quality assurance, and other best practices.

Advisor can be run for one page, a set of pages, or for all pages. Under **Checks to Perform**, review the selected checks. Enable and disable checkboxes as appropriate. Once executed, your previous settings will be recalled for the next use. You can also save the settings without executing using the **Save as My Preferences** task in the task bar.

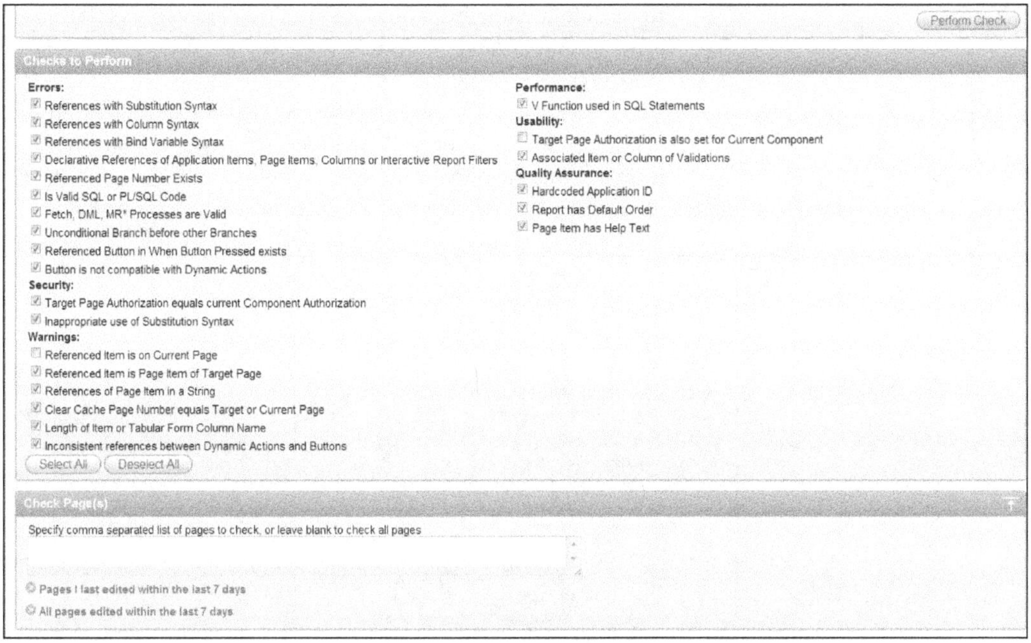

The preceding screenshot shows the different checks in the Advisor.

APEX has different tools and reports available to have a different view of the application.

Application Builder utilities	Remarks
Upgrade application	Not all the features are automatically upgraded when an application is upgraded. Features such as number field (updates a text field when there exists an IS NUMERIC validation), new date picker instead of CLASSIC date picker, ck editor (WYSIWYG editor in web pages), and flash charts (Upgrade SVG or flash chart to flash chart 5). Developers can choose the features to upgrade. So you have a choice what to upgrade; there is no obligation.
Database object dependencies	Database objects dependencies is a report of all database objects referenced in the application. Note: some objects can be missing, such as objects used in dynamic SQL. Public and APEX_040100 schema are included.
Attribute dictionary	You can use page item and report column definitions to update the attribute dictionary. You can also use the attribute dictionary to update page items and report columns.
Application Express views	`APEX_WORKSPACE_ACTIVITY` log. Highlight errors that occurred in applications. You can set up an application to monitor this Application Express view on a regular basis for example. This view can be queried to have a complete view of the error.

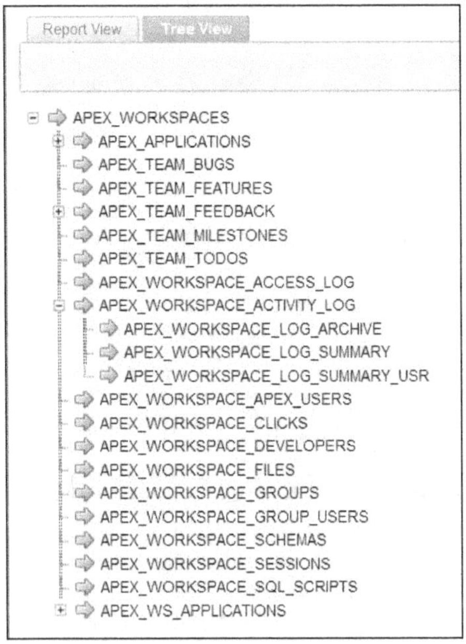

The preceding screenshot shows the available APEX views.

Summary

Debugging and troubleshooting in Application Express can be challenging because of different technologies used in Application Express. Each technology has its own set of tools for effective troubleshooting and debugging.

Fortunately, there is a variety of readily available options for debugging APEX applications. The key is to know how APEX generates pages, to know the tenets of the application, and to employ a variety of tactics to meet the challenge at hand.

Running the pages of the application in debug mode shows exactly which steps are taken. Use Oracle SQL Developer to not only debug your PL/SQL database code, but also to remotely debug the PL/SQL called from the APEX application.

There are numerous utility reports available that can assist you in the troubleshooting process. The Advisor can advise you before the trouble begins.

Specific web development tools, such as Web Developer, Firebug, and console wrapper, can assist with checking the HTML, CSS, and JavaScript code.

6
Deploy and Maintain

When you are done with the building phase of your application, you need to deploy it. Deployment can be done in several ways. One way is to create a packaged application. The deployment of a packaged application is very straightforward—simply follow the **import wizard** and you're done. However, the preparation to create a packaged application can be quite cumbersome.

Another way to deploy your application would be to separate all different components, such as database objects and JavaScript files, into a "deployment per type". This makes the deployment more complicated, but it is easier to patch or upgrade a small part of the application. In this way, the maintenance phase of your application will be easier. Both of these different approaches have their pros and cons.

Deploying your application to the users is only part of the job. After this step is done, your job is not over. At this moment, your users really start working with the application, and encounter issues they never thought of during the testing phase.

In this chapter, the following topics are covered:

- Considerations regarding packaging the application
- Version control
- Deployment
- Maintain the application: Active and proactive

Package your application, or not?

Oracle APEX allows you to create a self-contained application. This means that all necessary components are all bundled together in a single deployment script. All the database tables, stored procedures, images, JavaScript files, CSS files, and of course the APEX application itself, are bundled together. If all the components you need to install the application are in a single file, then deployment is very easy.

One of the new features that will be included in Oracle APEX 4.2 is an exchange of packaged applications. Packaged applications are not only created by Oracle itself, but also by independent developers. The Oracle packaged applications were previously known as **packaged applications**, and mainly served as example applications. Nowadays, they are fully functional and can be used as productivity boosters. Instead of having to develop your own bug tracking application, use the packaged application provided by Oracle. Oracle will support their own packaged applications and will be available when you use the Oracle Database Cloud service. The packaged application provided by Oracle will be locked when you install it into your own environment. It is not possible to edit and modify the locked application. When this is required, the application will need to be unlocked. Doing so will make the application ineligible for future upgrades and will no longer be supported by Oracle.

To create your own packaged application, you would need to navigate to the **Supporting Objects** page from within the context of your application.

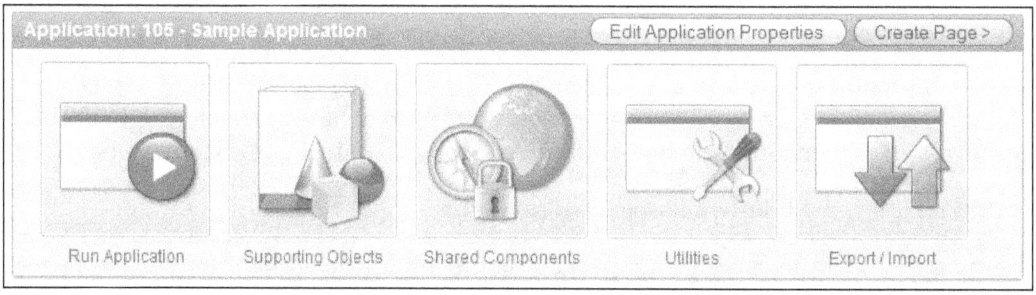

Figure 1: Main application builder menu

On the **Supporting Objects** page, you can create a packaged application. You can get to this page by clicking on the **Supporting Objects** icon on the application builder page (see *Figure 1*).

All of the different components required to create a packaged application are right here on this page.

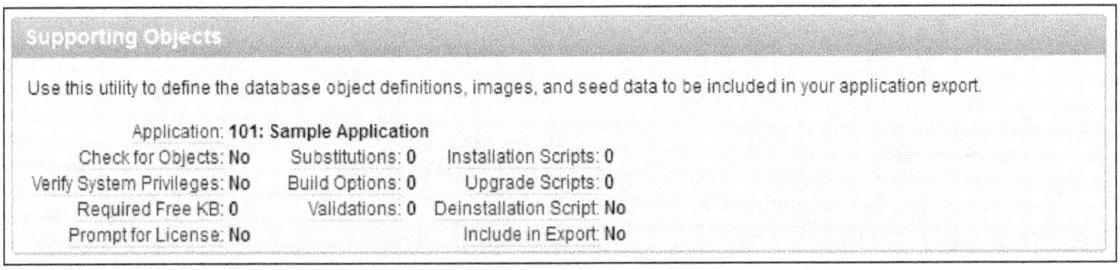

Figure 2: Summary of Supporting Objects

In the summary section, displayed in the preceding screenshot, there is an overview of the different settings and number of scripts you or your fellow developer have so far for the packaged application.

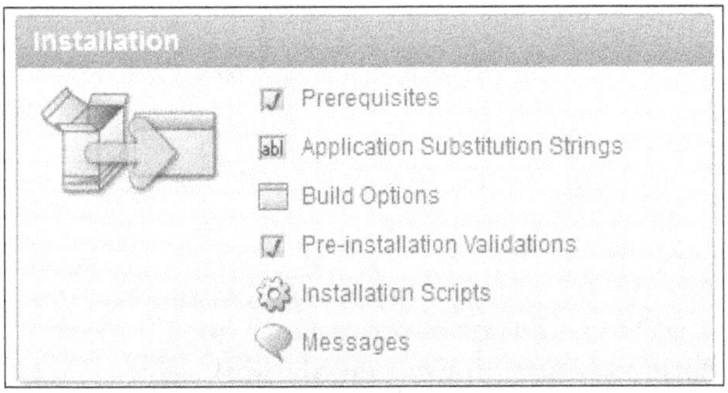

Figure 3: Installation Section

In the following region, labeled **Installation**, you can define all necessary scripts to make deploying your applications easy and straightforward.

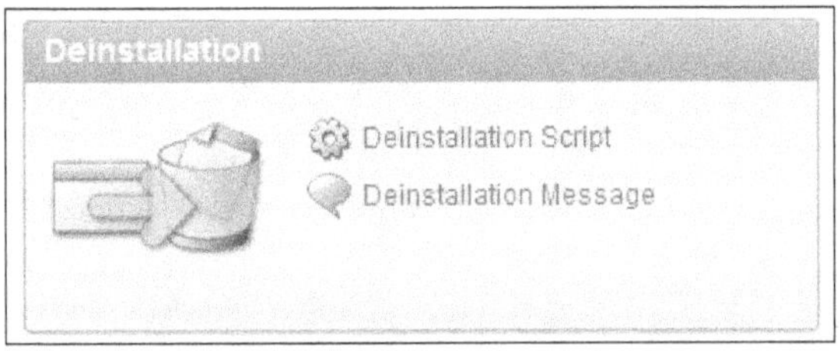

Figure 4: Deinstallation section

There is also a region to do the exact opposite, labeled **Deinstallation**. In this section, you collect all the script that will uninstall the application.

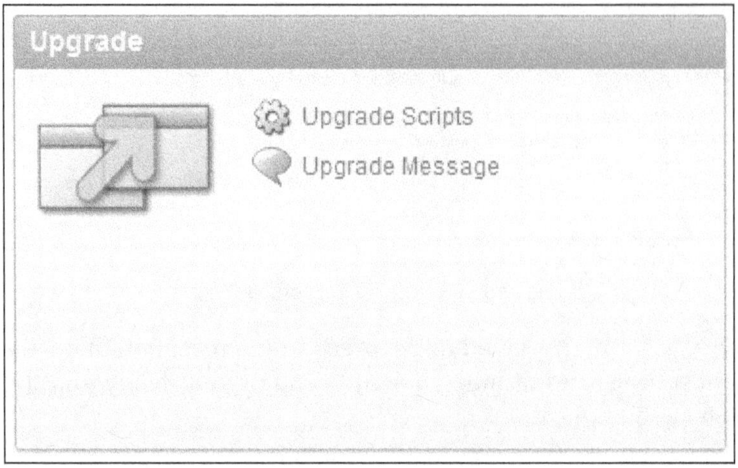

Figure 5: Upgrade section

The last section, labeled **Upgrade**, allows you to collect all necessary scripts required to upgrade your application. In this section, we will learn the most practical ways to use these options.

Gathering all the components to create a packaged application can be quite tedious. All your database objects need to be in scripts, and need to be uploaded through APEX in the **Installation** section, under **Installation Scripts**.

There is a utility available to make it easier to collect all database objects. Navigate from the application home page to the utility page—the icon is also visible in *Figure 1*.

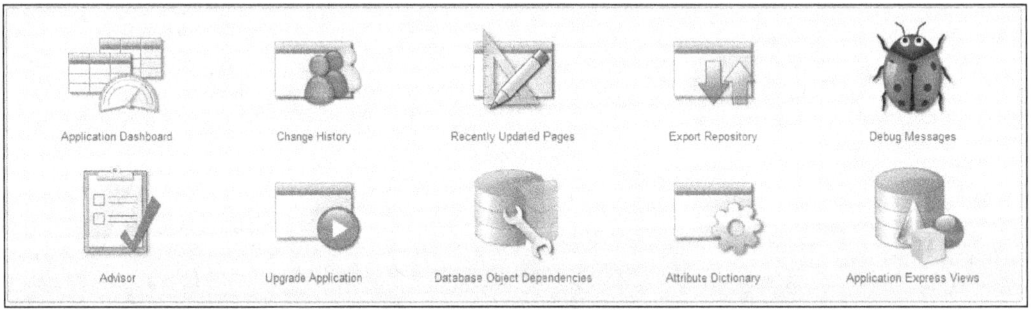

Figure 6: Utility Menu

There are a number of very useful utilities available on this page, but the the one that I want to point out is labeled as **Database Object Dependencies**. With this utility, you can let Oracle APEX do the hard work of determining which database object you absolutely need, to be able to deploy your application.

After you click on the **Compute Dependencies** button on the following screen, there will be a list of database objects shown. Both the button and the list of database objects are shown in the following screenshot. The list that is shown in the screenshot is based on one of the sample applications.

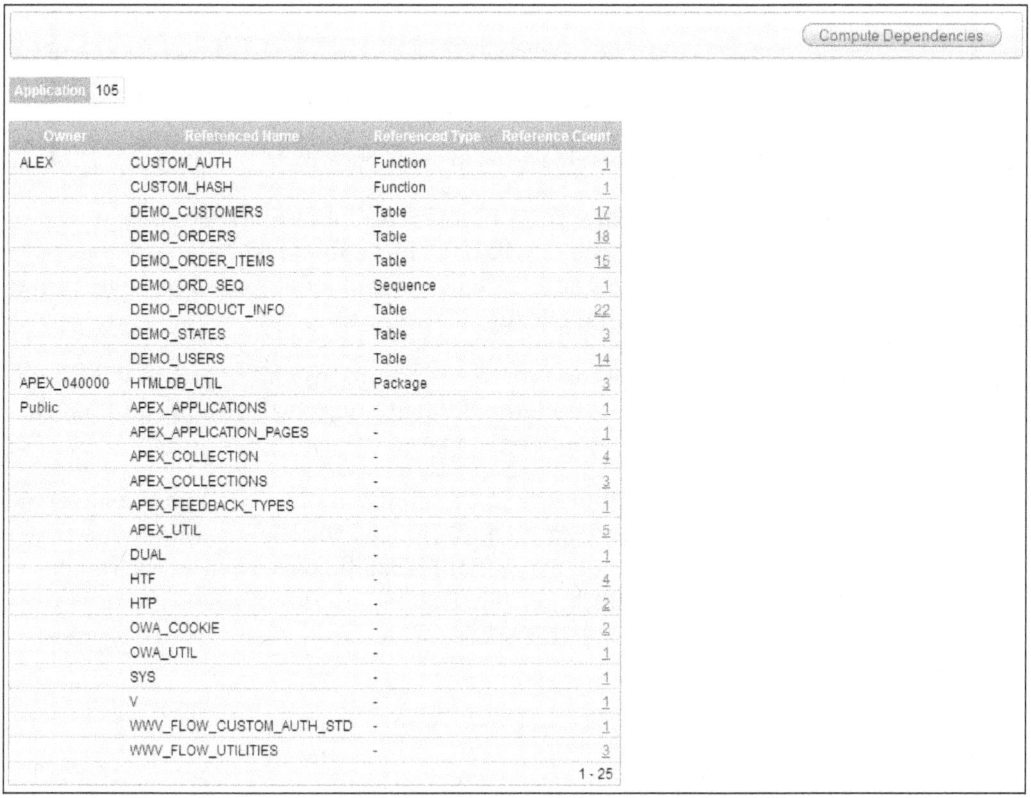

Owner	Referenced Name	Referenced Type	Reference Count
ALEX	CUSTOM_AUTH	Function	1
	CUSTOM_HASH	Function	1
	DEMO_CUSTOMERS	Table	17
	DEMO_ORDERS	Table	18
	DEMO_ORDER_ITEMS	Table	15
	DEMO_ORD_SEQ	Sequence	1
	DEMO_PRODUCT_INFO	Table	22
	DEMO_STATES	Table	3
	DEMO_USERS	Table	14
APEX_040000	HTMLDB_UTIL	Package	3
Public	APEX_APPLICATIONS	-	1
	APEX_APPLICATION_PAGES	-	1
	APEX_COLLECTION	-	4
	APEX_COLLECTIONS	-	3
	APEX_FEEDBACK_TYPES	-	1
	APEX_UTIL	-	5
	DUAL	-	1
	HTF	-	4
	HTP	-	2
	OWA_COOKIE	-	2
	OWA_UTIL	-	1
	SYS	-	1
	V	-	1
	WWV_FLOW_CUSTOM_AUTH_STD	-	1
	WWV_FLOW_UTILITIES	-	3
			1 - 25

Figure 7: Compute Dependencies

As you can see in *Figure 7*, not only are all database objects shown, but you can also drill down and see where the database object is used. You can drill down to see more details by clicking on the **Reference Count** column, where the number acts as a link.

There are two problems with this utility. The first is that only the directly referenced objects will appear in the overview, and the second one is that it doesn't help you with extracting the database objects into scripts. At least now you know which objects you need to include in the packaged application.

> There is a utility which can be used to extract all the DDL from an Oracle schema and spool the results to the file system. This utility is written and maintained by *Dietmar Aust* and can be retrieved from his website. You can download the utility from the following URL:
>
> `https://www.opal-consulting.de/apex/f?p=20090928:12:0::NO:::`
>
> You can also export database objects with Oracle SQL Developer. When you do, make sure to check the **Dependents** option on the export; this will make sure that all database objects referenced in the source code are also included in the export file.

As you can see from the previous description, it takes a lot of work to create a packaged application. Most applications will have more than just database objects; there will also be JavaScript, images, and CSS files, and they will need to be included in the supporting objects to create the packaged application.

There is also another way of deploying your application. Instead of creating a single script, which will contain the application, the database objects, the required images, JavaScript, and CSS, deploy each component separately.

This means that there will be multiple scripts to deploy. As you can imagine, this takes more work when you are deploying your application. The big advantage that you have with this method is that you can get all the static files, such as the images, JavaScript, and CSS, on the application server. The biggest downside is that it is very easy to forget a certain file. Therefore, it is advisable to create a shell script to assist you with this.

Why is it beneficial to place static files on the application server? These static files are needed very frequently in the browser. Instead of having these files in the database, and having to read them out of the database with each page load, the application server can serve these static files more efficiently than the database. The application server can also cache these files more efficiently.

So, should you create a package application or not? As with many things, it depends. I believe that it mainly depends on what you are going to do with the application.

If you are going to distribute the application, it might be a good idea to create a packaged application. If the application is going to be inhouse type (the application is for internal use), then it would be preferable that you deploy in separate files. This will give you a fine-grained control over which part of the application needs to be upgraded. For instance, if you have found a bug in your database code, then you can only redeploy the fixed database code, and only that database code and nothing else.

Each of the described methods of deploying the application has its pros and cons. The first described way makes it easy to deploy the application, and the second makes it easier after the application has been deployed. The choice is yours; the user just wants a bug-free application that works.

Version control

APEX doesn't have any built-in version control, at least not in versions up to 4.1. This means you will have to come up with your own plan of doing version control. The way we organize our application is outlined in the following section of this chapter.

We like to keep our database code, all the PL/SQL code such as packages, procedures, and functions, in files. Working in files has the advantage that they can be easily kept in under version control, like Subversion. The same is true for all other files necessary for the application, such as JavaScript, CSS, and images.

Subversion

Working with Subversion is very easy and straightforward. We will not discuss the complete installation of Subversion, but merely show you how to work with it from a developer's standpoint.

In order to be able to work with Subversion, you would need some kind of client tool to access the Subversion repository. There are many Subversion client tools available for various operating systems. One of the most popular client tools on Windows is **Tortoise Subversion**.

> **Subversion client**
>
> On this Wikipedia page, you can find a comparison between the different Subversion clients that are available: `http://en.wikipedia.org/wiki/Comparison_of_Subversion_clients`
>
> If you need a Subversion client on Windows, you can download the Tortoise Subversion client from the following website: `http://tortoisesvn.tigris.org/`.

After installing the Subversion client, you will need to make a connection to the Subversion repository. How to do this depends on the client that you are using. As I am using a Windows laptop, I use Tortoise Subversion as my Subversion client—the most widely used Subversion client on the Windows platform. The screenshots will therefore show how I use Subversion using this client tool; other client tools will more or less behave similarly. The Tortoise Subversion client tool uses overlays on the icons that represent the files and folders in the Windows Explorer, as can been seen in *Figure 5*.

> **Oracle SQL Developer and Subversion**
>
> The Oracle SQL Developer IDE has the possibility to directly connect to Subversion, without using a separate client installation. This makes it very convenient to work with Subversion directly from the IDE.

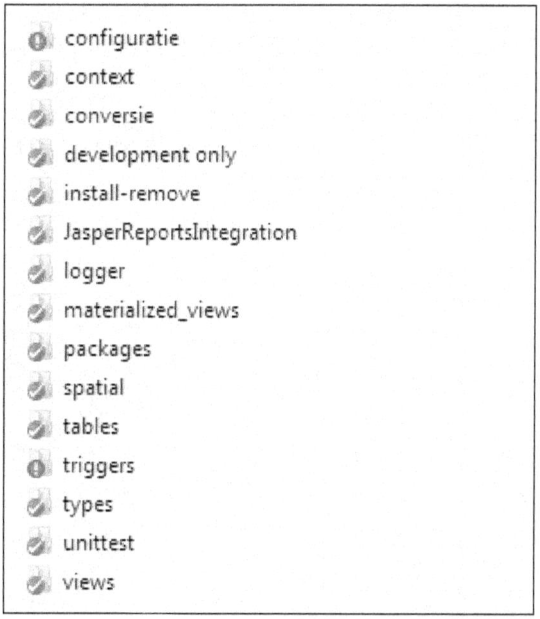

Figure 8. Directory Structure for Database Objects

In the preceding screenshot, you can see the directory structure that we use to keep our files under version control. Besides the structure you may also notice the overlay icons that Tortoise imposes. There are white checkmarks in green discs, and there are white exclamation marks in red discs.

The green icons in the preceding screenshot (*Figure 8*) indicate that the files within the folder are up to date, and not changed by you. When you start to change files, the icon overlay will change to the red icon. This will indicate that files are changed, and that you need to commit these files to the Subversion repository.

Subversion does not lock the files when you are working on them, although you can if you want to. When you change the file and want to write the changed file back to the Subversion repository (commit, see *Figure 9*), it will verify if someone else changed the file in the meantime. When this is not the case, your version will be the current version and all is well. When this is the case, and someone changed the file you were working on, Subversion will try to merge the files.

Of course, Subversion can only merge the files, the file from the repository and your changed file, when different sections are modified. When Subversion is not able to automatically merge the files, you will need to do this yourself. Tortoise provides tools to assist you with this. Right-clicking on the file or folder will show you all tools that Tortoise makes available to you. It is beyond the scope of this book to go into detail of all of Subversion's functionality.

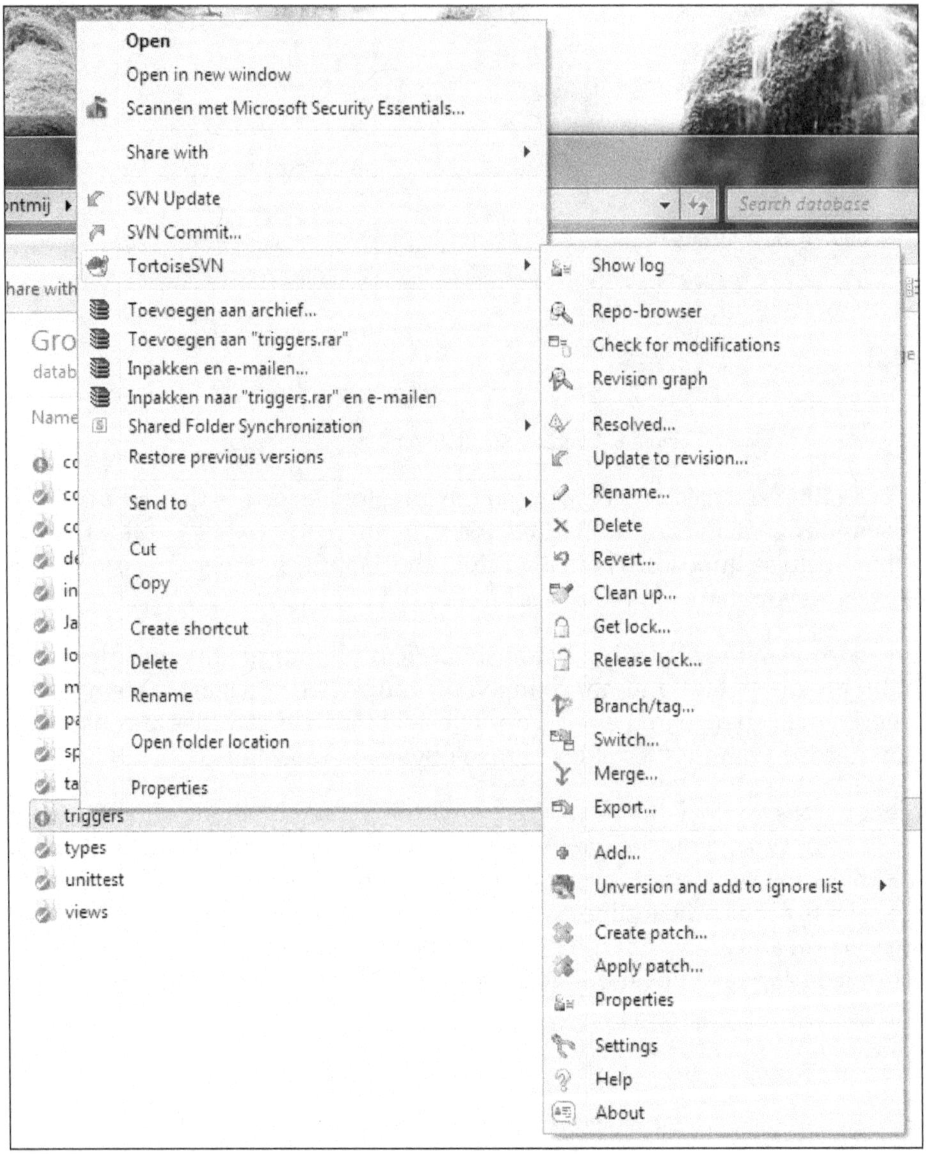

Figure 9. Tortoise Subversion Context Menu

To get your local folders up to date with the version that is available in the Subversion repository, you will need to perform an update. Right-click on the folder you want to synchronize, and choose the **SVN Update** option (see *Figure 9*).

Removing a file from your local folders will not remove the file from the Subversion repository. The next time you update your folder, the file will be "missing" in the eyes of Subversion, and will be placed back into your local folder. When you want to remove a file (or folder) from your local system as well as from the Subversion repository, you will need to do a "Subversion delete". Right-click on the file (or folder) and select **TortoiseSVN | Delete** from the context menu. This will mark the file as "deleted", and the next time you commit your changes to the repository, the file will be deleted from the Subversion repository. This option is visible in *Figure 9*.

> A **Sourceforge** project is started to combine the power of APEX with XMLDB, which allows you to use the Oracle database as your version control system. You can find more information about this project at `http://xace.sourceforge.net/`.

Deploying the database packages

When you keep all your files in folders, it is very convenient to generate a script with all the filenames in a single SQL file to be installed. That way, you will always know which files to call to install the database objects.

To generate the file to install the package specifications, we use a **BAT** file, which looks similar to the following. We have similar files for the other database objects.

```
@ECHO OFF
REM =====================================
REM == Prepare the Command Processor ==
REM =====================================
SETLOCAL ENABLEEXTENSIONS
SETLOCAL ENABLEDELAYEDEXPANSION
SETLOCAL

SET outputfile=%0
SET outputfile=%outputfile:~0,-4%.sql
set workdir=%~dp0
set currdir=%cd%

cd %workdir%
```

```
ECHO ------------------------------------------- > %outputfile%
ECHO -- Automatically created on: %date% -- >> %outputfile%
ECHO ------------------------------------------- >> %outputfile%
ECHO set define off >> %outputfile%
ECHO. >> %outputfile%

ECHO prompt ================================= >> %outputfile%
ECHO prompt ==== Package Specificaties ===== >> %outputfile%
ECHO prompt ================================= >> %outputfile%
ECHO. >> %outputfile%

REM ================================
REM == list the .pks packages ==
REM ================================
FOR /F %%a IN ('dir /b *.pks') DO (
  ECHO prompt Running %%a >> %outputfile%
  ECHO @@%%a >> %outputfile%
)
ECHO. >> %outputfile%

ECHO prompt ========================== >> %outputfile%
ECHO prompt ==== Package Bodies ===== >> %outputfile%
ECHO prompt ========================== >> %outputfile%
ECHO. >> %outputfile%

REM ==================================
REM == list the .pkb packages ==
REM ==================================
FOR /F %%a IN ('dir /b *.pkb') DO (
  ECHO prompt Running %%a >> %outputfile%
  ECHO @@%%a >> %outputfile%
)
ECHO. >> %outputfile%

ECHO set define '^&' >> %outputfile%
ECHO. >> %outputfile%

cd %currdir%

ECHO file "%outputfile%" created.
ENDLOCAL
```

This BAT file will gather all files within the folder with the `.pks` and `.pkb` extensions. This works as we keep our package specifications and package bodies in separate files, with the `pks` extensions for package specifications and `pkb` for package bodies.

The BAT file should be in the same folder as the package specifications and bodies. Open up a command window and navigate to the folder where you keep your package files. In the following screenshots, you will see examples of how to do this:

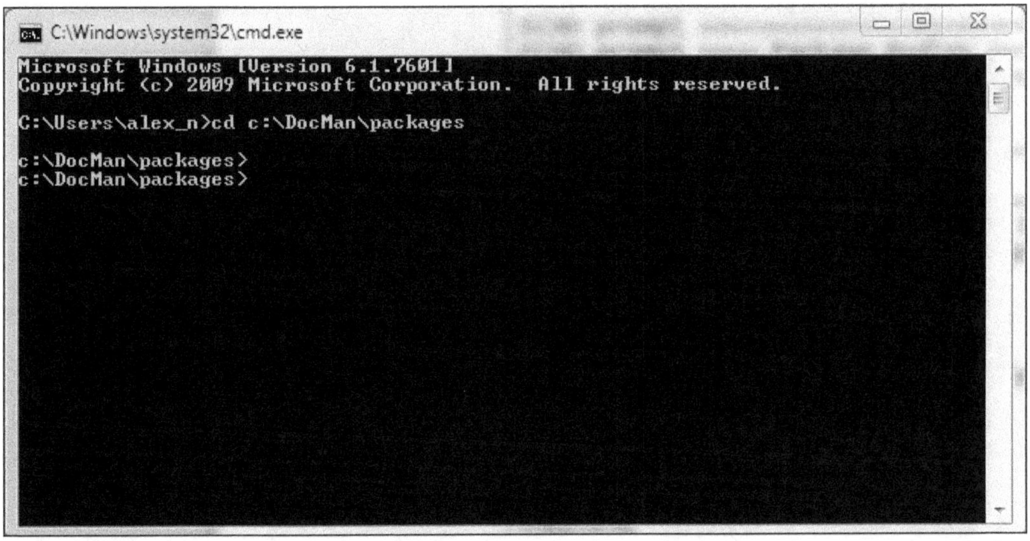

Figure 10. Change Directory in Command Window

Now, call the BAT file, and that is all. The BAT file will give you feedback that the `packages_all.sql` file is created in the same folder where all the package files are.

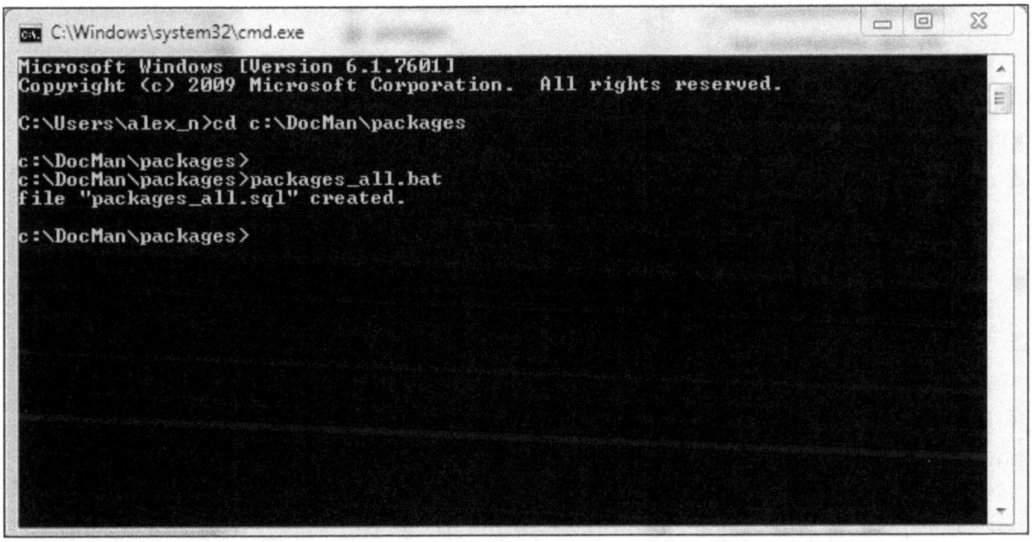

Figure 11. Run the BAT file to generate an Install script

The following listing shows what that the generated file will look like. The list of package specifications and bodies are shortened for display purposes.

```
----------------------------------------------
-- Automatically created on: Sat 12-05-2012 --
----------------------------------------------
set define off

prompt ================================
prompt ==== Package Specificaties =====
prompt ================================

prompt Running docman_autorisatie_apex.pks
@@ docman_autorisatie_apex.pks
prompt Running docman_autorisatie_pkg.pks
@@ docman_autorisatie_pkg.pks
prompt Running docman_context_pkg.pks
@@ docman_context_pkg.pks

prompt =========================
prompt ==== Package Bodies =====
prompt =========================

prompt Running docman_autorisatie_apex.pkb
@@ docman_autorisatie_apex.pkb
prompt Running docman_autorisatie_pkg.pkb
@@ docman_autorisatie_pkg.pkb
prompt Running docman_context_pkg.pkb
@@ docman_context_pkg.pkb

set define '&'
```

We deliberately included `SET DEFINE OFF` at the beginning of the generated script, to avoid being prompted for substitution variables when we run the script. Of course, we also included `SET DEFINE '&'` at the end of the script to reset `SQL*Plus`.

> Sometimes you will encounter `SET SCAN OFF` in `SQL*Plus` scripts. This will have the same effect as `SET DEFINE OFF`. The former is the older version to achieve the same, hence we prefer to use `SET DEFINE`.

Between each of the calls to run either the package specification, or the package body, we include a `prompt` command. This will help us when we run the `packages_all.sql` file to install the package specifications and bodies. When a package specification or body does not compile properly, we get the information that specifies the file that was executed.

Deploying the APEX application

Even though the database deployment is essential for the application, most users don't like to use an interface, such as `SQL*Plus`, to interact with the data. That is why they ask for the APEX application in the first place.

When the database side of the application is done, the APEX application itself also needs to be deployed. This can be done in different ways, through the APEX builder interface or through the command line. Both will be shown in this section.

My personal preference of deploying the APEX application is to do this through the command-line interface. This way I can deploy the database side, tables, packages, and so on, from the command line as well as the APEX application. There is no need to start up the browser and log in to the APEX environment. This whole process can also be scripted, so that installation becomes very easy.

Using the APEX environment

In order to deploy the APEX application using the APEX environment, you need to log in to the APEX Builder.

At the top of the page in the APEX Builder, there are options to create a new application, export an application, and import an application, as can be seen in *Figure 12*.

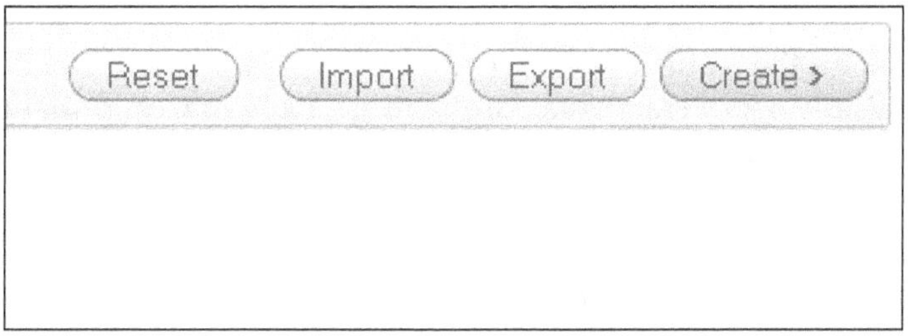

Figure 12. Import or Export through the APEX Builder

The **Reset** option in this menu relates to **Interactive Report**, which shows all the applications within the workspace. When you have filtered the results, the **Reset** button will remove all the customization you made to **Interactive Report**.

To deploy the application, click on the **Import** button. Then you will be prompted to specify the file which you want to import.

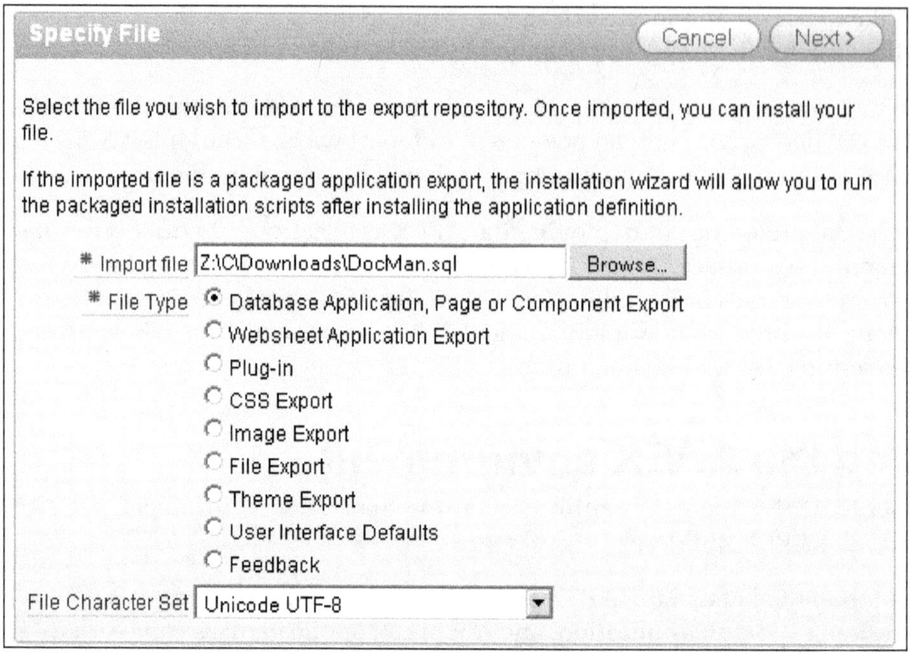

Figure 13. Specify the Import File

Because we click on the **Import** button from the **Application Builder** page, the file type is automatically set to **Database Application, Page or Component Export**. There is no need to change the file type.

After selecting the appropriate application file, click on the **Next** button.

The selected file will be uploaded to the APEX repository, and you will be shown that this has happened successfully.

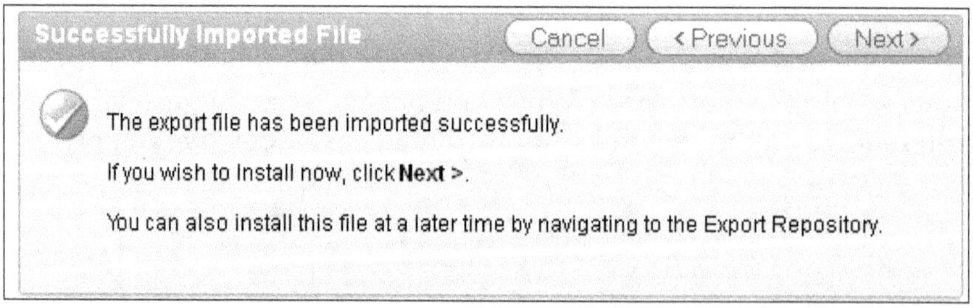

Figure 14. Successfully Imported File

Even though it might appear that you're ready, this is not the case. The application is not deployed yet. The application file is merely uploaded to the APEX repository. When we want to install the application, and that's what we want, we will need to press the **Next** button to start the deployment.

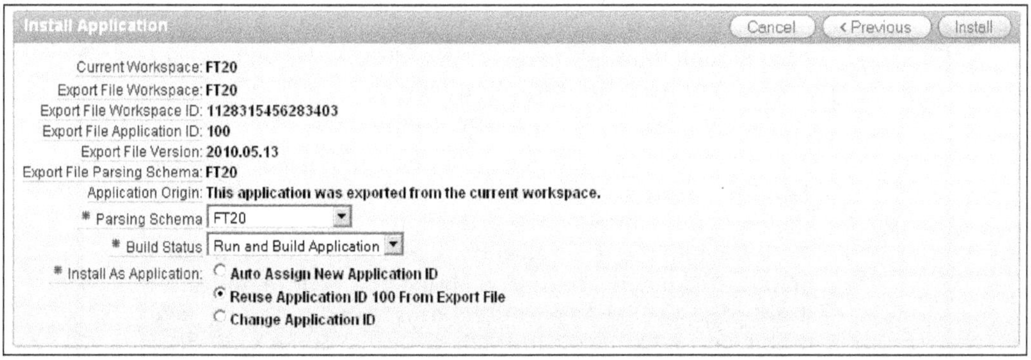

Figure 15. Install Options

First, we will be prompted with the information regarding the application, such as the current workspace, and the parsing schema from the export file.

Choose **Parsing Schema** for which the application needs to be deployed; in the screenshot (*Figure 15*), a different schema was chosen to deploy the `DocMan` application.

Also choose **Build Status** for the application. This can be any of the following:

- **No Build Status**
- **Run Application Only**
- **Run and Build Application**

The first option is a strange one. When you select **Build Status** as **No Build Status** and press the **Install** button, you will get an error, as shown in the following screenshot:

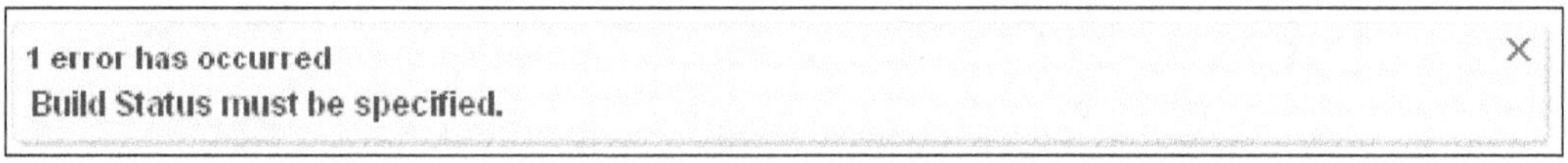

Figure 16. Error Message when Build Status is not Specified

Apparently **No Build Status** is implemented as null, but the item is mandatory, which can also be seen by the asterisk in the label of the item.

Run Application Only should be the option to choose when you deploy the application. This option deploys a run-only version of your application, just as the name indicates. Because the application is run-only, you are not allowed to make changes to the application after deployment. After all, you want to make changes to the development version of the application, and not to the deployed application.

> Even though the application is run-only, you can still switch it to the **Run and Build Application** mode at a later time. This needs to be done by the workspace administrator.
>
> Log in to the workspace as the administrator. Navigate to the **Administration** section, and select the **Manage Service** option. On the right-hand side of this page is a section labeled **Manage Meta Data**. In this list is an entry named **Application Build Status**. Clicking on this link will bring you to the **Application Build** page. On the **Application Build Status** page, you have the option to change the **Build Status** value of the application to **Run and Build Application** or to **Run Application Only**.

Run and Build Application will deploy the application in a similar manner as it was in the development environment. It allows you, as the name indicates, to run the application as well as to make changes to it. When deploying the application to production, this option should not be used. You don't want to have changes made to the production environment directly. Changes should always be made starting from the development environment to the test environment and eventually to production.

On the same page in the import wizard, the last option you have to choose is the application ID. There are three options:

- **Auto Assign New Application ID**
- **Reuse Application ID from Export File**
- **Change Application ID**

When you choose the first option, **Auto Assign New Application ID**, the first available application ID will be chosen for the application that you are importing.

The second option, **Reuse Application ID from Export File**, will use the application ID that is specified in the export file. This will be the same ID as the original application. When you use this option, the previously deployed application, if there is one, will be overridden. You will be prompted if you want to replace the existing application (*Figure 17*):

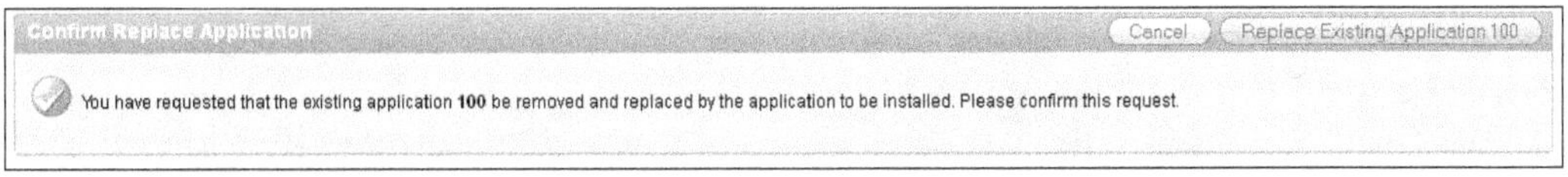

Figure 17: Confirmation Question to Replace an Existing Application

This should be the option you want to use. This way, you will only have one version of the production application in the production environment. There will never be any confusion as to which application is the "real" one.

If you auto assign a new application ID, the import process will also alter your application alias. Using an application alias is very convenient, because it allows you provide the users with a single URL, such as `http://xp-vm:8080/apex/f?p=DOCMAN`.

This URL doesn't need to change after you deploy the new version of the application.

The last option with regard to the application ID is to change it. When you choose this option, you will see a new text item where you can input your new application ID. There is a restriction, however. Not all application IDs are allowed. Oracle reserves the range between 3000 and 9000.

After you complete this form, the actual installation of the application will start:

Figure 18. Processing Animation when Installing

When the application is finally installed, a success message is shown as well as three options, with a choice of what to do next:

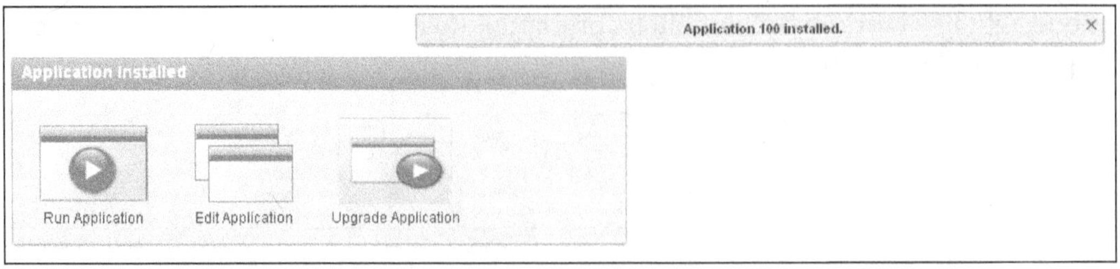

Figure 19: Options after Installation

These three options, shown in *Figure 19*, are only available when you have imported the application in **Run and Build Application**. When you have installed the application as **Run Only**, you will be presented with the following screenshot:

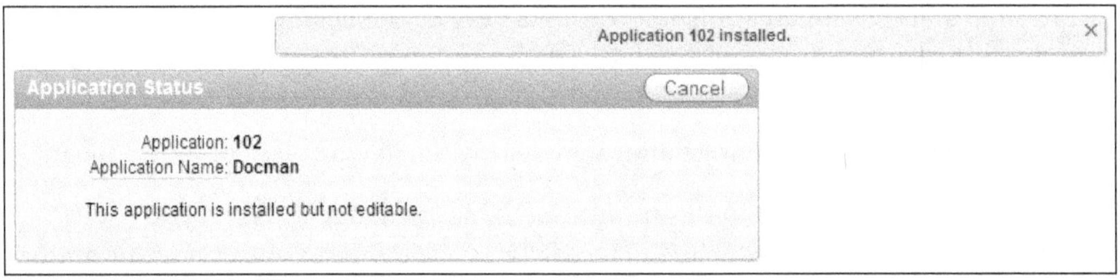

Figure 20. Run-Only Confirmation page after Installation

The only option that is presented now is **Cancel**. This will take you back to the application builder page. **Run Only** applications are easy to identify; they have a different icon from regular applications:

Figure 21. Run-Only icon

Needless to say that clicking on the icon will not show you the pages that make up the application. Instead, a message similar to the following is shown:

```
This application is installed but not editable.
```

The first and the second options are self-explanatory. The third option, **Upgrade Application**, was introduced with APEX 4. Since APEX 4 was a fairly extended overhaul, the APEX team provided you with the option to upgrade your application. Some of the functionality, which you had to implement yourself in earlier versions of APEX, have been standard pieces of functionality since APEX 4. For example, the **datepicker**; in earlier versions of APEX, the datepicker would open a separate browser window. Nowadays, it is a jQuery datepicker, which displays as if it were integrated in your application. The **Upgrade Application** option identifies the old-style datepicker and can convert these for you automatically, if you want of course—the choice is yours. There are many other features that can be enabled by a click of a button.

Using the command-line interface

When you know all the options that you want or need, it can be quite tedious to go through the APEX environment to deploy the application.

There is also the option to use the SQL command-line interface to deploy the application. The big advantage of this method is that the SQL commands can be combined into a complete deployment script, including the database objects (tables, packages, and so on) as well as the APEX application itself.

When you export an application, you are actually exporting the metadata that comprises the application. When you open the exported application, which is just a `.sql` file, you will see that the script consists of a number of PL/SQL anonymous blocks.

Some might be tempted to open up a SQL window and simply run the application export script. If you have ever done so, you will recognize the follow statement:

```
APPLICATION 100 - DocMan
Set Credentials...
Check Compatibility...
API Last Extended:20100513
Your Current Version:20100513
This import is compatible with version: 20100513
COMPATIBLE (You should be able to run this import without issues.)
Set Application ID...
begin
*
ERROR at line 1:
```

```
ORA-20001: Package variable g_security_group_id must be set.
ORA-06512: at "APEX_040000.WWV_FLOW_API", line 51
ORA-06512: at "APEX_040000.WWV_FLOW_API", line 304
ORA-06512: at line 4

Disconnected from Oracle Database 11g Express Edition Release 11.2.0.2.0
- Production
```

Even though it is a regular `.sql` file, you can not run it without undertaking some actions first. The following script generates the offset that is needed to install the application.

> This script has to be run as `SYS`.

```
declare
  l_workspace_id number;
begin
  select workspace_id
    into l_workspace_id
    from apex_workspaces
   where workspace = upper('&ws_name');

  APEX_APPLICATION_INSTALL.SET_WORKSPACE_ID(l_workspace_id);
  APEX_APPLICATION_INSTALL.GENERATE_OFFSET;
  APEX_APPLICATION_INSTALL.SET_SCHEMA(upper('&schema'));
 APEX_APPLICATION_INSTALL.SET_APPLICATION_ALIAS('&app_alias');
end;
/
```

There are a number of substitution variables in the script, which can be set when you run the script from SQL*Plus. The substitution variables are easy to recognize, as they have an ampersand (`&`) at the beginning of the name. You need to provide the actual names for the workspace name, the parsing schema, and the application alias. After running this script, you can run the exported application script from SQL*Plus.

Depending on your needs, it is also possible to create a workspace using the command-line interface, as follows:

```
begin
   begin
      APEX_INSTANCE_ADMIN.REMOVE_WORKSPACE(
        p_workspace          => upper('&ws_name')
       ,p_drop_users         => 'N'
```

```
        ,p_drop_tablespaces   => 'N'
        );
    exception
    when others
    then
       -- removing the workspace doesn't succeed
       -- most likely it is not there (yet)
       -- ignore the exception
       null;
    end;
    APEX_INSTANCE_ADMIN.ADD_WORKSPACE(
      p_workspace             => upper('&ws_name')
     ,p_primary_schema        => upper('&schema')
     ,p_additional_schemas    => null
     );
end;
/
```

The preceding script will attempt to remove the workspace if it exists, and then create a workspace with the given name. This script will also need to be run logged in as SYS.

When you create the workspace using the preceding method, you might get a message informing you that the workspace is inactive when you try to log in to the workspace. This bug only happens with APEX version 4.1.1, and should be resolved in later releases.

The exact message will be:

Error Workspace <workspace name> is inactive. Contact your administrator

To make the workspace available again, you need to run the following script:

```
-- Workspace can be disabled when the workspace
-- is created using the command line.
-- This can only happen with APEX 4.1.1
begin
  for l_workspace in ( select short_name
                       from   wwv_flow_companies
                       where  account_status='AVAILABLE' )
  loop
    apex_instance_admin.enable_workspace
       (l_workspace.short_name);
  end loop;
  commit;
end;
```

The preceding script should be run when connected as `SYS`, `SYSTEM`, `APEX_040100`, or any user who has `APEX_ADMINISTRATOR_ROLE`. In future releases of APEX, this inactivation of the workspace should not occur. This behavior was filed as a bug, number `13769526`.

Housekeeping the APEX repository

Importing applications into your workspace basically means that the files are uploaded to the APEX repository. When a lot of applications are uploaded, or at least a lot of files are uploaded, this will result in quite a large repository.

It is good practice to remove the older imported files from the repository, as they might be inadvertently installed. Since APEX version 4, the repository is automatically purged, but the time between each purge might still create an opportunity to mistakenly install the wrong application.

From the main menu, click on the little arrow next to **Application Builder**. A context menu will be shown. Select the second-last option on the list, labeled **Repository**:

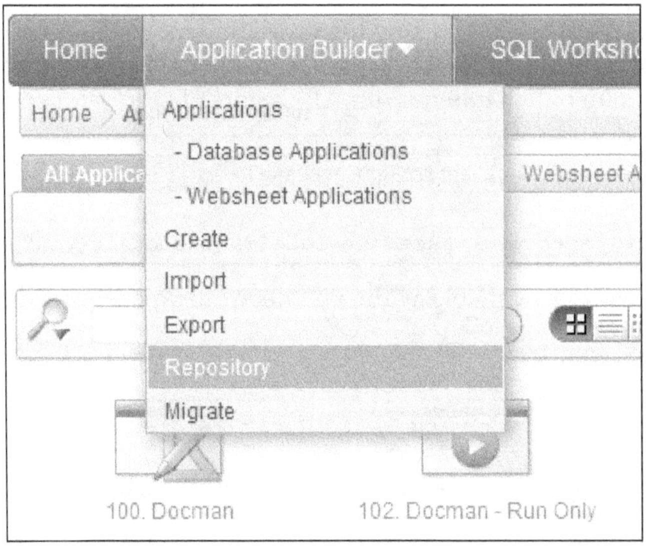

Figure 22. Navigate to Repository

This will take you to **Export Repository**, as shown in the following screenshot:

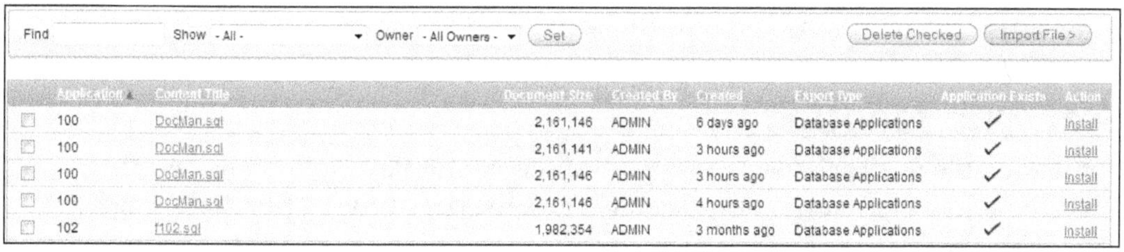

Figure 23. Export Repository

A list of imported files is shown. Not only imported applications, but all imported file types, such as plugins, Websheet applications, and themes will display.

Now, select the files you want to remove by selecting the checkbox on the left-hand side of the report, and click on the **Delete Checked** button. After the confirmation question, the selected files are removed from the repository.

Being active and proactive

The users expect the application to work flawlessly and the way they imagined that it would work. You do your best to create a flawless application, and implement all the wishes that the user wanted. You have taken care to test, test, and test some more. Your database code has gone through the harshest of scrutiny and has been deemed application quality code. Yet when the application is deployed, within the first millisecond, the user encounters a problem or just does not like the way the application works.

It seems like it does not matter how much effort you put into creating the ultimate application; there is always something that goes wrong, takes too long, or should have been implemented a different way.

Feedback

APEX 4 makes it really easy to enable feedback for your application. Before the APEX team releases their next version, they often ask the community to try it out, kick the tires so to speak. When they do, they always enable the **feedback** option, because the feedback the APEX team gets about bugs, requests for improvement, or general comment will improve the product before it is actually released.

You can do something similar in your own application, and it just takes a few minutes to be up and running.

Feedback is part of the **Team Development**, which is incorporated in APEX. In this section, we offer you a glimpse of what you can do with it. We strongly encourage you to discover all the ins and outs of Team Development.

Activate feedback

Activating the feedback for your application is as simple as following a wizard. Start the wizard to create a new page. Choose the page type as **Feedback Page** (see *Figure 24*):

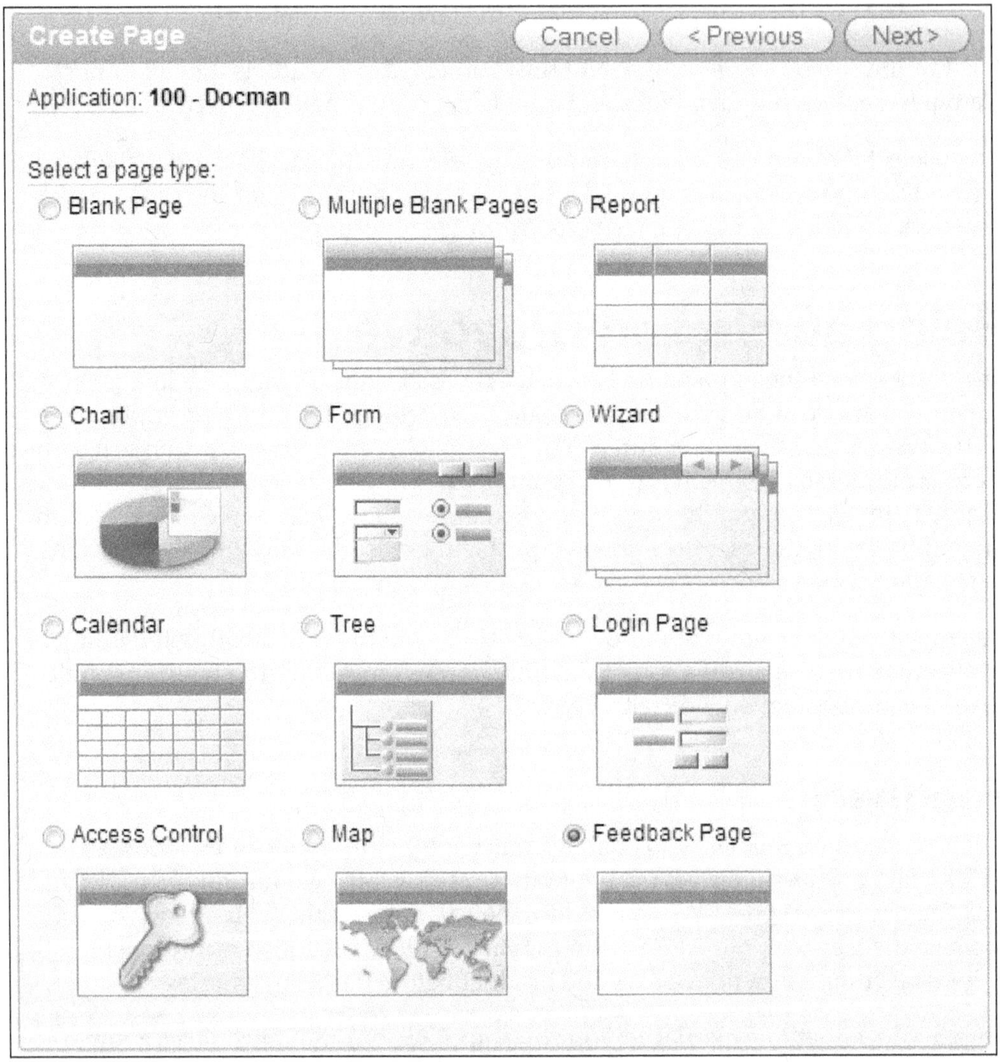

Figure 24. Create Page Wizard

Just like with any other page, you will see the regular properties, such as **Page Number**, **Page Name**, and two other sections.

The first section concerns the navigation bar. When you select **Yes**, there will be a feedback link added to the navigation bar (most of the times, in the top-right corner of your application where you also find the **Logout** link). You can define your own label for this navigation bar entry.

The second section gives you the option to enable feedback for the application. Most likely, you will select **Yes** here as well. You can also disable the feedback mechanism later on.

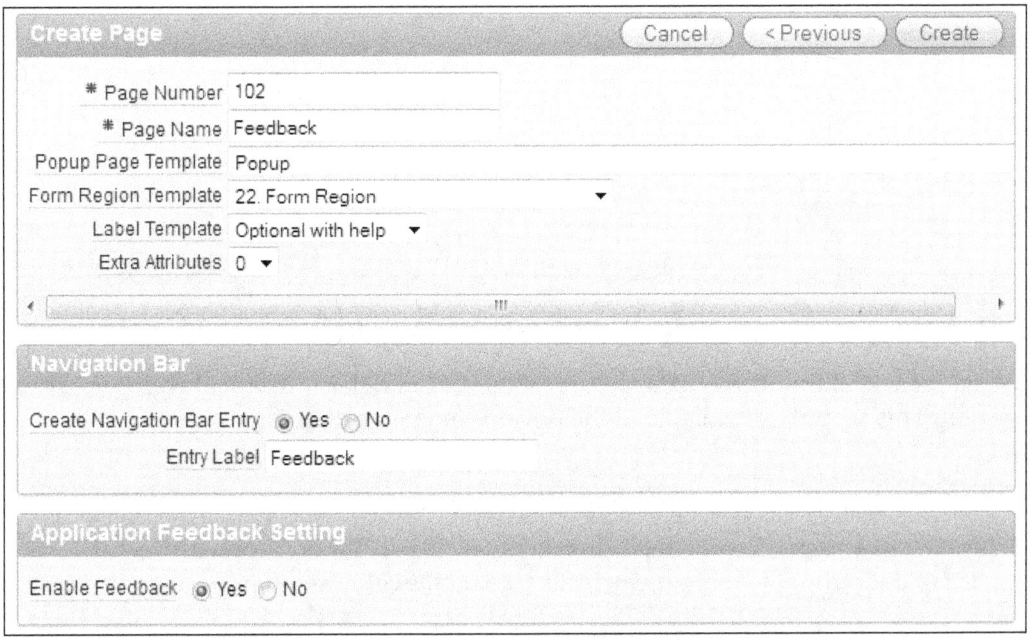

Figure 25. Feedback Page options

This is where the wizard ends. Select **Create**, and you will have activated the feedback option for the application.

When you run the application, you will notice the **Feedback** link in the navigation bar:

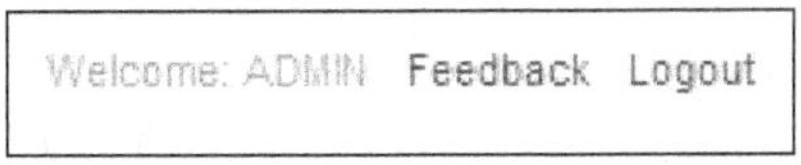

Figure 26. Navigation Bar with Feedback Link

When you click on the **Feedback** link, you will be shown the **Feedback** page (see *Figure 27*). Of course, you can customize this page, just like any other page. There are three different types of feedback: **General comment**, **Enhancement Request**, and **Bug**:

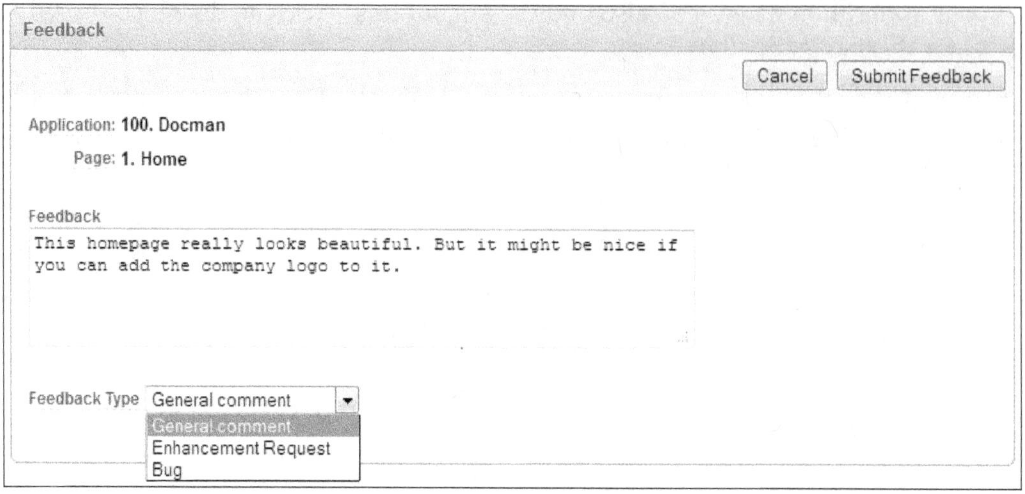

Figure 27. Standard Feedback Popup Page

When the user submits the feedback, it will be entered in the **Team Development** section. This section is available in the development environment.

Processing entered feedback

To see the feedback given by the users, log in to the APEX development environment. From the main menu, select **Team Development**:

Figure 28. Team Development Menu

As you can see, the **Team Development** section has a lot of options to keep a track of the project. Click on the large **Feedback** icon to navigate to the feedback section.

This will open up the **Feedback Dashboard**, where you get an overview of all the feedback that is provided to you:

Figure 29. Feedback section in Team Development

All incoming feedback can be viewed when you click on the **Feedback** tab page (see *Figure 29*). Here, you can see the feedback that we just entered through the application. Now, it is up to you to decide what to do with this feedback. Would you classify it as a bug, something that needs to be done, or would it be a new feature? Buttons at the bottom of the provided feedback allow you to classify them directly. Classifying the feedback will enter it into the **Team Development** environment, so that it can be incorporated into the project.

The type of feedback we got, in this example, would classify as a suggestion that will be put on the **To Do list**. Clicking on the button labeled **Log as To do**, will bring up the following page (*Figure 30*):

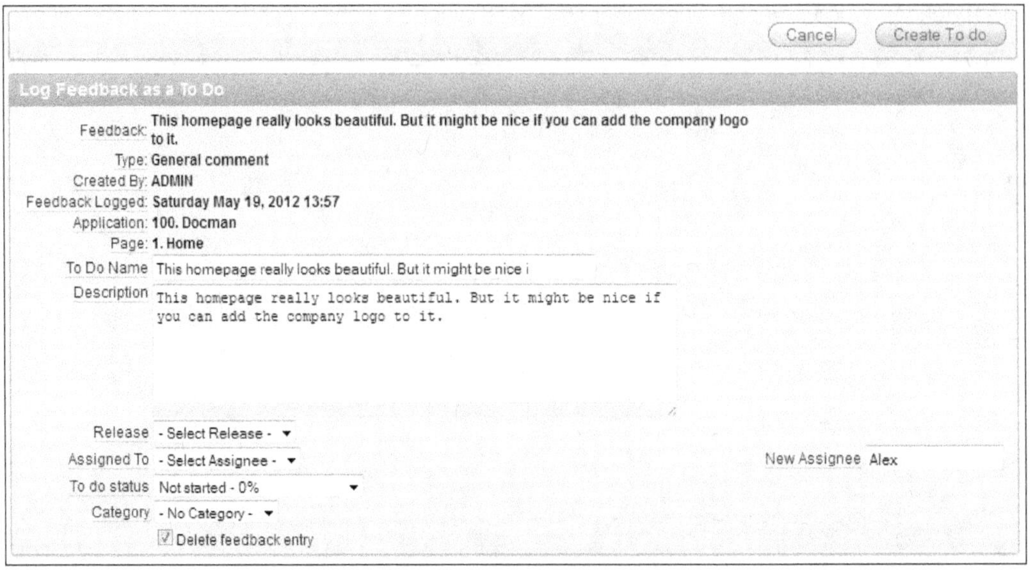

Figure 30. Log Feedback as To Do

On this page, we assign the task and provide the status. We can adjust all other settings later on, if we want to. Now that the feedback is registered in **Team Development**, we can keep a track of its progress.

The **Team Development** section offers a lot more functionality, which is worth exploring to aid with the development process, and we encourage you to do so.

Disabling the feedback for your application is even easier than enabling it. You can do this from the builder page of your application.

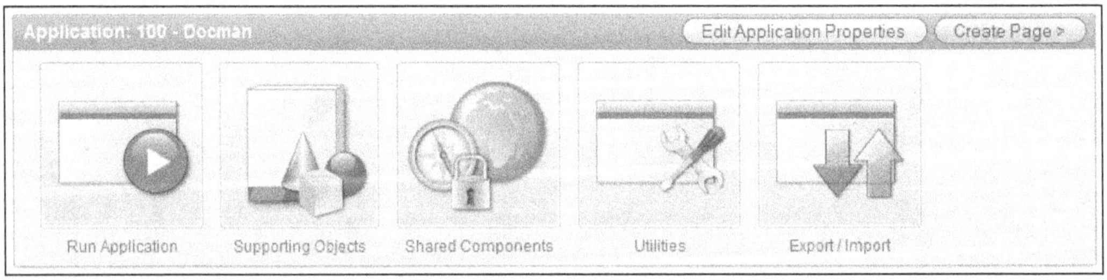

Figure 31. Application Builder Main menu

On the application builder page, next to the button to create a page, there is a button labeled **Edit Application Properties** (see *Figure 31*).

Clicking on this button will take you to the application's Properties page. On this page, there is a section **Properties** (see *Figure 32*). In this section, you can enable or disable the feedback for your application; simply set the value to **No** for the **Allow Feedback** property:

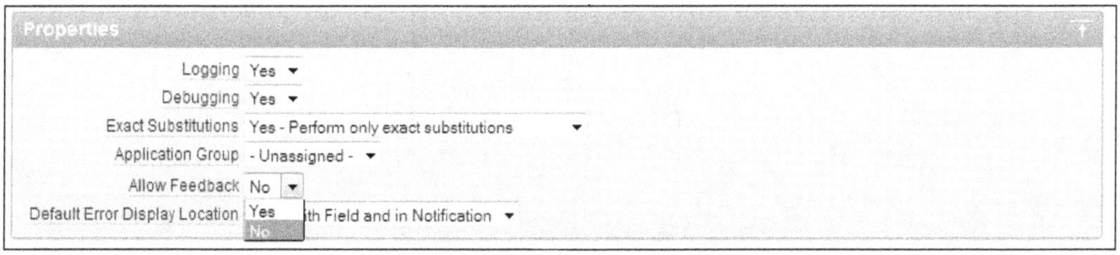

Figure 32. Application Properties

Apply the changes, and the feedback option is disabled for your application. Disabling feedback will automatically remove the **Feedback** link in the navigation bar.

Weighted page performance

One of the things that I really do not like is when the users of the application tell me that something "doesn't work" or that a certain page takes too long to load. While the first statement is less than helpful and needs more clarification, the latter is certainly easy to investigate. What is even better is that APEX can help you get proactive with identifying pages that take too much time to load. The fact that a certain page takes a long time to load is not necessarily a problem. Pages that are frequently visited, should be as fast as possible. Pages that are not visited very often, such as once a month, do not need to be blazingly fast. Users do accept that some pages take longer to load, as long as the pages that are needed most load very, very fast.

In the **Administration** section of the workspace, there is a report that can help you target the pages that are frequented often and take time to load.

Navigate from within your workspace to the **Administration** section, and click on the **Monitor Activity** icon:

Figure 33. Monitor Activity

There is also another way of getting to the **Monitor Activity** page. Next to the **Administration** menu item is a small triangle. When you click on that, you will see a drop-down menu, which also shows the **Monitor Activity** entry:

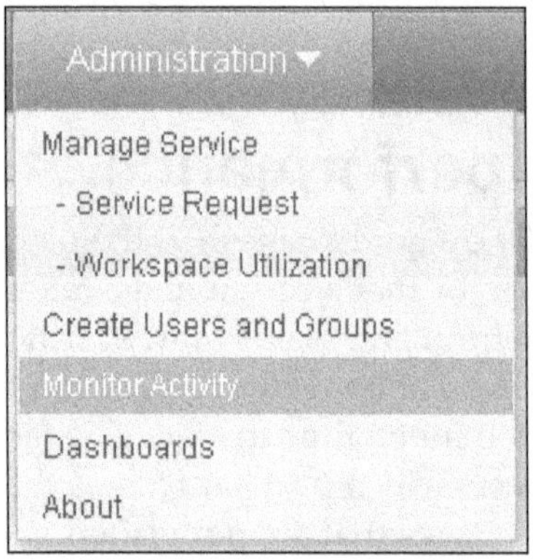

Figure 34. Monitor Activity Menu Option

Either way leads you to the page where you can find the report we were talking about.

There is a section on that page titled **Page View Analysis**, which has five different report links within that section. The one report we're interested in is called **By Weighted Page Performance**, highlighted in *Figure 35*:

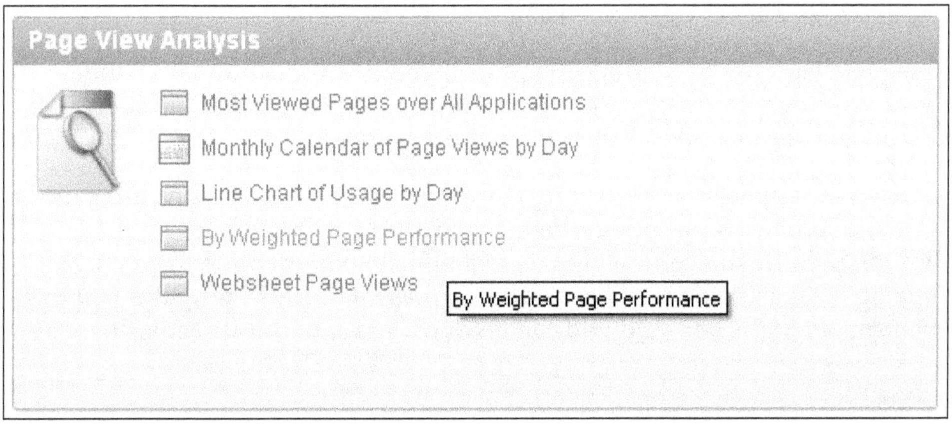

Figure 35. Weighted Page Performance Report

Clicking on that link will show you an interactive report like the one in *Figure 33*, which shows you the pages that are visited most frequently and their time to render. The pages with the highest value for the **Weighted Average** should get the most attention.

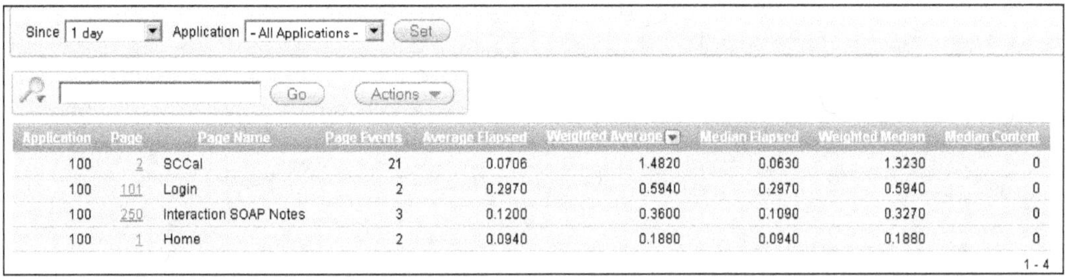

Application	Page	Page Name	Page Events	Average Elapsed	Weighted Average	Median Elapsed	Weighted Median	Median Content
100	2	SCCal	21	0.0706	1.4820	0.0630	1.3230	0
100	101	Login	2	0.2970	0.5940	0.2970	0.5940	0
100	250	Interaction SOAP Notes	3	0.1200	0.3600	0.1090	0.3270	0
100	1	Home	2	0.0940	0.1880	0.0940	0.1880	0

Figure 36. Weighted Page Performance Report

> Elapsed time columns are reported in seconds. Weighted average is calculated by multiplying page events by average page rendering time in seconds. Median average is calculated by multiplying page events by median page rendering time in seconds. Page events include page rendering and page processing events.

Summary

In this chapter, we looked at some different methods for deploying our application, including packaging your application as well as separately deploying the database objects and the APEX application, using the command line.

Enabling feedback for your application can engage the users more with the application, as they can provide direct feedback to improve the application and report unwanted functionality directly to the developers.

Monitoring the application, regarding performance, needs to be done proactively. Performance problems can be detected in an early stage by monitoring the application performance. Knowing where to direct your attention to when optimizing the performance of your application is vital. APEX provides you this mechanism out of the box, and you can take advantage of this directly.

A
Database Cloud Service and APEX 4.2

Cloud is the new pride of Oracle, announced during Oracle Open World in 2011. This addendum will give a short overview of the Database Cloud Service and the role of Application Express.

This addendum will discuss the following subjects:

- What is Oracle Public Cloud?
- Application Express features in the Database Cloud Service and APEX 4.2.

Oracle Public Cloud

The Oracle Public Cloud is a suite of Oracle applications, middleware, and database offerings delivered in a self-service, subscription-based, elastically scalable, reliable, highly available, and secure manner.

The Oracle Public Cloud includes the following services:

- Application Services
- Oracle Fusion CRM Cloud Service
- Oracle Fusion HCM Cloud Service
- Oracle Social Network Cloud Service

Platform Services:

- Oracle Database Cloud Service
- Oracle Java Cloud Service

For additional information, see `https://cloud.oracle.com`.

The Database Cloud Service, although based on the Oracle database, is a platform as a service product rather than a database as a service product. The Database Cloud Service combines the following products:

- Application Express
- RESTFul web services access
- SQL Developer
- Packages applications

Cloud computing is a little bit misleading. For Database Cloud Service, you interact with the Oracle database.

Packaged applications

The Oracle Database Cloud Service and Application Express 4.2 include a set of business productivity applications and sample code. All of these applications are easy to use, support mobile devices, and are installable in a few clicks. Productivity applications can be unlocked for customization and learning purposes. Of course, Oracle can only provide support for locked applications. Productivity applications are not the same as sample applications, because sample applications are unlocked by default.

Examples of productivity applications are the project tracker and checklist manager. Examples of sample applications are error handling, interactive reports, and the mobile sample application.

Plan for the future

In addition to these packaged business applications and sample code, the Oracle Database Cloud Service supports third-party applications. All third-party applications will go through a validation process to ensure the safety of the application and the protection of user data in the Oracle Database Cloud Service environment (Oracle Certification).

The following screenshot shows an example of the available packaged applications:

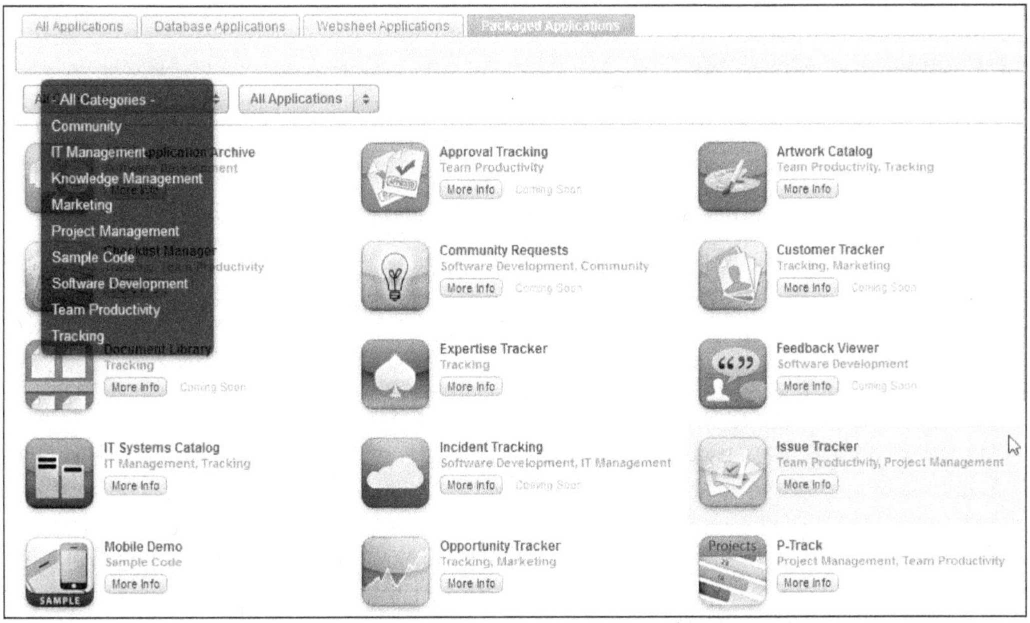

RESTful web services

The Oracle Database Cloud Service and Application Express 4.2 include the RESTful Web Services wizard that allows you to easily create a web service to access any SQL statement or PL/SQL program. This wizard makes it easy to create RESTful web services to be used by applications outside the Database Cloud Service.

RESTful web services have three main characteristics:

- The services use HTTP methods explicitly
- The services are accessible through URIs
- The services are stateless

Terminology used in the RESTful Web Services wizard are listed in the following table:

Terminology	Description
Module	The RESTful service module is used to group services.
Template	A template is identified by a unique URI, which also includes a portion based on the Database Cloud Service and the module.
Handler	A handler is based on a specific HTTP method, such as `GET` (select), `POST` (update), `PUT` (insert), or `DELETE`. You can only have one handler for each HTTP method for each template.
Source type	When you create a RESTful web service, the key attribute of the service is the source type. There are two basic categories of source types—SQL and PL/SQL.
Query	A query source type is defined as any standard SQL statement.
Query one row	The query one row source type only returns a single row from the `SELECT` operation.
Feed	The URL returned by the feed web service is formed by using the URI for the web service with the value for the first column in the SQL statement passed as the argument in the URI.
PL/SQL	The PL/SQL source type allows you to use any PL/SQL code to create and return data from a RESTful web service call.

The RESTful Web Services wizard

On the home page of the RESTful Web Services wizard, a report on web services modules exists. The module named **oracle.example.hr** is shown in the following screenshot. The home page can be reached through SQL Workshop/RESTful Web Services.

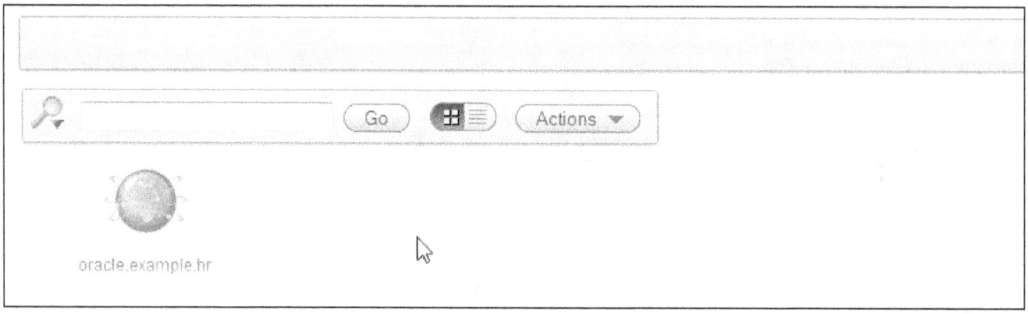

Click on the module and you will see two logical parts of the page. On the left-hand side, you will see a list of various templates within the module. On the right-hand side, you will see the attributes of this module.

The next example steps through the RESTful Web Services creation wizard are as follows:

1. Start the wizard by clicking on **Create Template**, as shown in the following screenshot:

2. Give the template a name, for example `empall/`.

> Remember that the forward slash at the end of the URI is required.

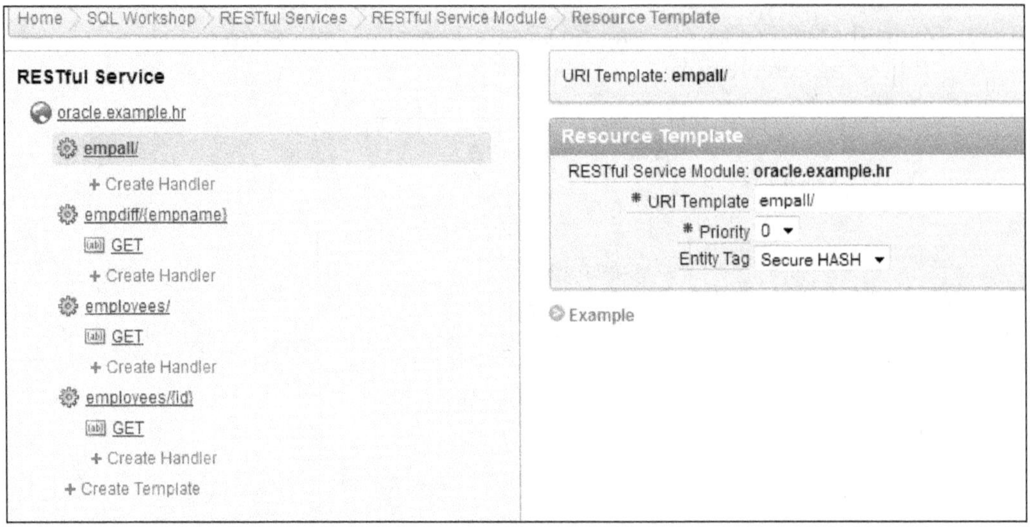

3. The next step is to create the handler.

   You can do that by clicking on **Create Handler** just below the RESTful service (**empall/**):

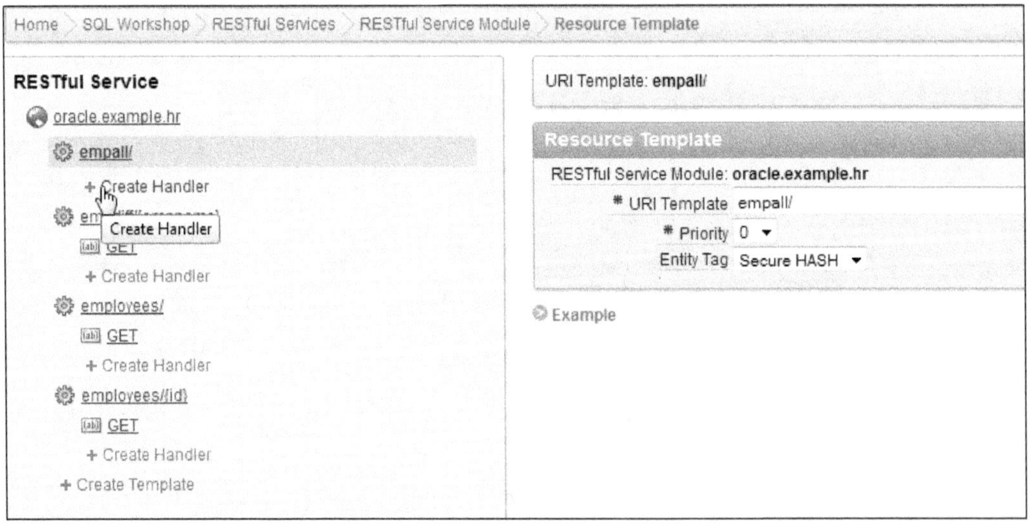

4. Now select the HTTP method for your RESTful service.

   The HTTP methods available here are **GET** (equal to select), **DELETE** (equal to delete), **PUT (equal to insert)**, and **POST** (equal to update):

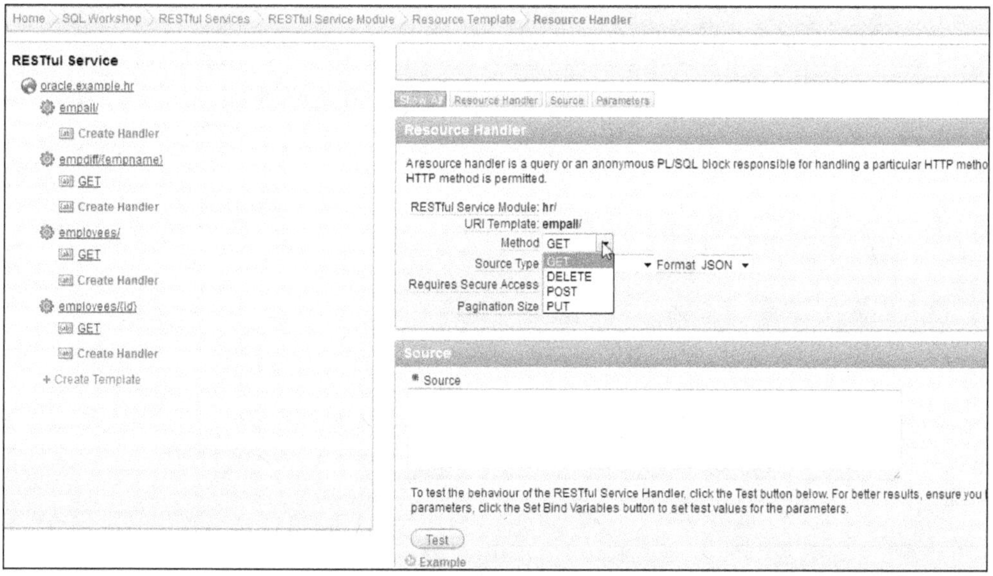

5. From the available source types, select **Query**. As the output format you can choose between **JSON** and **CSV**. Select **JSON**.

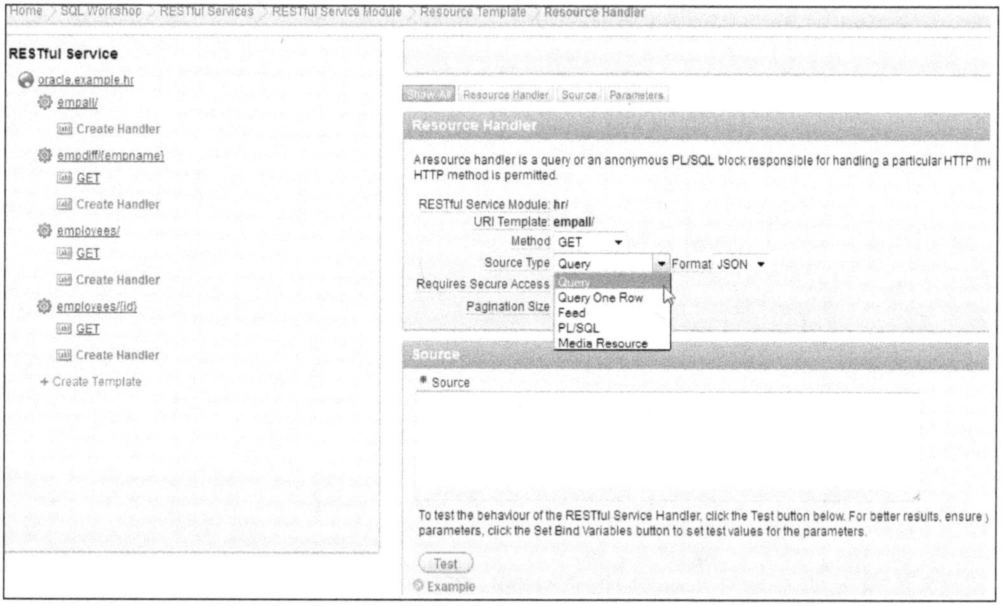

6. The **Source** field contains the source code, which will be executed when the web service is called. Enter the following query in this field:

```
Select *
From EMP
Order by deptno, ename
```

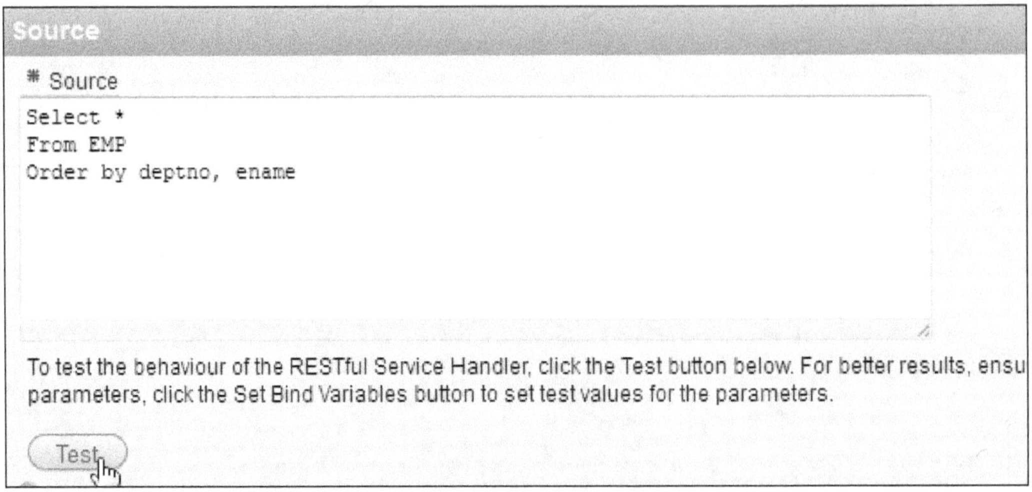

7. Click on the **Create** button to save the template.

   We can test the web service by clicking on the **Test** button and check the outcome of the web service. An example of a possible outcome, depending on your data, is shown in the following screenshot:

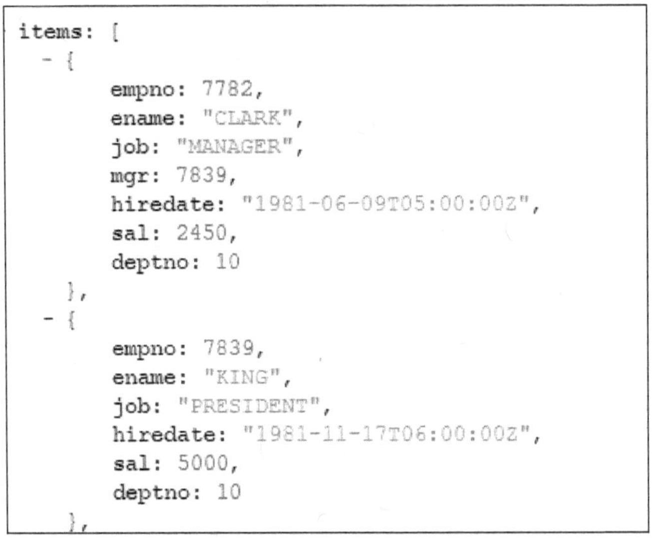

> **Remark**
>
> To have this nice layout, I installed the Firefox browser JSON viewer plug-in from `https://addons.mozilla.org/en-us/firefox/addon/jsonview/`.
>
> A report region can be created to show the output from the RESTful web services as shown in the preceding example.

Data load feature (SQL Workshop/utilities/data load)

The data load feature enables us to load or unload data from our Oracle Database Cloud Service. The utility enables you to upload data from a text file, an XML document, or a spreadsheet. This utility is accessed from the Application Express SQL Workshop.

Summary

Oracle Application Express is going to be an important tool in the Database Cloud Service. RESTful Web Services allows you to easily create a web service to access any SQL statement, PL/SQL program. The data load feature helps to upload or unload data from the Oracle Public Cloud.

Index

Symbols

32K limit
  bypassing, on reports 133

A

access control administration page
  creating 176-178
Access Control Lists (ACLs) 157, 158
accounts, APEX 19
ADF 8
administrator
  APEX, securing for 138
  creating 16, 17
  creating, in workspace 24
aggregate functions
  about 77
  frontend process, offloading 86
  GROUPING SETS 78
alternative quoting 147
analytic functions
  about 61
  examples 64
  syntax overview 61-63
Apache FOP
  about 102, 103, 120
  configuring 105, 106
  installing 104
  printing architecture 104
  using 106, 107
APEX
  about 7, 195, 205, 226
  accounts 19
  administrator, creating 16, 17
  administrator, creating for workspace 24
  and Firebug 215
  application, deploying 239
  background 7
  builders, enabling in 158
  characteristics 9
  command line 18
  database 19
  database environment, protecting 138
  database packages, deploying 235-238
  database tools 22
  developers, creating in workspace 24
  dynamic actions, debugging 215, 216
  error handling 217
  hidden items, protecting 186, 187
  history 8
  installing 9
  miscellaneous tools 22
  multiple applications, structure 30
  packaged application, creating 226-231
  Page Zero template 29
  password complexity rules 161
  remote debugging, performing 210
  repository, housekeeping 248, 249
  secure items 185
  securing, for administrator 138
  subscribe and publish mechanism 30, 31
  Subversion 232-235
  tools, for web development 22
  URL, for hosted version 9
  user interface defaults 25
  users, creating in workspace 24
  utility reports, used for troubleshooting 220
  version control 231
  versus WebDB 7
  VPD, implementing in 148, 149
  web interface 17

web server, selecting 12
workspace, creating 23, 24
APEX 4
feedback, activating for application 250-252
feedback option, enabling 249
APEX 4.2
features 226
APEX_ACTIVITY_LOG view 219
APEX advisor 192, 193, 221
APEX application
deploying 239
deploying, command-line interface used 245-248
weighted page performance 255-257
apex_application.g_debug variable 202
APEX_APPLICATION package 202
APEX application report
creating, with Business Intelligence Publisher 115
APEX Builder 239
APEX_DEBUG_MESSAGE.LOG_MESSAGE process 204
APEX_DEBUG_MESSAGE package 202, 203
APEX_DEBUG_MESSAGE procedure 202
APEX_DEBUG_MESSAGES view 200
APEX, dictionaries
about 25
attribute 25
table 25
APEX environment
entered feedback, processing 252-255
using 239-244
apex_fop.jsp 103
APEX, installing
full development environment, converting to runtime environment 11, 12
on development environment 10
on runtime environment 10
runtime environment, converting to full development environment 11, 12
APEX Listener
about 14, 15
plans, for future versions 102
APEX pages
data model, mapping to 37, 38
debugging 195-200
APEX repository
housekeeping 248, 249
ApexSec Security Console 193
apex_util.download_print_document 133
APEX_UTIL_DOWNLOAD_PRINT_DOCUMENT function 130
apex_util.get_print_document 133
APEX web interface 17
Application Builder utilities
Application Express views 222
attribute dictionary 222
database object dependencies 222
upgrade application 222
Application Context
about 144
manipulating 144
working with 144-146
application dashboard 191
application data 189
Application Express. *See* **APEX**
applications
creating 36
deploying 36, 225
feedback, activating for 250-252
report, linking to 119, 120
application services 259
Application Utilities 220
architectures
used, for deploying APEX 151
attacker 163
Attribute Dictionary 25
authentication 170, 171
authentication mechanisms
custom 172
database accounts 172
HTTP header variable 172
LDAP directory 173
no authentication 174
open door credentials 174
Oracle Application Express accounts 172
Oracle Cloud identity management 174
out of the box 172
Single Sign On (SSO) 174
authentication plugin 184, 185
authentication schema
creating, from scratch 175

authorization
about 174
access control administration page, creating 176-178
authorization plugin 184, 185
authorization schema
applying 178, 179
authorization scheme
about 174
creating 175
implementing 175

B

base tables
about 38
characteristics 38, 39
BAT file 235, 236
bind variable
using 169
breakpoint
about 207
defining, in procedure 209
browser attack methods
about 163
cross-site scripting (XSS) 163, 164
browser security attributes
about 183
Cache 183
database session attribute 184
Embed in Frames 183
builders
enabling, in APEX 158
Build Status option 10
Business Intelligence Publisher
about 109
APEX application report, creating with 115
main screen 110
print test, performing 111, 112
using 110, 111
Business Intelligence Publisher version 11
installing 109

C

characteristics, RESTful web services 261
chart
adding, to report 122-125
Cloud 259
cloud computing 9, 260
Cocoon 134
code instrumentation 201
Column Level Security 142
command line, APEX 18
command-line interface
used, for deploying APEX application 245-248
Computer Aided Software Engineering (CASE) 20
configuring
Apache FOP 105, 106
content
searching, in documents 97-99
credentials verification 172
cross-site scripting (XSS)
about 163, 164
rules 165
CSS 7
Cube clause 83
custom authentication schemes 172

D

database 138
Database 11gR2 11.2.0.1 158
Database 11gR2 11.2.0.2 158
database accounts 172
database, APEX
database objects, creating 21, 22
data model 19-21
tools 22
Database Cloud Service 260
database environment
protecting, for APEX 138
database modeling
guidelines 21
Database Object Dependencies utility
about 229
problems 230
database objects
creating 21, 22
database packages
deploying 235-238
database schema 179

database session attribute
using 184
database tools 22
data load feature 267
data model
about 19-21
mapping, to APEX pages 37, 38
Data Modeler 20
data model, mapping to APEX pages
base model 38, 39
intersection table 42-44
master detail 40, 41
other pages 46
simple report 46
datepicker 245
DBMS_DEBUG_JDWP 205
DBMS_DEBUG package 205
DBMS_LOB.SUBSTR function 127
DBMS_SESSION package 144
debug Advanced Programming Interface (API) 202
debug option, Oracle SQL Developer 207
deployment 225
developers
creating, in workspace 24
development environment
APEX, installing on 10
docman_ctx namespace 144
documents
printing, Print API used 130-132
dynamic actions
debugging, in APEX 215, 216
dynamic images
adding, to report 125-130
dynamic output
protecting 165

E

Embedded PDF plugin 13, 136
embedded PL/SQL gateway
about 153
URL, for info 154
ENABLE_DEBUG_MESSAGES procedure 202
entered feedback
processing, in APEX environment 252-255
error handling, APEX 217
examples, analytic functions
caveats 73-76
rank, assigning 70-72
rows, accessing in result set 69
running totals 64, 65
stringing 72
values, accessing from other records 67, 68
window, visualizing 66, 67

F

fake input 189
feed 262
feedback
activating, for application 250-252
feedback option
enabling, in APEX 4 249
Fetch Row process 43
file upload items 188
Fine Grained Access Control 139
Firebug
about 214
and APEX 215
URL, for downloading 214
fop.war file
deployment steps 105
form items
protecting 165
framework
creating 32
full development environment
runtime environment, converting into 11, 12
functionalities, login application 35

G

get_selectlist function 43
Glassfish 14
g_package 49
GROUPING SETS
about 78-81
Cube clause 83, 84
Rollups 81, 82
totals and subtotals, identifying 84-86

H

handler 262
heap table 54
hidden items
  protecting 186, 187
hidden items, APEX
  hidden 186
  hidden and protected 186
HTML 7
HTMLDB 8
HTML regions
  protecting 165
HTTP header variable authentication 172
HTTP methods, RESTful service 265
HTTP server
  about 151
  rewrite rule 152
  security considerations 152

I

import wizard 225
index-organized tables 59-61
installation process, APEX
  security measures 156
installing
  APEX 9
  Business Intelligence Publisher
    version 11 109
  JavaScript console wrapper 211, 212
  Subversion client 232
instance security
  managing 188
instrumentation, APEX code 201
intersection table 42-44
item encryption 186

J

JasperReports
  about 102, 135
  architecture 135
Java Runtime Environment (JRE) 105
JavaScript 7
JavaScript Console Wrapper
  about 211
  installing, steps 211, 212
jQuery datepicker 245

L

LDAP directory 173
Lightweight Directory Access
    Protocol (LDAP) 171, 173
LINT 192
List of Values (LOV)
  about 53
  creating 36, 37
logger_logs_5_min 50
logger_logs_apex_items 50
Logger package 48
logging
  about 218
  disabling 220
  enabling 219
login application
  about 33
  creating 33, 34
  examples, of pages 35
  functionalities 35
LOG_LONG_MESSAGE procedure 202
LOG_MESSAGE procedure 202
LOG_PAGE_SESSION_STATE
    procedure 203
lookup tables
  about 52, 53
  index-organized tables 59-61
  single-table hash clusters 53-58

M

master application
  about 33
  creating 33
master detail 40, 41
maximum session idle time 159
maximum session length 159
mod_rewrite module 152
module 262

multiple applications
framework, creating 32
structure 30

N

network services
testing 113
NO authentication 174

O

OC4J 102, 105
offloading process
about 86
images, using 95-97
one-off job 86-90
pipelined table functions 91, 92
pipelined table functions, in APEX 93-95
OHS 13
one-off job 86-90
On Load - After Header process 43
open door credentials 174
Open LDAP 171
Oracle
websites, based on APEX 9
Oracle Access Manager 171
Oracle Application Express
plugins 135
printing architecture 102
Oracle Application Express accounts 172
Oracle Application Express Listener
about 154
security implementation 155
SSL, enabling for web server 155, 156
Oracle Application Express, plugins
about 135
Embedded PDF 136
Reports 2 PDF 135
Oracle Application Server Containers for J2EE. *See* **OC4J**
Oracle Business Intelligence Enterprise Edition Plus (OBIEE Plus) 110
Oracle Cloud identity management 174
Oracle Database Cloud Service 9, 226
Oracle Designer 20
Oracle Flows 8
Oracle Fusion CRM Cloud Service 259
Oracle Fusion HCM Cloud Service 259
Oracle Fusion Middleware 133
Oracle HTTP Server. *See* **OHS**
Oracle Java Cloud Service 259
Oracle Platform 8
Oracle Public Cloud
about 259
packaged applications 260
patform services 259
services 259
Oracle Reports
about 133
integration 134
URL, for info 133
used, for creating reports in multiple formats 120-122
Oracle SQL Developer
about 205
debug option 207
URL, for downloading 205
Oracle SQL Developer IDE 232
Oracle Technology network
URL 109
out of the box authentication schemes 172

P

packaged applications
about 225, 226
creating 226-231
packaged applications, Oracle Public Cloud 260
page processing 199, 202
page rendering 199, 202
Page Zero 29
password complexity rules 161
password items 187
patching strategy 162
PDF printing
about 102, 120
alternatives used 133
pipelined table function
about 91, 92
in APEX 93, 94
pks extensions 236

platform services, Oracle Public Cloud
Oracle Database Cloud Service 259
Oracle Java Cloud Service 259
PL/SQL
about 7, 195, 262
guidelines 23
Print API
used, for printing documents 130-132
printing architecture 102
printing architecture, Apache FOP 104
printing issues
debugging 112
print test
performing, in Business Intelligence Publisher 111, 112
procedure
breakpoint, defining in 209
debugging 207
running 207
procedures, APEX_DEBUG_MESSAGE package
DISABLE_DEBUG_MESSAGES 202
ENABLE_DEBUG_MESSAGES 202
LOG_LONG_MESSAGE 202
LOG_MESSAGE 202
LOG_PAGE_SESSION_STATE 203
REMOVE_DEBUG_BY_AGE 203
REMOVE_DEBUG_BY_APP 203
REMOVE_DEBUG_BY_VIEW 203
REMOVE_SESSION_MESSAGES 203
Project Marvel 8
prompt command 238
p_scope parameter 50
pulling method 31
pushing method 31

Q

query 262
query one row 262

R

relations 20
remote debugging
about 209, 210
performing, in APEX 210
REMOVE_DEBUG_BY_AGE procedure 203
REMOVE_DEBUG_BY_APP procedure 203
REMOVE_DEBUG_BY_VIEW procedure 203
REMOVE_SESSION_MESSAGES procedure 203
report
32K limit, bypassing on 133
chart, adding to 122-125
creating, in multiple formats 120-122
creating, with Business Intelligence Publisher 115
dynamic images, adding to 125-130
linking, to application 119, 120
testing, against Apache FOP 108
report, creating with Business Intelligence Publisher
about 115
report layout, designing 116
report layout, uploading 118
report query, creating 115, 116
report layout
designing 116
uploading 118
report layout, designing
about 116
with RTF template (MS Word) 117
XML data, downloading 117
report query
creating 115, 116
Reports 2 PDF plugin 135
reports regions
protecting 165
Repository Creation Utility (RCU) 110
Representational State Transfer (REST) 9
RESTful web services
about 261, 262
characteristics 261
RESTful Web Services creation wizard
steps 263-266
Rich Text Format (RTF) 103
Rollups 81, 82
Row Level Security 139, 142
RTF template (MS Word)
report layout, designing 117

runtime environment
APEX, installing on 10
converting, into full development environment 11, 12
runtime exception
determining 149, 150
runtime installation, APEX 156, 157

S

save state before branch feature 191
schema 7
secure items, APEX
about 185
application data 189
fake input 189
file upload items 188
hidden items protection 186, 187
instance security, managing 188
item encryption 186
items, of type password 187
save state before branch feature 191
Secure Socket Layer. *See* **SSL**
security 137
security attributes 170
security considerations, for developer
about 162
authorization and authentication plugin 184, 185
browser attacks 163
browser security attributes 183
security attributes 170
SQL injection 166
URL tampering 179
utilities 191
security considerations, HTTP server 152
security implementation
in Oracle Application Express Listener 155
security measures, for APEX installation process
about 156
Access Control Lists (ACLs) 157, 158
builders, enabling 158
password complexity rules 161
patching strategy 162
runtime installation, determining 156, 157
session timeout 159
security patch 162
SELECT operation 262
services, Oracle Public Cloud
application services 259
Oracle Fusion CRM Cloud Service 259
Oracle Fusion HCM Cloud Service 259
Oracle Social Network Cloud Service 259
session state protection
used, for protecting against URL tampering 179-183
session timeout 159
session timeout settings
at application level 160
at instance level 159, 160
Single Sign On (SSO) 174
single-table hash clusters
about 53-58
URL 53
Sourceforge project 235
source type 262
SQL 195
SQL injection
about 166
avoiding 169
insecure use, of variables 167, 168
rules, for prevention 166
SQL*Plus 139, 239
SSL
enabling, for web server 155, 156
static areas
protecting 165
subscribe and publish mechanism, APEX
about 30, 31
benefits 30
Subversion
about 232
working with 233-235
Subversion client
about 232
installing 232
Sumneva 193
SVN Update option 235
syntax overview, analytic functions 61-63
SYS_CONTEXT function
about 146, 147
used, for accessing stored values in Application Context 146

SYS.DBMS_ASSERT package 169
system application 35

T

Table Dictionary 25
tablespaces
about 10
images directory 11
tablespace_apex 11
tablespace_files 11
tablespace_temp 11
team development 250
template 262
template application
about 33
creating 33
Template Builder
about 116
URL, for downloading 122
template workspace 36
terminologies, RESTful web services
handler 262
module 262
PL/SQL 262
query 262
query one row 262
source type 262
template 262
TKPROF 218
Tortoise Subversion 232
trace file 217
tracing 217

U

URL tampering 179
User Interface Defaults
about 25, 26
creating 26
using 26-28
users
creating, in workspace 24
utilities, APEX
about 191
application dashboard 191
utility reports
used, for troubleshooting in APEX 220
UTL_ENCODE.BASE64_ENCODE function 127
UTL_HTTP RDBMS package 103
UTL_RAW.CAST_TO_VARCHAR2 function 127

V

version control, APEX 231
Virtual Private Database. *See* **VPD**
VPD
about 139, 144
implementing, in APEX 148, 149
runtime exception, determining 149, 150
using 139
VPD policy
about 139
purpose 140
VPD policy function 139-143
vulnerabilities assessment
flowchart 167

W

WebDB
about 7
versus APEX 7
Web Developer form 214
Web Developer plugin 213
Web Developer toolbar 213
web listener
securing 151
WebLogic 14
web server
APEX Listener 7, 14, 15
EPG 7, 13
OHS 7, 13
selecting 12
SSL, enabling for 155, 156
weighted page performance 255-257
WHERE clause 142
workspace
administrators, creating 24
creating 23, 24
developers, creating 24
users, creating 24
WWV_FLOW_API.SET_ENABLE_APP_DEBUGGING 205

X

XML data
downloading 117

Y

Yslow
about 216
URL, for downloading 216

[PACKT] enterprise
professional expertise distilled
PUBLISHING

Thank you for buying

Oracle APEX Best Practices

About Packt Publishing

Packt, pronounced 'packed', published its first book "Mastering phpMyAdmin for Effective MySQL Management" in April 2004 and subsequently continued to specialize in publishing highly focused books on specific technologies and solutions.

Our books and publications share the experiences of your fellow IT professionals in adapting and customizing today's systems, applications, and frameworks. Our solution based books give you the knowledge and power to customize the software and technologies you're using to get the job done. Packt books are more specific and less general than the IT books you have seen in the past. Our unique business model allows us to bring you more focused information, giving you more of what you need to know, and less of what you don't.

Packt is a modern, yet unique publishing company, which focuses on producing quality, cutting-edge books for communities of developers, administrators, and newbies alike. For more information, please visit our website: `www.packtpub.com`.

About Packt Enterprise

In 2010, Packt launched two new brands, Packt Enterprise and Packt Open Source, in order to continue its focus on specialization. This book is part of the Packt Enterprise brand, home to books published on enterprise software - software created by major vendors, including (but not limited to) IBM, Microsoft and Oracle, often for use in other corporations. Its titles will offer information relevant to a range of users of this software, including administrators, developers, architects, and end users.

Writing for Packt

We welcome all inquiries from people who are interested in authoring. Book proposals should be sent to author@packtpub.com. If your book idea is still at an early stage and you would like to discuss it first before writing a formal book proposal, contact us; one of our commissioning editors will get in touch with you.

We're not just looking for published authors; if you have strong technical skills but no writing experience, our experienced editors can help you develop a writing career, or simply get some additional reward for your expertise.

www.ingramcontent.com/pod-product-compliance
Lightning Source LLC
LaVergne TN
LVHW062308060326
832902LV00013B/2103
* 9 7 8 1 8 4 9 6 8 4 0 0 2 *